FROM BANKS TO BLOW-UPS

FROM BANKS TO BLOW-UPS

Chicago Baseball in the 70's and Other Stories

John M. O'Donnell

ISBN: 1505755174
ISBN 13: 9781505755176

DEDICATION

The title of this book changed in January of 2015. Upon driving to our daughter's volleyball tournament, a radio disc jockey interrupted programming to inform us of the passing of Ernie Banks. To honor my boyhood hero, I altered book cover and title, dedicating this work to him. He was, is and will always be a role model for me. Many people said many kind things about the man, but I challenge us all to live more like him.

Shortly after revising the chapter that contains the interview with Billy Pierce, I learned of his death. In the brief time that I knew him, he helped me immensely by giving of himself and appearing at three book signings to assist in the promotion of my first book, Like Night and Day. Never have I met a human being so good at a craft and remain so humble. I shared with a friend that no matter what praise and tributes are sent his way, they will be inadequate and not do him justice.

To these two people, Ernie Banks and Billy Pierce, who were great people first and great ballplayers second, and to their families and legions of fans, this book is for you.

As a young baseball fan growing up in northern California, my older brother and I sneaked into the clubhouse of the visiting Chicago Cubs. There we had brief encounters with Ernie Banks, Billy Williams, and Ron Santo--a truly unforgettable experience. After reading John O'Donnell's book, LIKE NIGHT AND DAY, A Look at Chicago Baseball from 1964-1969, I realize that what I did at Candlestick Park all those years ago John and his friends could very well be doing in Chicago. As a broadcaster and baseball fan, I've come across many books on baseball. I can assure you that LIKE NIGHT AND DAY does justice to baseball in the 1960's.

Now John has written a second book, FROM BANKS TO BLOW-UPS, Chicago Baseball in the 70's and Other Stories. I find this book to be as stimulating as the first. This decade may not have produced any pennant winning teams in Chicago, but stories about great players and incredible games--like the 23-22 game between the Cubs and Phillies— appear on so many pages and allow the reader to travel back in time.

I think you'll find FROM BANKS TO BLOW-UPS a delightful read that has something for everybody. If you're a baseball fan who grew up in that era, you'll enjoy coming across events and players you haven't heard from in a while. If you're a Chicago fan, you'll appreciate the nostalgic stories from Old Comiskey Park and timeless Wrigley Field.

Even if you're not a rabid baseball enthusiast, you'll still appreciate the history lessons that this book offers.

As a person who loves baseball and its history, I like how FROM BANKS TO BLOW-UPS brings the 70's to life. I think you will too.

Pat Hughes

Chicago Cubs Radio Broadcaster

Table of Contents

Introduction

"Tell me this place is not a launching pad." TD's observation during his first trip to Wrigley Field coincides with yet another runner crossing home. TD, short in stature but long in baseball I.Q. shakes his head in disbelief as the sixth Cubbie scores in the *first inning*. Now they only trail the Phillies by one.

"Would you please not climb down the foul poles?" The man's voice on the PA sounded like a substitute teacher pleading against classroom chaos. He meant to sound authoritative, but it wasn't working. Too many wasted people, too much reckless abandon, too much toking and swigging to mind any requests or instructions. The promotion known as Disco Demolition Night brought out antics never seen since Nickel Beer Night in Cleveland. "Veeck as in Wreck" indeed. A fire soon spreads in Old Comiskey's spacious center field, canceling the second game of the doubleheader.

Both quotes capture two memorable events in Chicago baseball as the 70's drew to a close. It marks the second consecutive decade that both clubs fail to play in the post-season, making it 0 for 40 if you combine the two teams' performance. But there had to be other things to hold fan interest. So if the decade ends with run fests and demolition, how did it start?

1970

It starts with a question. What's worse, to lose in heartbreaking fashion at the end of the game as defeat is snatched from the jaws of victory, or to be completely bludgeoned by the other team? Which do you prefer as you leave the ballpark, to mutter a litany of "If only's," or to shout, "We're terrible," for the whole world to hear? If you were a Chicago baseball fan in the early 70's, you didn't have to choose. You got to see the worst of both worlds: the "if only" Cubs and the "we're terrible" White Sox.

The Cub fan knew that the Met thing of '69 would not happen again for a long, long time. Pitching is important, of course, but Met everyday players needed something beyond grit and luck. Like talent. The law of regression caught up with this club, at least for a couple of seasons. Outside of Tommie Agee (former Rookie of the Year with the White Sox), there's not one position where a fantasy fan would take a Met over a Cub.

And the Cubs tried to get better. All clubs say that, but the Cubs did attempt to upgrade their roster. They obtained Johnny Callison (another former White Sox player) to eliminate one outfield hole. Callison, a legitimate hitter albeit past his prime, produced runs. And it seemed that his professionalism and experience would be a good fit with Leo Durocher. To secure Callison, the Cubs parted ways with Oscar Gamble and Dick Selma. A couple characters—one who bashed his way into Chicago lore as a South Side Hit Man, and the other best known for his cheerleading skills that invigorated the left field bleacher bums. Both might be missed a little bit, but you figure that Callison would give the Cubs one more weapon to do battle against the sluggers of the Pirates. With Clemente, Stargell, Sanguillen, Oliver, Robertson, Hebner, et. al, there just weren't a whole lot of easy outs. So the Cub front office probably wanted more bats to give themselves a fighting chance. Pitching—it was in good Hands with Bill, Fergie and Kenny (we fans are on a first name basis), but what Cub fan gets excited about pitching? And of course Cub brass couldn't sleep on the Cardinals, just a couple seasons removed from two consecutive appearances in the World Series.

Another thing to consider was the mental approach going into the new decade. Having come so close to the post season would have to have an effect, wouldn't it? Would they be hungrier or deflated? Experienced or wary? Play with an edge or a hangover? Old school Durocher would likely pooh-pooh such mumbo-jumbo, but we saw where his approach got us in 1969. If Leo had his way, the roster could shed 5-7 players easily. If you're not tough enough to play every day, then you're not tough enough.

The White Sox, on the other hand, floundered. Their proud run of finishing in the first division for seventeen seasons in succession came to an abrupt and painful end after '67. Since then the Sox seemed to be scrambling for an identity. Pitching and defense as their cornerstones, but not knowing whether to go young or old. Luis Aparicio, Bobby Knoop, Tommy John, and Joe Horlen gave fans some familiarity, but were these players still good? Then throw in the hints of rebuilding with the youth of Bill Melton, Carlos May, and Ed Herrmann. How did this blend perform? Poorly. The Kansas City Royals in their inaugural season—made up of cast-offs and kids—finished one game ahead of the Sox.

Fortunately, there was another expansion club in their division to save the Sox the ignominy of finishing in last place. Can you name that expansion club which the Sox beat out? A gold star if you can. The Seattle Pilots, who after one year of ineptitude bolted for Milwaukee. Perhaps they thought that if we can't beat out the White Sox, we're outta here and leaving behind this Sick Stadium. (That was the name of the ballpark; you could look it up). So this ragtag bunch that included Steve Hovley, Don Mincher, Diego Segui, Tommie Davis, and Jim Bouton (the author) would now become neighbors just north of the Cubs. Here's another piece of Seattle Pilot trivia—which pitcher led the team in wins? Give up? A guy by the name of Gene "Tits" Brabender. I know of his nickname because a roommate of mine grew up an Oriole fan and Brabender broke in with Baltimore. I never asked how he got the nickname; some things are better left unknown.

So without the Seattle Pilots to kick around, how would the Sox fare? Worse. But at least now I wasn't worried that the Sox would relocate to Milwaukee. There were lean days in '68 and '69 when the Sox actually played "home" games in Milwaukee. Crazy, but just in a way. Why would people in Chicago have to suffer through 81 home games? Spread the misery around.

These were the days when the White Sox awarded free tickets to grade school students for perfect attendance or straight A's. An excellent mark in every subject stretched beyond my reach, but come what may, I was not going to miss school for anything. I don't care if I had triple pneumonia, I was going to get those Sox tickets. But in 1970, these tickets served as disciplinary measures:

Sister Aggie: Master Zorb, either you shape up or I'm sending a note home to your parents with six White Sox tickets.
Master Zorb: Oh no, Sister, not that. Make me clean erasers for a month, have me do a report on Catholics in the Partridge Family, but no Sox tickets, please, my folks would kill me! I'll be good; look—I'll give you some money right now for the missions.

The White Sox record in 1970: 56-106. Don't be deceived, they were not as good as their record indicates. Imagine finishing *nine* games behind the two clubs that were in *second-to-last!* My goodness, they could go undefeated for two months and still have a losing record. **50** games below .500. If they were a high school football team, they'd be the homecoming opponent for every single school on their schedule. Grade schools would try to schedule them.

My dad, the proud Sox fan, would have no part of this disgrace. We, the O'Donnell household, engaged in an unwritten boycott of the ballclub vis-à-vis my father that went something like this: "No way am I or any of you spending money to watch these clowns. If I wanted to watch a bunch of Little Leaguers, I'd go to one of your games, John, or up to Wrigley Field."

The good news is that the team would get a lot better and a lot more colorful and a lot more entertaining in just a couple of years. But my old man was not one to reinforce negative behavior by financially supporting a lousy team.

Sorry, he'd say, but get some ballplayers who can actually play and maybe we'll go back.

So while we have no games to report in 1970, we do offer something which serves as a more-than-worthy proxy: an exclusive interview with one of the White Sox television broadcasters from this season.

I'd like to take you on a tour. All this basement needs to pass for a museum is a ticket booth. There's an "Oh, my" exclamation with every photo and exhibit. Resting peacefully in the corner are five bats, authentic bats that were used in Major League All-Star games in the 1950's. The wood is pure, the brand is Louisville, and the feel is comfortable. I rouse one from its inverted vertical position, choke up about half an inch, and imagine taking cuts against Robin Roberts or Warren Spahn. I recognize the era from when this bat was created--not too many years later in the 60's I'd be using a similar make and model, less a few inches & ounces. I might have swung one in a Little League game; the one I'm now holding took swings against the best pitchers in the world.

Camaraderie. Find a team with a run of success, and you're bound to find the element of camaraderie. It's there in the photos before a game, with the smiles and mild horseplay among teammates. It's there in the photos after the game, with grins of relief and satisfaction. It's there in photos off the field, with teammates in suits and neckties posing at some kind of social function. I can't tell what the function is, but I can tell the subjects in the picture do enjoy one another's company. Then within these band of brothers was an even tighter connection—roommates. Back in the day when a player spent more time with his roommate than with his spouse, aloofness and space just weren't optional. Look at a picture with two roommates and you can only imagine the stories that each could tell about the other, had they not been sworn to secrecy. One story that can be told in mixed company goes like this: Nellie Fox, the roommate of the game's starting pitching, tries turning a double play. After the play, the pitcher (Fox's roommate) calls Nellie to the mound. The pitcher informs Fox that if only he had Fox's change-up, given the way he re-layed the ball to first base, he would win twenty games every year. Fox curses at his roommate and returned to his position.

Study these frames and the clichés come to life—how successful teams truly play for one another. And it had to be that way, if the team wanted any chance at all in competing with the mighty Yankees and other good teams in the American League.

Spiraling in a rack upon a bureau, baseballs line up in chronological order. Colored, too, are these balls that represent a successful pitching season. Studying them is like a cross between a kid in a candy store and Indiana Jones. Twenty balls for twenty wins. This in a season of 154 games. In baseball's Golden Age of Sluggers. I think that if I even thought of moving one ball out of this basement, or even out of its designated place, my face would melt away. Today these cold baseballs are historical artifacts—there, twenty wins. But I know that each one of those victories came with sweat, guile, talent, luck, and anxiety. And each, of course, is a team victory that a tennis ball or golf ball could only imagine. How can a ball share that with its holder? It just does.

Then the capper. In the center of a line of photographs on the basement wall, the subject of my interview grins ear to ear while he and Ted Williams point to the sweet spot on the bat. I fancy the captions that could fill the space underneath this picture. The finest hitter ever to play the game identifies where he aims to make contact with the baseball, and the pitcher next to him wondering how that's preventable. Then shifting your eyes five photos to the left, the subject relaxes in the clubhouse with the left arm of Willie Mays draped around him. I'm guessing this happens after a big late season victory in which both parties played an instrumental role. Maybe 1962? Just glancing at these two photos, in a sea of photos numbering fifty or so, I point out to my friend that posing with these two folks is comparable to a writer having a picture taken with Shakespeare and Dickens. He, as he often does, smiles a little and nods.

Bill Pierce had one heckuva baseball career; his life has been even better.

And you couldn't be happier. I know over the years Leo Durocher has been beaten up, unfairly, over the line attributed to him, "Nice guys finish last." He didn't exactly say it that way, but statements such as those require one to pause, if just for a moment, to consider its validity. Upon further review, I'd have to say there's some truth to it, yes. It's the age-old conflict—nice guys will likely have the Golden Rule within them to some degree. And if you're competing, that principle may be a hindrance and not a help. As General Grant said about war, in the end it's only butchery. Couldn't some realist, such as Durocher, say the same about sports: in the end, it's about winning and whatever it takes to get there?

Consider the mindset of two pitchers: Early Wynn and Bill Pierce. Their careers intersect with the White Sox for a few seasons, including the pennant winning year of '59. Legend has it that Wynn, who won 300 games, would throw at his mother if she was batting against him. Pierce, on the other hand, is quoted as loving the game of baseball, but there are certain things he would not do. Without being overly dramatic, he mentions how difficult it would be to live with himself if he curtailed another ballplayer's career through a beaning. Two highly successful pitchers, two radically different approaches. If nice guys finish last, then gentlemen like Pierce are an aberration. And it just so happens that when Pierce gets traded to San Francisco in the twilight of his career, the Giants and LA Dodgers have a best-of-three playoff at the end of the '62 season to decide the pennant. Pierce wins a game and saves another propelling Frisco to the World Series. And guess who was a coach for the Dodgers that year? Leo Durocher.

1970 was hardly a pennant winning year for the White Sox. But it was the year that Bill Pierce was pressed into duty as a broadcaster. Mel Parnell did broadcast White Sox games previously, but couldn't in '70 due to health issues. So the Sox brass offered the position to Pierce, and he accepted. What follows are his reflections about that season.

Q: What is the fondest memory of an otherwise forgettable 1970 season with the White Sox?

BP: Working with Jack Drees. He was a first class gentleman and a great announcer. His knowledge of baseball was limited, so that's where I came in.

Q: What do you recall from that 1970 team? Its record was not good, but could you see good things on the horizon?

BP: Baseball back then really didn't operate that way. If you were in the middle of a bad season, it was a bad season. I remember filling in a lot of dead time by promoting our sponsors—especially a car dealership in Chicago. I even remember the address: 3535 N. Ashland Avenue.

Q: What holes did you see the White Sox needing to fill?

BP: No team ever won without good pitching. And it seems that the White Sox had trouble securing corner infielders—seems like the first basemen and the third basemen did not stick around.

Q: The starting shortstop from that team was a player you played with for a long time, Luis Aparicio. Was it strange to be broadcasting games for a former teammate?

BP: Some fellows can hang in there a long time. Looie was one of those guys. Good shortstop. (editor's note—Aparacio led the team in hitting with a .313 average. At the age of 36, he also led the team in salary, earning 38 K that season).

Q: I'd like to go through a little litany of the players from that team. For each, share a comment or two as to what you remember, okay?

BP: Okay

Q: Carlos May (.285 avg., 22 years old)

BP: Good ballplayer, good hitter.

Q: Bill Melton (33 HR's, 24 years old)

BP: Hit a lot of homers, but then he hurt his back.

Q: Ken Berry (.276)

BP: Very good centerfielder.

Q: Bobby Knoop ('71 was his only full-time season with the White Sox. This second baseman was the second highest paid player with a salary of 35 K)

BP: Didn't know him very well.

Q: Ed Herrmann (at 23, he hit 19 homers. Frequently during broadcasts, Harry Caray would challenge him to a foot race)

BP: He could hit you the long ball.

Q: Tommy McCraw (age 29, part-time first baseman. He and Carlos May led the team with 12 stolen bases).

BP: Good ballplayer, good runner, good hustler.

Q: Tommy John (at 27, he led the team with 12 wins and 269 innings pitched)

BP: Real nice young fella. Not a great fastball, but did win games.

Q: Joe Horlen (age 32, 6-16 record)

BP: Good curveball

Q: Bart Johnson (age 20, struck out 71 batters in 90 innings)

BP: He could throw the ball.

Q: Wilbur Wood (2.81 ERA. One year away from being a starter and beginning a string of four 20 win seasons. One year pitched over 376 innings).

BP: Knuckleballer. He could throw it all week long. Real quiet guy, you'd never think of him as a ballplayer.

Q: The primary manager for this season was Don Gutteridge (49-87). At the end of the season, Chuck Tanner took over as skipper. Any thoughts on Gutteridge?

BP: Gutteridge had a tough deal. Managers don't lose 100 plus games a season. A manager, with a decent team, may win 7-10 games per year. Likewise, the manager can lose 7-10 games a year with a bad team. The White Sox were fortunate to have Paul Richards in their system. He was very astute and helped develop a lot of the players.

Q: Do you recall any particular conversations you had with the players?

BP: One day I asked Tommy John why he threw a particular pitch (and I wasn't second guessing, I was first guessing at the time when the pitch was thrown). He said that Herrmann doesn't always call the right pitches. I told him that you can always shake him off.

Q: Did you ever get the feeling that when watching the game from the broadcast booth, you could get these guys out?

BP: No, I stayed away from "Back when I played ..." because the people want to hear about today's game. I never felt comfortable going to the clubhouse after my playing days. You don't belong there. Some former players as broadcasters, the way they talk about themselves I started to think that they batted .600.

Q: You covered the Sox when they played people like Al Kaline. You also pitched against Al Kaline. Being from Detroit originally, what do you remember about him?

BP: There was this bird dog scout who says I got a kid who'll be a good ballplayer. I told him that I'll tell the White Sox people about him. Turns out to be Kaline. During his first year up (editor: Kaline went straight from playing high school baseball to the Tigers) you could overpower him. But after his rookie season, you couldn't do that anymore.

Q: During your year as a broadcaster, did anything catch you by surprise—either in a pleasant or disappointing way?

BP: Truthfully, I enjoyed it. I knew the players—for us and against us. There wasn't as much homework as there is now. And I felt I could help Jack (Drees). There was one time when there was a man on first for the other team and the count was full. I said he probably will be running here. He did and they got him out at second. Well, later in that same game there was a man at first with a full count and Jack says they'll probably be running here. I nudged him under the table and shook my head. This time there wasn't a base stealer on first base but the first time there was.

Q: How did you like interviewing?

BP: I enjoyed it. One time I planned on talking about hitting with three totally different hitters—Frank Thomas (ed.--not the "Big Hurt" but another Frank Thomas), Nellie Fox, and Ted Williams. I wanted these three because they each were good but different when it came to making contact and hitting for power. Well, I had it all set up but it fell through at the last minute. So I asked Ted if he'd do it again some time with me and he said "Sure, Billy, any time." So we tried it again and it came off well.

Q: Who are the baseball broadcasters that you've appreciated over the years?

BP: Jack Brickhouse. He was always involved in the community, and came without expecting to get paid. He came to every Little League function (editor: Billy coached Little League baseball in the town of Evergreen Park after he retired) and every event for our cancer charity. I thought he was a fine announcer, as is that fellow still announcing out in Los Angeles (Vin Scully). Earlier announcers used to have their own distinctive voice. Now they all sound the same to me.

Q: Thoughts on Bob Elson?

BP: He was a great interviewer. He had this popular show he did from a fancy place called the "Pump Room" in downtown Chicago. He invited my wife and me to be on this show one day. In the Pump Room they had this custom of seating celebrities in a special booth called Booth One. When we get there, my wife looks around trying to locate the celebrities. She keeps looking and looking, trying to figure out which booth holds the famous folks. Finally, she asks Bob where Booth One is. He says, "You're in it."

Q: I've got to get one thing off my chest. How can you retire from the game with a strikeout total of 1,999? That would drive me nuts. Couldn't you finagle a deal that allowed you to get one more strikeout in the first week of the season and then retire?

BP (chuckling): Numbers didn't matter that much to me. When it was over, it was over—I was through with baseball. I had a family to raise (three kids) and I would be making a lot more money in the envelope business than playing baseball. Besides, if you include my numbers in the World Series and All-Star games, I struck out over 2,000 batters.

Q: One last question about your playing days. The 1962 World Series. Game 6 & 7 in San Francisco where you and your Giant teammates host the Yankees. Got any stories?

GP (Gloria Pierce, Bill's wife, handles this one): I woke up planning to go to Game 6. I read in the papers how everything rests on Bill, since he was the starting pitcher. On the elevator lots of people tell me how important this game is and they sure hope Bill pitches well. I start to feel sick, so I head back to my hotel room and listen to the game there. Well, Bill pitches well and the Giants win. Now I'm feeling a lot better, so I plan on meeting up with Bill after the game. He sees me and says something like, "Oh sure, now you come!"

So the next day it's Game 7. This time I feel fine, Bill's not pitching. And it's a very close, tense game between the Giants and the Yankees.

BP (stepping in): It's the late innings, and our manager, Alvin Dark, looks to me in the dugout and asks if I could pitch an inning. I said I'll give it a try, and I head from the dugout to the bullpen.

GP: So here I am in the late innings of Game 7 of the World Series, and I see Bill heading toward the bullpen. I couldn't help myself. I stand up and holler at him, "Sit down, you idiot."

(Editor's note: Baseball Encyclopedia describes Pierce's performance as "masterful" as he defeats the Yankees in Game 6, 5-2. He throws a complete game, allowing only 3 hits. In Game 7, much to Gloria Pierce's relief, Bill does not relieve. With two on and two out in the ninth inning, Willie McCovey lines out to the second baseman Bobby Richardson, ending the game and the Series).

GAME 1: SAN FRANCISCO GIANTS VS. CHICAGO CUBS
SATURDAY, JUNE 6, 1970

Were you a Scout? Boy Scout, Girl Scout, Brownie, Cub Scout? I wasn't, but sometimes I wish I was. I'm well aware of the controversy surrounding this institution over the years, and I'm not going down that path. My frame of reference is scouting in the 60's and 70's.

Two impressions I had of scouts—one favorable and the other not. To address the latter first, I never saw scouts as the most athletically inclined people. And since sports were pretty much my life, I didn't seriously consider what scouting had to offer. Many folks have expounded on the life lessons to be learned by playing sports and I don't disagree. But had I been a little wiser and a little braver, I would have taken a more serious look at the scouting life.

Which takes me to my second impression—independence. Scouts seem to have a better handle on things. Call it a greater sense of adventure, a more welcoming approach of a challenge, even a little more serenity—I noticed this in scouts and envied it. To this day I shy away from outdoorsy activities like lighting campfires, pitching tents, or even tying knots to secure things. A former scout jumps right into this stuff, while I almost always defer to them. Kind of like they have a "Can do" spirit, while I'm sometimes stuck with a "Don't screw this up" mindset.

Scout trips often move away from urban areas to camp and hike, but today it was movement to the city to catch a game. My two brothers were Scouts and didn't pass on the opportunity to see the Cubs play the Giants. I probably would have gone too, but Little League obligations stood in the way. However, since I came across the scorecard, I'd like to pass on a few recollections from the game.

Number one—it's chilly, especially sitting in the upper deck. I don't think a t-shirt and shorts are the standard until mid July, and even then it's not a sure thing. But Scouts are rugged, so what's a couple hours of frostiness and Frosty Malts when you're used to days and days of exposure to the elements. If Scouts weren't so well-behaved, I could see them starting a campfire with some wood from empty seats in the upper deck so they could cook up their S'mores.

Number two—it's my dad keeping score. Poor guy gets roped into being a chaperone, at chilly Wrigley Field, no less. So his way of passing the time is to make marks on the scorecard as play proceeds.

Number three—not one, not two, but three Hall-of-Famers in the visitor's lineup. Willie Mays, who will drive in a run; Willie McCovey, who will club a three run homer in spite of the elements, and Gaylord Perry, who will scatter 11 hits over nine innings. Plus, there's one who's not pitching today—Juan Marichal. Can the Cubs match that? Not quite. One Hall-of-Famer isn't playing, Ernie, and another isn't pitching, Fergie. But Williams and Santo, along with Hickman and Callison and Beckert batting, with Bill Hands pitching, could provide stiff competition. In fact, I like their chances.

Number four—those chances took a big hit in the 3rd inning as the Giants collect three little hits and a long blast by the aforementioned McCovey. The huge slugger propelled Frisco to a 4 zip lead. Not a Gigantic deficit, but daunting with the chill of the weather and the saliva of Perry. A couple of late inning rallies shaved the lead to one, but that's as close as it got. The Giants add an insurance run in the 9th and the Cub scouts watch the Cubs lose, 5-3.

Number five—Wise baseball folks say it's not what you hit, it's when you hit. That being said, it's time to throw a Cub legend and Hall-of-Famer, Ron Santo, under the bus, at least for today. On paper, Ronnie had a good game: 3 for 4, and was not the reason why the Cubs lost. However, his 3 hits came with no one on base and 2 outs—hardly clutch hitting. The only time he failed to hit safely came in the 6th as the Cubs were mounting a comeback and had two runners aboard. I bet Ron would trade those three hits for one knock with runner(s) in scoring position. But you can't just pick and choose when you get hits, can you?

GAME 2: PITTSBURGH PIRATES VS. CHICAGO CUBS
FRIDAY, JULY 3

"Great," my dad cried out somewhere in the middle innings, "go to a Cub game and spend a whole weekend at Wrigley Field."

This game had to be torture for my dad. Not just watching his least favorite professional baseball team in Chicago play, but having to endure a 3 hour and 45 minute marathon slugfest. On the day when the virtue of patience was handed out in various degrees for people to use throughout their life journey, I think my dad was sick and didn't get any.

Now today, marathon games aren't that big a deal—especially in postseason. With the disappearance of the complete game, relief specialists in the bullpen taking forever between pitches, umpteen commercials between innings, batters having rituals before every pitch, good hitters working the count, and other factors, games are longer than ever. In 1970, games did not have these impediments and therefore took less time to play, usually. But when two teams combine to score 30 runs, pitching coaches, relief pitchers, and restroom facilities get a work out.

The game's length did not bother me, but the final score did. The good news: Cubs rock Buc pitching to the tune of 14 runs. You already know the bad news. I guess kudos to the Cubbies for giving PR people the opportunity to use the cliché that "this team battled back," or "they never quit." Heck, it's their job, isn't it? I mean if you are going to play, you might as well give it your best, right? So why do people keep stating the obvious when a team getting hammered doesn't forfeit?

Anyway ... an oddity of sorts. Now in baseball history practically everything has happened, except this. For the first four innings, the Pirates scored in this fashion: 1-6-0-2. For the first four innings, the Cubs scored: 1-6-0-2. What do you think the odds are of having two teams put up those same numbers throughout the first half of the contest? I'm not talking of 8 goose eggs or both teams scoring once in the first and zeroes for the next 3 frames, but to score 1, then 6, then 0, then 2; and to have your opponent duplicate those numbers?! Please get back to me if it's ever happened.

Weird things happen at Wrigley Field. Bill Madlock once said that, and he ought to know. And in this game, a 7-1 deficit heading into the bottom of the second was not promising. But a grand slam by Billy Williams picked up the crowd's spirits (you know your pitching is struggling when the number 3 batter bats for the second time in just the second inning with the bases loaded). It got better as the Cub offense got over the hump by snatching leads in both the 5th and the 7th. But alas, *two* three run innings in the 8th and 9th by the bad guys sent us home deflated and defeated.

But we're getting a little ahead of ourselves. Here's an assignment for you—first, find an old-time baseball fan. Someone who remembers baseball from the 50's or at least the 60's. Then, ask her or him who was the finest player they have ever seen play. Then call me up for a wager. I'll give you 2:1 odds that the ballplayer's initials are R.C. (hint: neither Rocky Colavito nor Rod Carew). I've done my own informal research on this, and I've asked about a score of people this question, and except for a few old-timers who mention Ted Williams (Bill Pierce says it's Willie Mays) the overwhelming choice has been Roberto Clemente. TD, who you met at the outset of this book, claims that the only reason that Clemente gets mentioned is because he died heroically in a plane crash in a humanitarian project. I respond by saying that TD is full of manure. If you choose someone else, fine, this is still America, but quick—name me a person who matches Clemente in both talent and intensity. Ah-hah, not so easy, is it?

Please note: I was **not** a Clemente fan as a kid. In fact, I didn't like him at all. One simple reason, which you can probably guess—he *abused* the Cubs. Case in point—this game. First time up, Clemente homers (either to right or left, I don't remember). Second inning, Clemente homers again. I do remember that it was the opposite direction of the first. So I predict that after a homer to left and a homer to right that the center fielder better move back in his third at bat. I also point out that he's on pace to homer nine times in today's game and drive in 18 runs. But the Cubs hold him in check until he singles and scores in the ninth.

Pity Bill Hands. I'm scared spitless of the Pirates and I'm sitting some thirty rows up in the grandstands. Imagine facing these sluggers from 60 feet away with the wind blowing out. Yikes. And then there's this matter of logos. How in the world can a cute little baby bear compete against the nefarious pirates. Really, what chance do they have? Even Pirate uniforms are scary, they wore those black and white "death to you all" uniforms with the intimidating sleeves. The only things missing were for their coaches to have eye-patches, wooden legs, and parrots perched on shoulders. I bet their pitching coach was hitting the rum, giving the outlay of this game. I wonder if anyone on the pitching staff walked the plank back to the minors after today's performance.

Fortunately for the rest of the baseball world, these Pirates can't bat and run the bases forever. Inevitably, the third out will come and the Pirates have to take the field. Why, I don't know. When it came to pitching and defense, let's say that the Pirates have an explosive offense. Nicknamed the "Lumber Company" made sense, with their big wooden bats and what seemed like wooden mitts in the field. Just don't hit the ball to right field or to second base (Bill Mazeroski) and your chances of reaching aren't half-bad. Pittsburgh simply had trouble hiding six or seven mediocre defenders.

So as the Lumber Company taketh, they also giveth away. Cubs did some scoring of their own and all was well until the top of the eighth. Then with all the sluggers on the Pirates, who would have ever guessed that the light hitting shortstop, Gene ("Don't go down the …") Alley would crush two taters in the alley over the last two innings. (With all do respect to Chris Berman, my friends and I played with players' names three decades before there was an ESPN. Too bad we didn't have a patent). If you like symmetry, and who doesn't, Alley and Clemente made wonderful bookends for the Pirates this day. One homered in each of the first two innings, and the other in the last two. And when Gene Alley almost hits for the cycle, you know it's not your day.

One final observation. This happened to be the first time I ever saw a baseball game through binoculars. It was pretty cool until I focused on Al Oliver crushing a pitch well into the bleachers. Seeing the ball practically go splat up close and personal could make a kid lose his appetite. I dropped the eye aids as quick as I could, only to see Mr. Oliver circling the bases. This came just moments after Clemente made the same trip. Let's move on to the next game …

GAME 3: LOS ANGELES DODGERS VS. CHICAGO CUBS
FRIDAY, AUGUST 14

Numbers and baseball have enjoyed a long and fruitful marriage. Show me a player or fan who isn't up on numbers and I'll show you a neophyte to the sport. The list is too long to get into now, but it's hard to hold any significant or insignificant conversation about baseball without getting into things like stats, goals, and records.

For instance, one of my goals as a kid was to see each major league team play at least once. As a seventh grader averaging about four games per year, we were making steady progress. I also had this thing about seeing the more traditional teams (read better). Seeing the Yankees, Tigers, Redlegs, Giants, Pirates, Indians—now that's baseball. And today I will, for the first of many times, witness the Dodgers pound the Cubs.

What's the matter with me? The Cubs for many years would struggle against Triple A teams, and I expect them to beat the best? No wonder my won-lost record was horrid for the 70's. Take today, for instance. Did I really think that the Cub's pitcher, Jim Colborn, was going to get the best of Don Sutton? Why didn't we take more seriously the probable pitchers for these games?

Ladies' Day, that's why. In 1970, the Cubs offered my mom and my sister free admittance on certain days. So be quiet, and see if the Cubs can get to Sutton. After all, you are seeing one of the classiest organizations in baseball, whether you like them or not. It seemed that certain teams just understood the game better, and the Dodgers, along with clubs like the Orioles (and for a while, the Chisox) knew how to compete with pitching, defense, and speed against teams that had superior talent. And what superlatives can you add about where the Dodgers play, Chavez Ravine. What a masterpiece for baseball— with mountains and palm trees outside the ballpark, and Koufax and Sutton and Wills and Willie Davis within the ballpark, the experience could not be any more aesthetic.

Don Sutton. I had the chance to hear him in person at a coach's convention many years later. These were his highlights:

1. "I'd rather sell snow to an Eskimo than pitch in Wrigley Field." His lack of success in Chicago (with today's game as a perfect example) proves that. He did not pitch well in Wrigley for most of his career.

2. When asked to show us the proper grip of a spitter, he coyly responded, "Why don't you ask someone who threw a spitter?" I responded, "I am." Then the subject was changed.

3. When asked who the best hitter was that he ever faced, he did not hesitate: "Roberto Clemente."

4. He stressed, over and over, the psychology of baseball. He appreciates how catchers call games to bring the best out in you and to even enjoy the experience of pitching. (At this point I was hoping he'd change the subject again—it was getting a little too weird for me).

5. He did not want to be interrupted when he was pitching. He even went so far to say that visits to the mound were by "invitation only" once he matured as a pitcher.

6. This one I got from a newspaper account that relates to # 2 and # 5 above. One day an umpire came to the mound in an attempt to inspect the baseball. (Gee, Don, why would he do that?) Anyway, Sutton instructed the ump to "get your fat ass behind the plate." Strangely enough, the ump did not take kindly to that remark, and Sutton got the rest of the day off. If memory serves, the ump did get the ball, but only *after* he tossed the ball into the dirt in front of his catcher.

Unfortunately for Sutton, on this day he wasn't making sales pitches to Eskimos but fat pitches to Cubbies.

Gopher balls, no less. In the first inning, mind you. Yes sir, singles by Beckert and Williams preceded a walk to Hickman, and Joe Pepitone, he of hair dryer fame, put the Cubs up 4 nil. Two walks later and Mr. Sutton could shower up and pass on pitching responsibilities to Fred Norman (former Cub). The little lefty (ever notice how it always seems to be a little lefty but seldom a little righty? Must be an alliteration thing. Maybe we should start calling pitchers from the other side rugged righties, or if they're the Reuschels, rotund righties) restored order as the Cubs did not score again until the 6th.

For the Cubs, was this game a case of too much too soon? How can competitors not let up at least a little when holding a significant advantage so early in the game. Anyway, by the time the Cubs did score again, they were on the wrong side of a 7-6 game. They muscled three more homers in the latter innings, and did win home run derby that day, 4-3. Unfortunately, the Dodgers won the game, 13-9.

A few memorable things about that ballgame. Ernie Banks was at the game but not in uniform--he did some color commentary in the booth with Jack Brickhouse. My dad shared with me one comment from Mr. Cub: as Maury Wills reached base for the sixth time in six at bats, Ernie revealed that it was likely a case of showing off for the ladies (amusing at the time, maybe not so much after reading Ball Four). Talk about place setters, the top two slots in the Dodger lineup were retired *once* in twelve plate appearances (Bill Russell—the shortstop-to-be who was in right field that day—reached on an error, three singles, and a walk. Wills walked, doubled, and singled four times). But the story of this day was the long ball. Callison, Hundley, Williams and Pepitone all homered for the Cubs, and each had ample power. Now look at who homers for the Dodgers: Billy Grabarkewitz and Ted Sizemore. Billy G., a write-in candidate for the All-Star game, nailed two homers on his way to a seventeen home run season. He ended his career with 28 long flies, and I happened to see 7% of his career total on this one day. But wait, it gets better. Guess how many homers Ted Sizemore hit in 1970? I'll give you a clue—I happened to be present for all of them. Yes, one homer for the entire season, and it came with two outs and Willie Davis on base. That was pretty much the ballgame. When one team enjoys tremendous on-base prowess of the table setters and the power surge from the most unlikely of hitters, it's not too surprising that they win the game.

And though the home team has plenty of baserunners, hits, and runs, the inablility for any Cub pitcher to record one perfect inning in the contest screams incompetence. In fact, not one no-hit inning. More evidence to support Sutton's claim about selling to Eskimos.

GAME 4: NEW YORK METS VS. CHICAGO CUBS
FRIDAY, SEPTEMBER 4

A lot to discuss here. A pennant race, sort of. The Cubs are in the mix, as are the Mets. And we have one last trip to make to the ballpark at the outset of Labor Day weekend. One last trip to garner a victory. One last trip prior to the demands of school. And some Billy Williams news to spice things up—he returns to the lineup after taking the day off yesterday. At that point in time, he set the National League record for most consecutive games played, and trailed only Lou Gehrig in the history of the game. This impressive NL record would eventually fall to Steve Garvey, but Billy's dependability and durability take a back seat to no one.

All that being said, I think the biggest attraction of the day is the starting pitcher for the Gotham team. A young and sensational fireballer by the name of Nolan Ryan. Perhaps you've heard of him. Looking back, I think all in the NL, and perhaps all of baseball, are delighted he didn't hit his stride with the Mets. Could you imagine Seaver-Ryan-Koosman at the front end of the rotation for a decade or so? Mercy.

At this point in his career, Ryan had yet to find command of the strike zone. In this game he walks five in the first four frames. Cubs scratch out a couple tallies with a Hundley double in the second, and three free passes in the 3rd.

For the Cubs, it seems as though #49 had matters well in Hands until the 6th. That's when a three run bomb by Art Shamsky puts the Mets ahead, 3-2. Now with the famous Met pitching, the chances of going O-fer 1970 loomed large. (If you're keeping track, the O'Donnells have already seen Cub defeats at the hands of the Giants, Pirates, and Dodgers to stand at 0-3).

But hooray, a three run homer in the 7th by a clutch hitter, Jim Hickman, propels the Cubs to an eventual triumph, 7-4. In a game of bullpens, the Cubs came out on top. In fact, when examining the numerous changes made by both managers, one could see that both clubs saw themselves in the heat of a pennant race. Hardly going through the motions, Durocher went to his bullpen four times over the last three innings. Normally, Leo's stance toward pitchers likely took this tone, "Here's the effing ball, kid. Now get the eff out there and get those effing hitters out because I don't want to effing use our effing bullpen. Got that?" If the relievers were used, it would be a case of Phil Regan coming in for the final 2-3 innings after Fergie, Holtzman, or Hands went deep into the game. And Cub pitching had to be good when you consider who's in the outfield. The Cubs had folks like Pepitone and Hickman in center field. My gosh, I think 70% of the fans on senior citizen day ran faster than Hickman. Callison, a fine fielder in his day, was about 3-4 years removed from his day. And Williams gave you decent but not exceptional defense in left.

The Mets' skipper, Gil Hodges, not to be outdone, employs 18 players this day with Joe Foy the only position player on the roster not used. The quantity and rapidity of substitutions demonstrate a desire for these managers to give their team every edge possible in order to find a way to win. Five pinch-hitters in a nine inning game slowed the game down but heightened the drama. Unlike the last time I saw these two teams do battle in '64, this match was well played and well coached with talent on both clubs. Watching the dreaded Mets lose was sweet, and their lineup commanded some respect because of the 1969 experience. Agee, Jones, Clendenon, Shamsky, Boswell, Grote, Harrelson, Swoboda, to go along with their renowned pitching staff, proved their mettle against great odds. Theirs was a team not nearly as frightening as the Bucs, but still one that you couldn't underestimate. Just ask the Orioles.

Would this victory with less than a month to go over the reigning World Champs get the Cubs going, drive them toward the pennant, and exact sweet revenge on the Mets?

POSTSEASON

Nope. Neither the Cubs nor the Mets, but the Pirates take the division. No surprise, and neither is their opponent in the NLCS—the Big Red Machine. They say that good pitching beats good hitting, but with these two teams it's more a case of mediocre pitching against great hitting. And Cincy prevails, clubbing the Buccos in three games (when the series was a best-of-five). In the Series, they'll face the Orioles who knocked off the Twins, just as they did in '69.

This time, we won't have to hear about that Amazin' team from NY ad naseum, just two really good teams with stars galore. In truth, I doubt if any team could hit with the Reds, but the Orioles could pitch and defend better than Cincy. Baseball is a team game, supposedly, but sometimes one person can completely dominate, especially on the sport's biggest stage. This series belonged to Brooks Robinson. Whereas Agee and Swoboda shared the defensive spotlight from a year ago, Robinson was a one person highlight sensation. *Everything* hit his way resulted in an out. Robbing Lee May, robbing Johnny Bench, going to his right and throwing from foul ground, diving to his left to snare a liner—it approached the absurd. Throw in some clutch hitting (.429 average with 2 HR and 6 RBI in 5 games) and you have a performance for the ages ... or at least until next year. Maybe the second most remembered memory of Brooks and a few of his mates was the eye black rubbed under their eyes. As a kid I thought it looked so cool, and I just remember Robinson, Davey Johnson, and Mark Belanger always seemed to be wearing it. I was told that it helped to minimize the glare from the sun. Heck, the way the Oriole infielders fielded, I'd put the stuff on for night games. Cincy proved no match for the Birds this year, just too much Brooks. Baltimore sprinted to a 3-0 lead in the Series, dropped the 4th game, and clinched in five.

1971

He has the aura. Today they'd call it swag. Some might see it as cockiness. Frequently it's referred to as a presence. Whatever the word, Randy Hundley has it. Not arrogance, for he truly is a humble man, but not in want of confidence. He's probably used to heads turning toward his direction as he walks into a room. You wouldn't associate Carly Simon's "You're So Vain," with him, but having strangers stop and look your way for the majority of your adult life has to do something to one's psyche.

It would be a stretch to say he could still play today, but I'd guess that his current weight, some thirty-six years after he caught his last game, falls within 20 pounds of his weight when he played for the Cubs (that is, his weight *before* catching both ends of a July doubleheader). His hair lights up the room, not a drab gray but a striking white. A ruddy complexion suggests a healthy lifestyle with ample time on the links. But the most memorable feature has to be the drawl. Not a whole lot of folks from the Midwest talk like Randy Hundley. He'd have a devil of a time trying to impersonate a teammate—he'd have to use mime. My daughter, hardly a baseball fan, heard him speak twice. The second time she heard his voice was on the radio, and within moments she proudly proclaimed, "Oh, that's Randy Hundley."

Hundley, catcher for the Cubs in those spirited seasons of the late 60's through the mid 70's, bears no malice toward his skipper Leo Durocher who at times has been vilified for using and abusing his players.

"He was a good manager," Hundley freely attests. "I had no problem with playing as many games as I did." So take that, all you Leo bashers. If anyone's opinion carries weight on the controversial issue of playing time, it should be the players. And while Hundley did not gleefully speak of Durocher with a smile on his face and a twinkle in his eye, he matter-of-factly praised his managerial prowess and supported his decisions.

Games Played. This is one Hundley stat that necessitates a double take. One year he caught 160 games. Please don't gloss over that number—160 games in the intense daytime heat and humidity of Chicago. This topic is dear to his rebel heart: "I'm most proud of this record—there have just been a few catchers that have caught as many as 150 games in a season (editor's note #1: I believe the number is 14). I've done it three times and my son Todd has done it once" (editor's note #2: one more game caught in 1966 would make it four times).

In convincing fashion Hundley accepts the wear and tear on his body. It's been frequently noted how ballplayers from this era got scared. Not between the lines, not that at all, but fear from the bench. The likelihood of a player not playing and the backup taking your place and keeping your place is more than myth (ask Wally Pipp). Talking to Hundley one gets the sense that ballplayers, while relishing the perks of a big leaguer, did not presume a whole lot. Epitomized by Hundley, they worked hard at their craft. It was a game, a job, a passion, and a sport they loved, but it was also played with an occasional glance over the shoulder. Therein lies the reason why veterans did not always embrace and welcome rookies. Ed Farmer, White Sox broadcaster, speaks of the competition at the major league level when he saw other players as "trying to take food from my family's mouth."

Here's Hundley on a variety of players he played with and against ...

- On Fergie Jenkins, "He gave up some home runs, but hardly with anyone on base. What helped him out is that he could also hit." (He went on to suggest that Jenkins, because of his adept hitting, did not have to be lifted for a pinch hitter in the late innings of a close game).
- On roommate Bill Hands, "A good pitcher, but couldn't hit a lick." (Hundley and Hands were traded together to the Cubs from the Giants in December of '65. In return, the Cubs sent Lindy McDaniel, Don Landrum, and Jim Rittwage to San Francisco. I think Rittwage was the key to the whole deal).
- On Ken Holtzman, "I told him to take that slider of his and stick it." When asked if he found it unusual for a pitcher to have a good slider and a good curve, Hundley agreed. As Jack Brickhouse would

say about Holtzman's curve, "it was like trying to hit a ball falling off a table."

- On Ron Santo, "Sometimes I'd just have to say to him, 'Will you shut the dang up?!' People may not know this, but there were threats made on his life. If these happened to occur on the road, we (his teammates) would make sure to sit nowhere near him on the bench."
- On Joe Pepitone, "The funniest guy I ever played with. He imitated a woman one time as he came on the plane and it had me in stitches."
- On Bob Gibson, "The best pitcher."
- On Willie Mays, "The best all-around player."

Etched in my mind is one play from the infamous '69 season. The fading Cubs were playing the surging Mets late in the season at Shea Stadium. A Met runner was trying to score. The throw home looked to beat the sliding runner, easily. After the play at the plate, the catcher (Hundley) turns to see what the other base runner is doing. Dramatic pause. Then Hundley, in a delayed reaction, jumps like I've never seen a catcher jump before or since. The runner at home was called safe.

Hundley's version: "I tagged that runner so hard coming in from third I was afraid the ball was going to pop loose. Then I turned to see what the other runner was doing since it wasn't the third out. I didn't hear the umpire's call, but I did hear the roar of the crowd. When I turned and saw that the ump called him safe, I went nuts."

Randy Hundley. You know how that saying goes about mediocre players, something like statistics don't tell the whole story. With Hundley, it's not just a polite thing to say, it's the truth. His lifetime numbers fail to overwhelm, starting with a .236 lifetime batting average. I'm guessing that the average Cub fan from that era would guess Hundley's average to stand 15 points higher, at least. But his clutch hitting, his durability, his leadership, his ability to call a game and handle pitchers, and his competitive spirit don't show up on the back of a baseball card, nor would they likely impress sabermetric disciples. With three Hall-of-Famers in their everyday lineup, the Cubs needed role players and supporting actors. None played his role better than Hundley.

GAME 5: ST. LOUIS CARDINALS VS. CHICAGO CUBS
WEDNESDAY, APRIL 7

Lots of ways to tell public school talk from Catholic school talk. For one, public schoolers don't moan and groan about Sister Mary Agatha. She was tough. I liked her though and being good at math and being a relatively good kid scored me some benefits that other kids didn't enjoy. Some kids have street cred; I had nun cred. I'll never forget the time this one classmate and I were caught red-handed doing something naughty. I mean there was no way to alibi out of this one. I thought to myself this ought to be good—one of her favorites (me) and one of her not-so-favorites (him) doing the same thing. Is my reputation going to lessen the punishment for him, or is his bad rep going to get me in trouble? After a dramatic pause of looking at both of us, you could hear the wheels churning. Then Sister gave *him* a thorough scolding. Me, never a word. I used this example with my kid brothers to tell them to be good, so you won't get into as much trouble when you do get into trouble.

Public school lingo consisted of school boards, school districts, middle school, and junior high. I really had no clue what the first two meant, and not once did we ever call it middle school or junior high; it was always the nominal grade level. Moreover, we had a huge advantage over Catholic kids who attended public schools—we didn't have to take any religion classes on our time. Back then it was called CCD (Confraternity of Catholic Doctrine) and it was a pain. Think about it--subjects during the school day aren't torturous enough; these poor fools had to go at night, while some even went on Saturday. They had to be getting massive plenary indulgences that we could only dream of.

So for this outing we're not in junior high but in eighth grade, and we're feeling like pioneers. For the first time, no one is going to the game from our party over the age of fifteen. A bunch of us, about five or so, bug our parents enough so that we can see the second game of the year. (The opener, of course, is impossible to snag tickets, so we decided to go to the next game). No school due to Easter break (publics would call it spring break) and we plan to bask in our newfound freedom. That is, once one of our parents drives us to the bus stop—we weren't *that* free. I recall the parent talking to his son on the way to the bus. The conversation went something like this:

> Dad: I hope you have a nice day.
> Kid: I will if the Cubs win (I swear this isn't me speaking).
> Dad: Can't you just enjoy the day regardless if the Cubs win or lose?
> Kid: (Silence, disgruntled silence).

My sentiments lie with the kid. The parent makes more sense, they always do, but the kid speaks the truth. Here's a question I asked a lot back then, and still do today: if you knew in advance that the White Sox/Cubs were going to lose, would you still go? Conversely, if the team you're rooting for is assured a victory, to what lengths would you go in order to witness this triumph? For me, the answer to the first question is a "No" and I'm tempted to respond with a "Whatever it takes," for the second one.

The CTA bus cruises down Addison Street, averaging a solid 14 MPH. I heard that these vehicles can do zero to sixty in a day and a half. If the infinite stoplights don't nail us, the incessant bus stops do. And should we get on a roll for a couple of blocks, undoubtedly some son-of-a-buck driver in front of us will want to turn left in a single lane of traffic. No left turn arrows back then, mind you. A junior high student could board the bus as an 8th grader and exit as a sophomore, in college.

But what's the rush—friends, fun, Cub game, no adults and no school. No snail-moving bus, no pollutants in the nostrils, no standing in the aisle and lurching forward upon every stop could ruin this day. I wondered what could possibly bring us down.

Try this, 14-3 Cardinals. That's the baseball Cardinals, not the football Cardinals. They limited the Cubs to a mere field goal. By the time the baby Bears batted in the 3rd, they have zero and the Deadbirds have six. Steve Carlton, working his way toward super-stardom, held the Cubs in check, while the Cardinal offense constantly harassed Cub pitching without decimating it. In fact, if this were a game of home run derby, the Cubs would be triumphant by a score of 2 nil (courtesy of Messrs. Pepitone and Williams).

Not much to say about this woeful game, but the Cardinal lineup deserves some acknowledgement. The first surprise to me is who is NOT batting first, and that would be Lou Brock. He's hitting third, but it's tantamount to having two lead-off men come to bat in the first inning. The actual leadoff hitter is one of the Alou brothers, Matty. Batting second is Ted Sizemore, and with his power he could use more size. The cleanup dude is Joe Torre. Yes, that Joe Torre. A slam dunk Hall-of-Famer as a manager, but back in the day he was a splendid hitter. He was on his way to having an unconscious season with 230 hits, 127 RBI's, and a batting average of, are you ready for this, .363. Joe would never approach those numbers again, but he ended his career with a lifetime average of .297. And from his catcher days in Milwaukee to the corner infield position player with the Cards, it seemed as Torre lost about half his body weight. One more surprise in this lineup: Joe Hague hitting before Ted Simmons. I don't get that, especially with Simmons being a switch hitter. But that day Red Schoendienst, long-time Redbird manager, looked like a genius as Hague knocks out three hits to Simmons' one. Julian Javier, the second baseman with specs, bats 8th, one slot ahead of Carlton.

The day did have its light moments. To some people, like my friends and I, sneaking down into the box seats to watch the game was part of the baseball experience, just like the 7th inning stretch. On this particular afternoon, we didn't mess around. As the Cubs were getting clobbered, we placed our bottoms in seats which were directly behind home plate about five rows from the field. We watched the game in peace for about an inning. That's when an Andy Frain usher spotted us and strikes up a conversation that went like this:

Usher: Excuse me, but can I see your tickets?

Us: Sorry, but we misplaced them.

Usher: I'm afraid you'll have to leave. These seats are reserved for Mr. Wrigley.

Us: And you'll never guess who gave us our tickets!

It was the first and only time I'm chased by an usher who was laughing.

What started as a slow and deliberate trek to the ballpark results in an even slower commute home. Rush hour traffic in full swing now, on top of everything else. But at least we're a little more grown up, handling this "adult-less" rite of passage with ease. And when tomorrow comes, we still won't have school.

GAME 6: ATLANTA BRAVES VS. CHICAGO CUBS
MONDAY, JUNE 14

"The coldest winter of my life was a summer in San Francisco."

I wonder if sitting in the grandstands in Wrigley Field on this summer afternoon would change this person's opinion. It was so chilly my mom purchased Cub sweatshirts from the souvenir stand for her kids. A noteworthy transaction because these white "noodies" (some kids call those sweatshirts without the hoodie) cost three times as much as our general admission tickets, and more than six times our typical hot dog lunch. Worth it, though, because with that lovable teddy bear engulfing the famous red Cub logo in a sea of white cotton, the shivering stopped, numbness evaporated, and scorekeeping duties resumed.

But the shivering resumes hours later, and this time it's due to nerves. Cubs bat late in the game and trail the Bravos, 2-0. Pitching for Atlanta is the Hall-of-Famer-to-be, Phil Niekro. Last time I saw him pitch here he was on the down side to Kenny Holtzman's no-hitter. He pitched well that day, too, allowing just a 3-run homer to Santo in the first inning. Today, it looks like his turn to claim a masterpiece, knuckling his way to a 3 hit whitewash.

The third time through the lineup, though, Cub hitters show some life. Back-to-back safeties from Johnny Callison and Chris Cannizzaro (remember him? A former back-up catcher on the Mets) may signal a weakening Niekro. Then crunch time in the 8th: 2 on, 1 out, and Billy Williams batting. One hall-of-famer vs. another. A bouncer to the pitcher results in only one out, not two, and the Cubs still have life. Had it not been for Williams' hustle to first to beat the double play, the Cubs don't have this opportunity. Randy Hundley's favorite cut-up, Joe Pepitone, bats. First time up for Pepi, he fans. Ditto in the fourth inning. 7th inning, he flies to center. Now it's the eighth inning—and the fourth look at Niekro's knuckler. After allowing just 4 baserunners in the first six innings, the Cubs have had several reach in each of the last two. Time for a bullpen change sponsored by _____ (fill in the name of your favorite oil change). Isn't that what you would do, change pitchers?

Nope, and thank you very much, Luman Harris, manager of the Braves. With one swing Pepi launches the ball through the chilly breeze and we have a one run lead. Much happiness as Pepi and his toupee bounce around the bases. I just love it when the home team that you're rooting for takes the lead in the bottom of the eighth. The only thing better would be the home team taking the lead in any inning that followed.

But with batsmen like Garr, Aaron, and Cepeda as your 2-3-4 hitters, the Cubs still have work to do. Who ya gonna call? Cub closer!

Wrong again. The Cub closer, Phil Regan, happened to be the Cub starter on this unorthodox day. It would be his only start of the year. To whom does Mgr. Durocher turn?

I'll give you a few clues—and I'll give you a dollar if you get the right answer. He pitched for the Kansas City Athletics in 1965, and then for nobody at the major league level until 1971 (this year). Need another hint? OK, his nickname is "Stretch." Yes sir, Willie McCovey comes in and gets the save. Just kidding, it's a guy by the name of Ron Tompkins. He pitched in the big leagues for two seasons and finished with as many wins as you and I put together (that would be zero, I'm assuming).

But Tompkins finishes with three career saves, and on this frosty afternoon I happen to witness one-third of them. A Cub sweatshirt and a game winning rally in the last at bat all on the same day. Not bad.

GAME 7: PITTSBURGH PIRATES VS. CHICAGO CUBS
MONDAY, JULY 5

I'm sure you've come across folks that demand order, stability, and control. They often take the form of coaches and mothers-in-law. Their players must be at practice two minutes early, every day. They have to sit in the same chair, every night. They have to frequent the same restaurant and order the same thing, they have to make so many shots before they leave the gym, and they have to take the same route to work. In short, the order freaks can be a pain to us as we, I'm sure, are a pain to them.

The wrap-around game sticks in the craw of these folks; I know it does because they're on record for saying so. If a weekend series lapses into Monday, they get uneasy. I'm serious. Most of the western world wouldn't notice nor care if they did notice, but that wrap-around game bugs these folks like a piece of steak lodged in a molar.

It's not the wrap-around game that bugs me today; rather, it's the Pirate lineup. Why do I go to these games? Where's my logic? Do I think that the Titanic is not going to sink if I see the movie often enough? Then why do I think the Cubs have a chance against Pittsburgh?

1969 gets all the attention, but truth be known, the Cubs fielded better teams than that one. Take a look at this model, for instance. Who would you rather have, Don Young or Joe Pepitone? Rich Nye or Milt Pappas? Al Spangler or Johnny Callison? (Answers: Pepitone, Pappas, and Callison). Throw in the core group from '69 with no one past his prime save for Ernie, and you have visions of pennants. So what went wrong?

Today's opponent, that's what went wrong. The Pirates were to the Cubs as the Bulls were to the Cavs during the MJ years. Just couldn't get past them, no matter what. And there's no shame to that, not when you're trying to beat a team that has Al Oliver batting seventh. *Batting seventh.* Seventh is the spot reserved for a weak hitting catcher who's followed by the weaker hitting shortstop. At one time during the 70's, Red Sox propaganda boasted that their ninth hitter was Butch Hobson, a 30 HR guy. I never did buy the Bosox hype, however, for this reason: how did the team perform, especially on offense, on the road? Comparable to the Cubs in this regard, take them out of Fenway/Wrigley and they're just another team.

The Bucs, on the other hand, seemed to mash the ball on the road and in Pittsburgh with equal ferocity. In case you forgot, today's lineup had Al Oliver, one of the finest hitters in my lifetime, batting seventh. And Pops Stargell isn't even in the lineup! Lions and Tigers and Pirates, oh my.

A quick recap of this game shows the Cubs scratching out a run in the first and the second, which is where the game was lost. So many times it's not the zero runs in an inning that kills you, but the lone run when the team should score three or four. They had a chance to knock out Steve Blass early—six hits in two frames (and five of those coming with 2 outs) and only two runs to show for it. I'm guessing that 99% of the people at the ballpark felt that two runs were not going to beat the Pirates. Leading the way with this thinking was probably the Cub pitching staff. One of the cardinal rules in baseball—in the vast majority of games (close to 90%) the winning team scores more runs in one inning than the losing team scores in the entire game. Single tallies are like field goals in football—better than nothing, but often not enough.

Nevertheless, Ken Holtzman cruises through the lineup twice, retiring 11 straight Bucs at one point. But lightning from the Lumber Company strikes Holtzman in the sixth. In this frame my scorecard reads like a tennis match for the visitors: double-single-double-single. Game over? Hardly. The Pirates do an encore performance the next time up, with a double and a slew of singles (the pitcher himself knocks in two). The good news is that on offense the Cubs on-base percentage is tremendous with twelve hits; the bad news is their slugging percentage is weak—only one extra base hit and that's a double. A lot of hits, a lot of base runners, a lot of runners stranded, but not a lot of runs. Final score: 6-2, bad guys.

Has this ever happened to you as a kid: you're going up against an excellent opponent in something, say ping-pong, and you're shocking yourself by being extremely competitive? Heck, at some point it looks like you're going to win with ease. Then you notice something. Your opponent has been playing you with his weak hand. So he switches hands and skunks you. I kind of felt this way watching the Pirates. Were they teasing us by not scoring anything for five frames? Like trying 50% or so until the middle innings, and then the lights go on (figuratively speaking, of course, for this is Wrigley Field) and they start competing at a higher level. How else do you explain nada for the first hour and a half, then in a span of ten batters, eight hit safely? Sandbagging, that's what I think. Cruel, too.

My friend Pete and I trudge to the el tracks behind Waveland Avenue after the game. His trudge is livelier than mine, for he's a sincere White Sox fan who won't lose sleep over this loss. But to get our minds on happier things, we play a game called "Name those players." It goes like this: name four current Sox players who used to be on the Angels. I'll be hanged if Pete doesn't come up with Rick Reichardt, Tom Bradley, Jay Johnstone, and the toughie, Tom Egan. For his turn, he'll ask which Cubs used to play for the Dodgers. This will take a while, so I stall by pointing to something outside the window (possibly a kid wearing an Orioles hat or a cute girl. Believe it or not, our heads would probably turn more quickly if we see the Orioles hat). "Okay," I clear my voice and rattle off, "Paul Popovich, Phil Regan and .... (dramatic pause), Jim Hickman," quite proud of myself.

"Not quite," my friend retorts, "you forgot Durocher."

"Coaches and managers don't count," I reply. "Besides, he was terrible."

"True."

We take a break as the el makes yet another stop. No pretty girls nor Oriole hats, but this one big black dude came on wearing a Pirate hat.

"Hey," I whisper to Pete, "Stargell took the day off to ride the el?!"

We laugh for a moment, than back to business. "Okay, name two Pirates who used to play for ..."

GAME 8: PHILADEPHIA PHILLIES VS. ST. LOUIS CARDINALS
THURSDAY JULY 22

Watching a ballgame in a foreign city compares favorably to sampling a new flavor at Baskin-Robbins. You don't quite know what you're going to get, but it'll probably be good. Baseball and ice cream, hard to mess up either.

One dark episode on this journey to St. Louis—there is this photo of me wearing a Cardinals' cap. Why? Of all the irresponsible and immature things I've done in my youth, of all the things that can be held against me as black-mail, why can't I have this one back? Why did I let someone take a picture with this horrid thing on my head? What can I possibly say if this image gets into the wrong hands? What could I possibly tell my grandkids? Something like, "No, kids, grandpa didn't rob banks, do drugs, or forget to recycle, but he did wear a Cardinal hat once. Please kids, think before you act. Remember, you're representing our family." Oh, how the iniquities of our youth can haunt us.

On the bright side, there was the *Arch*. The *Arch* was, is and forever will be cool—one of the best landmarks. And it's surprisingly old. I'm thinking the average Joe or Joan would be off by several years if he/she guessed when it was constructed (answer: the mid 60's). Like the *Needle* in Seattle and other splendid architecture, it is a decade or so ahead of its time, and ages gracefully.

Then there's something else we could never do in the western suburbs of Chicago—take a trip on the country's most famous river. I'm thinking that the steamboat would be the second best way to navigate these waters; unfortunately, nobody that day was selling sight-seeing tours on a raft. The steamboat ride was nice, but I can't recall how many times I received reprimands from the parental units for pretending to throw my younger brothers over the edge—had to be close to double-digits.

One evening on this trip my folks tried to incorporate some religion during our secular vacation by reserving a room at the retreat grounds called "Our Lady of the Snows." I believe it was in Belleville, IL—home of tennis ace, Jimmy Connors. Anyway, this setting was not a good fit for my adolescent hyperness. As my folks left me and my brothers in the room for the evening (not one of their wisest decisions) neither the management nor my folks (usually one-in-the-same, but not tonight) appreciated my constant rough-housing with my siblings. Fortunately, there was a bit of a distraction to mini-mize the carnage: on TV the Annual College All-Star Football Game from Soldier Field. For many years the Chicago Tribune sponsored this game in late summer that pitted the reigning NFL champs against a conglomeration of fresh grad All-Americans from the finest football factories across America. This game, promoted ad nauseam by the Trib, was seldom competitive. Think about it—a bunch of talented college kids whose team chemistry stretches a whole three weeks versus the best team of professionals. Now who do you think is going to win? I do remember the Bears playing in this game when I was a tike, and being a little surprised that my old man did not root for the home team. I understand now but didn't then. And another lasting memory is watching the Green Bay Packers play in this game, again and again it seemed.

But this is a baseball book, so it's time to leave the touristy stuff and turn our attention toward Busch Stadium. I shall now follow the sage advice of Thumper's mother and if I can't say anything nice, I won't say anything at all. So here are the nice things about Busch Stadium: you can see the Arch from our seats in the upper deck, and it's cool when the Cardinals do something good, like hit a home run, because this electronic Redbird on their jumbo scoreboard (how quaint) flies around, lands back on his perch, and tips his cap. So there, all you Cardinal fans, I just said more nice things about your organization than I have ever heard Cardinal fans say about the Chicago National League ballclub. It feels good to be the bigger person.

Then there is the team itself. It pains me to acknowledge this, but this team, like so many other Deadbird teams, plays the game well. I will never admit this to a Cardinal face-to-face, in a bar, at the ballpark, or in a court of law, but the Cardinals over the years know what they're doing. They've had some lemon teams, like any other franchise, but as a rule they do okay. And why shouldn't they? You've got names like Lou Brock (at this point in the sea-son hitting .336), Joe Torre (sizzling at .353 in the midst of his batting champ year. FYI—Glenn Beckert would place second), and Ted Simmons (the long-haired Simba batting .299) Add a couple of pitchers like Bob Gibson and Steve Carlton, and you should be in the running, at the very least.

Gibson actually pitched a gem that nite. I don't know what was sharper—his pitching or those home Cardinal uniforms. Very white and very red. It was helmet nite, so my brothers and I leave the stadium (I hesitate to call it a ballpark) with free enemy stuff. At that time in my life I collected hats and even a few helmets from different major league teams, and pretended to be my favorite players from those teams.

This game itself was not a fair fight—not when you have the last **three** Phillie batters under .200 facing off against the best pitcher in my lifetime (anyone from the Clemens, Maddux, Palmer, Hunter, or even Koufax camp care to argue? No, I didn't think so). Inexplicably, Gibson's record this nite was 6-9. Honest, that's what it was. I understand that he was dealing with a lot of injuries this year, but Gibson at 6-9 is akin to Einstein getting a 74 on a math test. But this night proved to be different. Gibby yielded four hits--two to Larry Bowa--and no runs in a complete game whitewash (fitting, for this is Tom Sawyer territory).

The highlight for me came when Brock homered in the 3rd inning. His ball barely missed the left field foul pole. (I thought of this location when I saw Mark McGuire drive his 62nd homer of the year some 40 years later). Brock's heroics set off the aforementioned bird on the scoreboard. Not as cool as the White Sox exploding scoreboard, but not bad either.

We probably were Gibson's good luck charm as his fortunes changed dramatically at this point in the season. Counting this game, he wins 10 of his last 14 decisions to end up 16-13. Just too much pride and intensity to have a losing record. The other Hall-of-Famer on that staff, Lefty Carlton, would wind up with a 20-9 record. But neither stat would matter, as Pittsburgh won the division easily.

St. Louis: hot temperature, friendly people, fine baseball team, but no Wrigley Field. Not even close. Does a good team without Wrigley Field trump a mediocre squad with Wrigley Field? It depends who you're asking. If you ask my head, he says "yes." If you ask my heart, he says "no." If you ask me, I say heart wins. It's not all about wins and losses.

GAME 9: BALTIMORE ORIOLES VS. CHICAGO WHITE SOX
SUNDAY, AUGUST 15

As a little kid, family members tell me that I pronounced the last name of the baseball team from Baltimore just like I pronounced the name of a famous cookie. Makes sense, because while I didn't know much about birds, I did enjoy cookies almost as much as I liked baseball. The Orioles and the Oreos both get high marks.

Very few teams I liked outside Chicago as much as this Baltimore franchise (the Twins and Tigers make the short list as well). I see the O's as the A.L.'s version of the LA Dodgers. Pitching, defense, and class—three terms that come to mind immediately. Think back to that cocky animated bird perched upon the head of Earl Weaver. I think that either one (the bird or Weaver) would give this club a distinct advantage. To have both on the enemy side, mixed in with the Robinsons, the Palmers, the McNallys, the Powells, the Cuellars, etc., seemed unfair. But back to that bird logo—it was baseball's version of the Ram helmet. How were you ever supposed to beat such a smug creature; just like how were you ever supposed to tackle that battering ram? Both seemed indefatigable, and in Baltimore's case it practically was. If logos could talk, this one wouldn't. Its silent, silly grin is deafening. Its taunting smirk suggests: "do you *really* think your team has a chance?"

When using the word "class" to describe this franchise, one must be careful. If class means something along the lines of Cary Grant, we have a serious disconnect with the manager. I think the only way class and manager would be used in the same sentence would be something like this: "Earl Weaver finished second-to-last in his conduct grade for kindergarten class, and it went down from there." If I had been in any position of authority that claimed Weaver as a subordinate, I'd give serious thought about changing professions. He seemed downright cruel to umps, and this statement has been validated many times over by the late umpire, Ron Luciano. So class for the players, the front office, and the Oriole product. Some would say take off the first two letters of class, and then you'd have the O's skipper.

But think of other words when discussing Weaver. I'm guessing that any except "loser" would set well with Weaver. As long as his team won, he could give a rat's bottom about labels. Jim Palmer, Weaver's love-hate ace, put it like this: "No other manager had a greater will-to-win than Earl Weaver."

And win they did—World Series participants in '69,'70,'71. What surprises me is not this consistent level of success, but rather grabbing the Series Crown just once in three tries. Regardless, this team taught me what it takes to win at the highest level: a few superstars, a bunch of players knowing their role and selflessly fulfilling it, and a manager who can maximize players' performance over the long haul. The Orioles got great mileage from personnel that paled in stardom compared to other clubs (think of the Angel teams in the 80's, the Indian teams in the 90's, or even, ahem, the Cubs of '69). I learned for the first time that a team of inferior talent who plays the game well and for each other will defeat superior talent who pays little attention to detail and puts stats ahead of W's.

Okay, so given that adulation, what chance do the Sox have on this glorious Sunday afternoon? Believe it or not, they out-Orioled the Orioles. They pitched and defended themselves to a victory. A sweet 2-1 win over the Oreos.

These Birds in this season had something that the baseball world will probably never see again: a quartet of twenty-game winners on the pitching staff. Let that sink in. In an era when all of baseball won't have four pitchers with 20 win seasons for an entire year, the O's had *4 on one team **in one season.*** Mercy. Fortunately for us, the Ringo Starr of this foursome, Pat Dobson, hurled against Chisox ace, Wilbur Wood. His knuckleball baffled many a hitter this season, as we'll see later. So with excellent pitching and solid defense, another ingredient that figures in nicely to the winning recipe is scoring first. So just imagine what the Sox did in the first inning? Bill Melton tripled in lead-off man Walt Williams, who had walked. That's right, Bill Melton tripled. That represented one-half of the triples he'd hit for the entire season, and one-ninth of the triples he'd blast in his career. Must have been one of those Ron Santo triples in which any other ballplayer would have an inside-the-park home run. But Sox score first, and let's take comfort in knowing that the team that scores first wins more often than not.

The score remained 1-zip until the Oriole fifth. That's when F. Robby singled and Boog Powell doubled him home. Tension grew, as the Sox had to figure out another way to score. Time now to speak out of both sides of my mouth. Did you ever notice that teams with an early lead seem to have difficulty scoring later? Maybe it's complacency, maybe it's a sense of sportsmanship of not wanting to run up the score, maybe it's the other team buckling down, maybe it's me imagining things… but I've seen teams with early leads have to figure out a way to regain some momentum later. As mentioned, teams that score first do usually win, but it's seldom easy.

The White Sox did score again (I already gave you the score), and here's how it happened. Perhaps the flakiest player of the 70's, Jay Johnstone, doubled leading off the sixth. What followed is something that Manager Weaver disdained: the sacrifice bunt. He once said you only get 27 outs, and why give one away by bunting. His offensive strategy, repeated many times, is the three run homer. Could you imagine Frank Robinson bunting a man over when he's already in scoring position? Seems absurd, but that's precisely what Mgr. Chuck Tanner of the Sox had his 3rd place hitter, Mike Andrews, do. (Yes, the same Mike Andrews of World Series infamy when he later played for Oakland). So now the situation is this: home team batting in the sixth in the midst of a pitcher's duel, man on third and the clean-up hitter steps to the plate. A twenty-game winner in the making against the team's leading RBI guy, Melton, who had already tripled. Fun stuff, no?

Dobson wins this time, as Melton grounds out to Mark Belanger with Johnstone holding third. If I'm an Oriole fan I'm thinking, "Whew, dodged that bullet. Let's put this next hitter away and let our offense win the game." Possibly Dobson let up after retiring the Sox best run producer. A walk follows to a decent hitter, Rick Reichardt, but then a considerable downgrade is next in the person of Steve Huntz. A part-time player at best is Huntz, but he's a full-time hero at least for today. He singles in what is to be the winning run. Tough game to figure out.

The Orioles don't have Wood figured out, with Wood retiring eight in a row in the later innings. Wilbur walks Powell again, and then it's five more consecutive outs. Wood has his complete game victory over the "best damn team in baseball", according to Weaver. A well-played, well-earned victory over a great team.

GAME 10: DETROIT TIGERS VS. CHICAGO WHITE SOX
WEDNESDAY, AUGUST 18

My oh my, for the first 13 years, 8 months and 7 days of my life I saw neither the Baltimore Orioles nor the Detroit Tigers, two of my favorite teams, play in person. Now in a span of eighty hours I'll be seeing them both. Not only that, but we get to see the Sox ace, Wilbur Wood, which gives us the best chance to see another win for the home team.

Now have you been paying attention? There is a definite abnormality in these opening lines, can you tell us what it is?

Okay, you in the back wearing that bright red White Sox cap, what do you have?

Did I write August 18? Why, yes I did. Very good attention to detail, and for your keen observation, you win a prize--here are three baseball cards. Look carefully, because each card is a White Sox shortstop from 1971: Rich Morales, Luis Alvarado, and Bee Bee Richard. Truly a three-headed monster if there ever was one.

The kid with the Sox hat knew. Wilbur Wood, after chucking a complete game victory against the World Champs, is on the mound with *two days rest.* Granted that the knuckleball does not put a great strain on one's arm, but still—two days rest? Tells me two things: 1) the resilience of Wood, and 2) the lack of depth in the Sox starting rotation.

But the Sox did have quality pitchers, honest they did. Bart Johnson, Tom Bradley, and a young Terry Forster can bring the heat. Toss in a couple of seasoned vets like Joe Horlen and Tommy John and you have some reputable performers. No doubt, though, that Wood's the unequivocal ace. How good was he? Try on some of these numbers he put up in '71: 334 innings pitched (today 200 is considered a workhorse). 22 complete games. An ERA of 1.91. 22 victories (the first of four consecutive 20 win seasons).

He better be good, because the lineup he's facing would make Walter Johnson wince. Detroit features pretty much the same characters from the '68 team, which won it all. Imagine for a moment that you're the Detroit manager, Billy Martin. How comfortable would you feel if you had these players <u>not</u> playing: Norm Cash, Dick McAuliffe, and Jim Northrup? Household names, at least in my house, on the bench and at the ready. Then look at the players who are going to get the four at-bats or so: Al Kaline, Willie Horton, Bill Freehan, and Mickey Stanley. Guys whose baseball cards I covet. For you old-school fans who appreciated the lineups on the Old Comiskey scoreboard, here's how the heart of the Tiger lineup read: 6 RF, 23 LF, 11 C, 24 CF. And don't forget 3, 5, 25, & 26 on the pines just waiting for a righty to relieve the left-handed Wood. That would be, in order, McAuliffe ("nuts"), Northrup, Cash, and the Gator—Gates Brown.

Perusing the scorecard, you know Wood did not have his best stuff when he faced 7 men in the first inning, but allowed just one run. From then on, he was in command. Six hits and one run sprinkled over the last eight frames. Would that be good enough to win?

I haven't said anything up to this point about the Tiger hurler, but I should. He was second banana to Mickey Lolich, who for many years was second banana to Denny McLain. This banana in '71 happened to be Joe Coleman, who's known for a couple of things: he won 20 games in '71 (so a battle of 20 game winners this evening) and to prove it was not a fluke, he earned 23 wins in '73. But perhaps of more interest to Cub fans, Joe Coleman fathered a son who has pitched for the Cubs, Casey Coleman. I doubt he'll ever enjoy the success of his old man, but you never know.

The White Sox knot the game at 1 in the third when Pat Kelly delivers an RBI double with his "soul pole." The soul pole is what PK called his ebony bat. Then pitching took over as the score remained tied heading into the bottom of the sixth. I recall how in the span of just a few days I witnessed *three* twenty game winners mow down batsmen in short order. Thanks to Pat Dobson, Joe Coleman, and Wilbur Wood, vendors, relievers, and babysitters didn't have to work very long.

Four highlights from this contest stand the test of time. In ascending order, they are ....

1. PK of the White Sox scores the go-ahead run from first *on a single.* My old man, who gets excited once every leap year when it comes to baseball, enthusiastically praises Kelly with these words, "Now that's

moving!" May not seem like much to you or me, but for him it qualifies as an impassioned cheer.

2. Kaline, the great Al Kaline, the future Hall-of-Fame Kaline, claims the bonehead play of the game. Tied at 1, #6 of Detroit leads off with a clean single to center. Then the unthinkable. As Kaline rounds first base and nonchalantly retreats to the bag, Chisox flake Jay Johnstone throws behind the runner. A shocked crowd and an even more shocked Kaline stare in disbelief as Mike Andrews applies the tag before Kaline's foot reaches the base. Fortunately the visitors' dugout is on the first base side thereby minimizing the shameful return to his mates.

3. Bill Melton, in a tight race for the home run title, slugs a two run bomb in the 6th. This lights up the scoreboard, and gives Melton one more homer than the Bengal on the bench, Norm Cash.

4. Now for crunch time. The Tigers claw back with a run in the 7th on a Mickey Stanley triple and a two out pinch hit single delivered by Jim Northrup. Heading into the ninth, Sox cling to a 4-2 lead. Then an entertaining game becomes very dramatic. The first two Detroiters (Freehan and Stanley) reach. Decision time for the White Sox. Should Manager Chuck Tanner chuck Wood or continue to let Wood chuck? Remember, he's tossed 17 innings over the past three days against two outstanding lineups. If not physically spent, there's a good chance that mental fatigue is an issue. Tanner opts to stay with Wood, and strikes gold. Ike Brown (no relation to Gates Brown or Ike Turner) grounds into a double play. So it comes to this ... all that stands in the way of a Sox triumph is the man who is vying Melton for the league lead in taters, Norm Cash. Now he rates high on the Cool chart for a sundry of reasons. First, his name—he's CASH. Second, his humor—he once brought a piano leg rather than a bat in an attempt to hit Nolan Ryan (the humorless umps didn't allow it). Third, his stellar career highlighted with an incredible .361 batting average in 1961. Fourth, and foremost in this boy's estimation, was his batting helmet. It was so old

school. It was a fielder cap that had protective lining on the inside. Cash wore one, Tony Taylor wore one, and if memory serves correct a catcher by the name of Bob Montgomery wore one. If you think of any others, give me a holler.

Back to the game. So who has the advantage: a fresh bat off the bench, or a knuckleballer who's thrown a bunch of knuckleballs? Wood vs. Cash. Vet vs. vet. Guile vs. power. Warm vs. cold. Lefty vs. lefty. The last and most lasting image of the game is this: Cash viciously tossing his helmet toward the Tiger dugout immediately following the third strike. Norm storms off the field, vanquished.

"Dad, when can we see Wilbur Wood pitch again?"

I'm not a Tiger fan, but from what I gather, this Tiger team (circa 1968) has the same enormous fan appeal as the '69 Cubs. I watched with interest as members from this club got together for a reunion. I saw McLain and Lolich spin yarns (McLain sharing how he decided to give Mickey Mantle a present during the Mick's last season and groove a batting practice fastball). But an exchange between Kaline and Stanley trumped all else. It went something like this ...

Kaline busts into the room and informs the audience of news regarding Mickey Stanley's uniform.

Kaline exclaims, "I just heard that the Tiger organization has finally agreed to retire Mickey Stanley's number after all these years. Yep, just as soon as Miguel Cabrera is done wearing it, that number 24 is going to be retired!"

GAME 11 & 12 KANSAS CITY ROYALS VS. WHITE SOX (2) FRIDAY, SEPTEMBER 3

"It was the third of September. That day I'll always remember, yes I will. Cuz that was the day that the Sox dropped two."

The temptation is to keep on with the lyrics, but baseball beckons. In every baseball season a little rain must fall. Tonight we have the melancholy of enjoying a twi-nite doubleheader after completing the first few days of high school. Already feeling melancholy as the school sentence resumes, within me lies some serious alienation as I begin my high school career. I undoubtedly speak for millions as I confess a less-than-gleeful transition from 8th grade to freshman year. No matter how hard the adults in your world try to ease the transfer, the overwhelming awkwardness descends daily at different times and in different ways. Nothing is routine. With days loaded with foreign faces, teachers, and structures, it's only fitting that one of my classes should be a foreign language. Now I can dislike school bi-lingually. If I didn't like school when I ruled the world as an 8th grader, what is it going to be like now? When will I be on firm ground again? A report not too long ago singled out the loneliest person in our society as a fourteen year old girl. I don't doubt that, but maintain that a fourteen year old boy can't be far behind. Adults have facades and a plethora of ways to cope and deal with social discomfort; 9th graders aren't so skilled.

Even the visits to ballparks in this late summer are laden with some sadness. In Chicago, the home team must play out the string as a Greek character must accept his fate. The hum of happiness dims; the hope of April and May deteriorates into the resignation of August and September. Kids called up from farm teams swell the rosters. Most players act, if not perform, professionally in these lame duck days, and fans sense it. The football teams dominate the sports pages and the air waves; baseball clubs out of contention get the scraps. Die-hard football fans who may barely tolerate baseball in the most interesting of times either scorn or ignore what little life the sport has left. In a scene from <u>Canterbury Tales</u> Geoffrey Chaucer presents cold villains in this fashion—they come upon an elderly gentleman they ask him why he isn't dead yet. Sometimes I feel that way hanging out in ballparks in September.

Combating this fall baseball dreariness and the insecurities of high school stand friendships. A friend from grade school, Jud is his name, and his mom invite me to Comiskey Park. There I am on familiar ground and with familiar people. Hah, take that, you freshman demons.

The games didn't matter much to me, honest. Since we arrived late I didn't even keep score, which was a first. I always kept score, much to the chagrin of my cooler friends. Weird sensation, this was. Kind of like auditing a class; I got something out of it but didn't feel much of a kinship with what transpires. Good thing, too, as the Sox lose to the lowly Royals, 3-1. But who cares because I didn't keep score (how's that for putting me ahead of the team). Now the nightcap better be better because I've got my pencil ready and the lineups in the scorecard.

On paper a mismatch. Like a point guard trying to stop a center in the paint, the Royals are outclassed in the heart of the lineup. Check out the White Sox 4-5-6 batsmen: Bill Melton 3B, Rick Reichardt LF, Carlos May 1B. Not too shabby. Now with the Royals taking the opener they go with their JV lineup: Ed Kirkpatrick CF, Joe Keough RF, Paul Schaal 3B. (Poets must love a couple of the Royals players like Paul Schaal and Amos Otis. Too bad they didn't trade for Don Hahn). And if those names weren't inadequate enough, consider who hit in the third spot on this "B" team: Gail Hopkins. You may remember him as a Sox part-timer in the late 60's. He did hit for a decent average (as 3 hits in his first three AB's suggest), but only 25 homers spanning a seven year career. This evening had split written all over it.

After a four run outburst in the 1st, highlighted by May's home run with Melton on board, this had the makings of a slaughter-rule game. But Joe Horlen, the capable righty who seemed to struggle when I saw him pitch in person, got nicked for 3 in the 3rd and 2 in the 4th. Horlen departs with his team down by one.

But not for long. A hit, an error, and three walks in the fourth results in the Sox reclaiming the lead, 6-5. Things settle down, and when my buddy's mom suggests that it's time to leave for a pizza joint, I have no doubt that the

Sox have this well in hand. But alas, some leaky relieving dooms the home team. Sox lose, 8-6.

The good news is that I have nothing of the KC comeback on record, so Joe Horlen and I have the same outcome—a no-decision. I can't get rid of the melancholy completely, but the pizza was good.

GAME 13: KANSAS CITY ROYALS VS. WHITE SOX
SUNDAY, SEPTEMBER 5

Rain delays. How do you handle them? Options include: go home, stay and drink beer, get something to eat, drink more beer then slide on the wet tarp, or seek autographs. Today I chose the last one.

Heavy precipitation dissolved into a drizzle. Several Sox fans, probably inebriated, soon let their displeasure be known with the continued delay. Since management was slow to respond, they took matters into their own hands. A handful of customers hopped onto the field and began tugging at the tarp—a subtle hint that they wanted play to resume. They failed in removing the tarp—either it was too heavy or they were too drunk. In short order, security and ushers rushed through the mist to move this voluntary grounds crew off the premises. Though stymied in their attempt, this intoxicated entertainment earned the fans' biggest ovation of the day.

But as mentioned in the opening paragraph, I chose another course of action. Swooping down the stairs while dodging the rain and the ushers (who had bigger concerns on the field) I snuck down to the home team's dugout. An adolescent rush of adrenaline and rebellion led me to poke my head into the players' hangout—I figured I couldn't get into that much trouble since I'm neither on the field nor drunk. My brashness led to a close encounter with Sox skipper, Chuck Tanner. He seemed to be somewhat amused by the antics on the field, with a relaxed presence that put me at ease. What the heck, I thought, being the only sober fan anywhere near the playing area, I contorted my body around the dugout and casually requested, "Hey, Chuck, can I have your autograph?"

As the Good Book says, "ask and you shall receive." The next couple moments loom large in the memory banks. Chuck replies, "Sure," takes the ball and pen, and signs with his left hand across the writing of the ball. Not the open sweet spot, mind you, where so many skippers less-than-humbly sign, but the counterpart where it reads, "Official Pro League." I'm sure handwriting analysts would have something to offer regarding Tanner's un-even penmanship, with his two names and eleven letters bouncing legibly across the ball. This helped to confirm my opinion that lefties are indeed different—a righty's signature would be so much more serious. As I expressed my thanks, I felt boosted by this brush with celebrity and pursued more signatures.

Lo and behold players started to emerge in the dugout in an amiable mood. Maybe it was because of the lead they enjoyed, or maybe the snacks in the clubhouse were tasty. Whatever the reason, I was to soon enjoy one of the finest autograph bonanzas in my young career. Pat Kelly, another lefty, agrees to sign on. Thanks, PK, and I like your soul pole. "Bee Bee" Richard, who can neither hit nor field, but can rocket the ball as a bee-bee as it leaves his hand, obliges. Terry Forster, labeled a "fat tub of goo" once by David Letterman, lightly adds his signature. Forster must have been all of 19. Bart Johnson, owner of a blazing fastball and crazy hair fashion, adds his name to the collection. Johnson one year had long curly locks, and another year sported the Yul Brynner look. Steve Huntz, utility infielder, says yes. White Sox flake, Jay Johnstone (bats lefty) writes his name with gusto. And the crown jewel of the day, Tommy John, is kind enough to sign my ball too. Heck, with a little more rain I could get the whole team.

But all good things must end as I return to my grandstand seat with a lot less empty space on my ball and watch the Sox pummel the Royals, 8 zip. A three hit blanking by Wilbur Wood. This makes the third time we've watched him pitch this summer, and the third time we went home happy. Hardly a coincidence.

I think there's something to karma, and Johnstone lends credibility to this theory in the later innings. He slugs a three run bomb in a 5 run 7th *after* signing my ball during the rain delay. Doing a nice thing for me results in a nice thing happening to him—one swing and three RBI's.

In the BB days of Kansas City ("Before Brett") the Royals were far from contending. But they did have a few noteworthy names, such as Bob Lemon who managed this team and would later take the Yanks to the World Series (he also had a brief stint managing the White Sox). And you may have heard of the Royals' clean-up man this day, a fine hitter by the name of Lou Piniella.

Seeing that this was the last trip we'd make to the ballpark for the season, it was a heck of a way to go out. I clutched a winning scorecard—three in less than two months, and a ball loaded with **<u>legible names!</u>** Names that did not require the number of the jersey to be included because you could actually read the first and last name of the ballplayer. Today you simply can't. It would be a long, cold winter—it always is—but the memory of this last game would be replayed and might just be enough to get me to the next opening day.

POST-SEASON, '71

Surveys. Wise tool, good business, and very American. Lots of folks wanting to know what you think on anything from the trivial such as presidential candidates to the important such as baseball uniforms. There's money to be made on what people know, like, and want.

For reasons unknown I remember, even though a kid, responding to a high number of such survey instruments in the late fall and early winter months of 1971. One such questionnaire was at church. And I also remember being politely asked on more than a few occasions if I had any final comments. My standard reply was, "Yes, I think the Baltimore Orioles should have won the World Series." Hey, they asked.

Could there be any greater contrast than what the Bucs and O's offered the world in this championship? Four twenty game winners versus none. A huge white slugger, Boog Powell, versus a black basher, Willie Stargell. A pitcher on the radical side known to wear curlers in the bullpen, Dock Ellis, versus a model who posed in underwear, Jim Palmer. A sedate manager who rocked on a rocking chair, Danny Murtaugh, versus a manager who rocked umpires, Earl Weaver. A cute and cocky little bird versus a perilous pirate. Two similarities— both are championship teams and both right fielders are very good.

Yet all these intriguing matchups would take a back seat to the performance of the greatest baseball player in my era.

At the outset of this series, I'm all smiles. The O's hold service at home, and Mr. Murtaugh mentions from his rocking chair after the second game how delightful it would be for his team to embark on a four game winning streak. "Ain't gonna happen," I hoped.

Game 3 changes the world as we know it, or at least my world. It was the first ever World Series game at night. Too bad. No more sneaking transitors into the classroom. No more pleading with teachers to allow the class to watch a game (or at least a few innings). No more rushing home from school to catch the last few outs. And no more going to bed at a decent hour. When it comes to World Series evolution, we've gone from having no games at night and everyone I know tuned in, to having all games at night and having no one interested. Shucks. I guess the pro$ outweigh the cons.

So as I'm trying to memorize my Spanish vocabulary for tomorrow's quiz ('gato' is cat, 'perro' is dog) an umpire convention down the first base line distracts me. They need to know if the ball hit by a Buc is a home run or a foul ball. As kids we'd solve this problem with a do-over, but adults don't care for this kind of justice. I remember that this ruling went against the Birds, as did all three games in Pittsburgh. Now what?

For me, it meant a trip to the DL. In a pick-up football game Friday after school, I fall on my finger with all my weight. In the course of my childhood I fell countless times. No sooner would my mom buy me new pants than I'd have a hole in the knee and matching grass stains. But this fall was different from all the others. I got up with my pinky bent at a weird angle. In the emergency room, I didn't mind the injury a whole lot as a kind and cute nurse fussed over me. At first the treatment was a splint, but it soon grew to an entire cast covering most of my right hand. No more sports—at least for a while.

The timing was okay, however, as I got to watch Games 6 & 7 without too much interruption. Game 6—tight, tense, and in the end, terrific. With the score tied at 2 in the bottom of the 10th inning, Frank Robinson reaches third base with one out. On a 1-2 pitch, Brooks Robinson lofts a fly ball to shallow center field. Vic Davallio has just been inserted in the game, and he releases the ball homeward after the catch. From my vantage point on the couch, it looked like the ball, the runner, and the catcher (Manny Sanguillen) would all intersect simultaneously. Bracing myself for a collision of epic proportions, I knew this was going to be thrilling. But something happened to the ball on its flight homeward, something that you don't see a whole lot. The thrown baseball hit the infield grass and bounded high in the air. Sanguillen leaps to catch it, and as he returns to earth, F. Robby slides in safely. He comes up a little woozy as Sanguillen foots connects with Robinson's head. Brooks races by him with palms pointing upward at the waist as Frank obliges with a low ten (instead of a high five). As Jack Buck would say, "We'll see you tomorrow!"

Game 7 ... where legends leave their legacy. Brooks Robinson owned the World Series in '70, but his team dominated with a near sweep and did not have to deliver in a Game 7 (or 6). This year, Roberto Clemente, in a classic, down-to-the-wire affair, took his rightful place among the legends; not only because what he did, but when he did it. He homered in Game 6 and then homered off the O's screwball lefty, Mike Cuellar, to account for a third of the runs scored in Game 7. A big hit by Jose Pagan and a masterpiece hurled by Steve Blass sealed the deal. Final score: Pittsburgh 2, Baltimore 1. Pirates take Series, 4 games to 3. Too bad, but I do remember watching pure greatness in the person of #21 for Pittsburgh. His hustle, his arm, his bat, his leadership, his spirit, his pride, his performance in the clutch—Clemente may not have been the best at any one of these vital characteristics, but if you consider the entire package, he's without peer.

1972

GAME 14: MONTREAL EXPOS VS. CHICAGO CUBS
MONDAY, MAY 29

Years ago, an ad jingled: "Red and yellow and green and blue; purple and orange too; I can build a rainbow, build a rainbow, build a rainbow, too." I think the promoted product was Jello.

These verses reminded me of the Montreal Expos, especially their baseball caps. Seeing this expansion team for the first time was an experience in color overload—not so much in the quantity of colors, for red, white and blue, especially blue, made up the entire uniform. Yes, not so much the number of colors but the way the colors were coordinated upon Les Expos—the mingling of the red and blue and white on the cap was not just colorful but colorful in a way you just didn't see among **visiting** outfits. By 1972 the bland grays of the visiting uniforms had given way to a powder blue for some clubs (see Cardinals and Phillies) but no other team in the league resembled this Canadian club, at least for now. Colorful, neat, and original come to mind—definitely out of the mainstream for a city out of the mainstream. A kid in the neighborhood tried to explain the cap to me once after he had seen it live, but it made little sense to me—why would professional ballplayers subject themselves to such silliness, methinks. Still, this uniform would soon meet its match with the "Aquarius-looking, sunshine-kissed, horizontal-striped" configuration of the Houston Astros attire. Why did real pros like Nolan Ryan, Terry Puhl, Jose Cruz, and Joe Niekro agree to wear them?

But we're getting ahead of ourselves. These Expos, all of four years in existence, had some legit players. Leading off was a former Met who got hit by the pitch a lot. And his name was … Ron Hunt. I suppose announcers' pun fun compelled them to wonder if age would ever catsup to Hunt, or if Hunt could ketchup to a blazing fastball. Then there was Boots Day, a former Cubbie, and Bob Bailey, a former Dodger. Another former Dodger, Ron Fairly, and a former Met, Ken Singleton, hit in the middle of the lineup. Singleton would eventually enjoy productive years with the Orioles. A strong switch-hitter, Singleton would surprise you with his swiftness. He didn't have any. Along with a former Cub and Cardinal, Ken Reitz, they had to be the two most un-suspecting runners—both had average to above average size, average to above average skill, and way below average speed.

But it wasn't the "wearing it" of Hunt, the Dodger duo of Fairly and Bailey, nor the plodding of Singleton I remember most about this team. Nope, it was the way the announcer at Jarry Park in Montreal would announce the name of a former Cub and current Expo part-time catcher: John (pause) **BOCK ...OOO...BELL...*AAAHHHH!!!*** Never in the history of the game would a journeyman player receive such a grand introduction. We'd delay our play for a few seconds if we saw Boccabella was going to hit next just so we could hear the PA guy scream his name.

And the manager for this interesting squad? Perhaps the most heralded skipper to have never managed in a World Series. His name is Gene Mauch. Seldom has anyone this side of Ralph Branca been linked to heartbreaking failure as much as Mauch. The cerebral style of his management notwith-standing, his catastrophic collapses with the Phillies in '64 and two decades later with the Angels in '86 are part of baseball lore. He would also manage the Twins, but at this point in his career, he succeeded in making the Expos a Fairly competitive club. Much more competitive, it should be noted, than their expansion mates in San Diego. In fact, 1972 marked the second con-secutive season that the Spos would <u>not</u> finish in last place—that distinction would fall to the Phillies. San Diego, by contrast, owned last place by double-digit margins from '69 to '73.

On the mound for Montreal, with his bright ginger hair peeking out un-der his colorful cap was Carl Morton. How would he and this band of throw-aways compete against the Cubs this day? Too good, I'd say. For through five innings, Morton had a no-no. And the Expos claimed an early lead after Singleton doubles home Fairly and Bailey homers ("Won't you touch home, Bob Bailey?"). But with two doubles and four singles in the later frames, the

Cubs jumped ahead by three. Milt Pappas, a fine pitcher and hitter, gave up as many runs as he had hits—two. Final score: Cubs 5, Expos 2.

Now if you're taking the time to read this book, I scarcely have to explain to you the charms of baseball or the wonders of attending a game in person. For instance, the pace of the game enables you to engage in different things at the ballpark. For my first fifteen years or so, I (and often my brothers) would go for a walk. Pass on the scorecard to another family member or friend, and get lost for a few minutes. Sometimes to the concession stand, sometimes to the box seats, sometimes to the bullpen, but somewhere we'd go exploring. Could you just go walking around at other sporting events so freely?

Not only that, but baseball allows you to wander at times without leaving your seat. Take this game, for instance. My brother and I were bored, so we pretended we were the managers of the upcoming All-Star game and our task was to name the pitching staffs for each league. Here are my selections, given the pitching performances up to this point in the season: Fergie Jenkins, Cubs; Carl Morton, Expos; Tom Seaver, Mets; Steve Carlton, Phillies; Steve Blass, Pirates; Bob Gibson, Cardinals; Phil Niekro, Braves; Don Sutton, Dodgers; Juan Marichal and Sam McDowell, Giants; and Dave Roberts, Padres. I'd expect some texts from irate fans over some hurlers not selected; names like Koosman and Matlack (I hated the Mets); Bill Hands, Bill Singer, Larry Dierker, Chris Short or Don Gullett. Sorry, can't take everybody.

In the junior circuit, I'd go with Dave McNally and Jim Palmer of the Orioles; Sonny Siebert, Red Sox; Gaylord Perry, Indians; Joe Coleman and Mickey Lolich, Tigers; Clyde Wright, Angels; Bert Blyleven, Twins; Kenny Holtzman, A's; and Wilbur Wood, White Sox. You could have a second All-Star staff made up of folks like Mike Cuellar, Paul Splittorff, Nolan Ryan (remember that this is '72 and not '82 or '92), Andy Messersmith, Vida Blue, Catfish Hunter, Jim Kaat, Jim Lonborg, Mel Stottlemyre, and Tom Bradley. This "B" squad would probably match, if not surpass, my choices. You could argue for hours, and why not? And if you look at those names again you'll notice something—not one reliever in either league. Pitching in the early 70's revolved around a four man starting rotation which also happened to be the four best pitchers on the team. Relievers on a pitching staff were like the utility players among the regulars. Besides, how important could some relievers be when starters like Jenkins and Gibson and Lolich and Wood gave their team over 300 innings?

How did my selections compare to the real managers' picks? Pretty close. Manager Earl Weaver used these folks in the actual All-Star game: Palmer, Lolich, Perry, Wood, and McNally (5 for 5). In the National League, Danny Murtaugh of the Pirates and I agreed upon Gibson, Blass, Sutton, and Carlton. The only differences were Bill Stoneman of the Expos and Tug McGraw of the Mets. You may be wondering how either league could score with such great pitching. Good question. Somehow, in ten innings, the two teams combined for seven runs, with the National League getting four of them. Hank Aaron, in front of the hometown fans, belted a two run dinger, and Joe Morgan of the Reds had the walk-off hit.

GAME 16 & 17: MILWAUKEE BREWERS VS. CHICAGO WHITE SOX SUNDAY, JUNE 11

"They just sit over there, expecting to win." (*Chicago Tribune, June 12, 1972*)

Take a sport, any sport. Now think of that sport played at the highest level. What are the first words that come to mind to describe this phenomena? I'll bet that the word "easy" does not make the list.

Now please take another look at the opening quote. Anyone who's been involved in a lengthy winning streak can recognize the sentiment behind the statement. Sport, especially baseball, is not easy, but there are the blessed times when as a player, a coach, a fan, or even a casual observer, you just *expect* to win. What "the zone" is to an individual's performance, the winning streak is to the collective performance. The experience transcends hopes to the level of expectations and even knowledge that a favorable outcome is inevitable. This team is just going to win. Don't ask how, to what extent, or why; just accept that there's going to be a happy ending.

That's the good news. The bad news has to do with a most popular song at the time. The group was Climax, and the band's one smash single was "Precious and Few." These moments, whether spending time with that special someone or in the midst of a special winning streak, are indeed precious and few.

Surprisingly the opposing team knows this feeling, too. The dreaded doom in the pit of your stomach appears and won't go away. No matter how much fortitude you can muster, and sports demands that you muster a lot, sometimes it's just not meant to be. You can be the brave warrior, but ultimately you are Hector facing not just Achilles but the gods on his side. Meanwhile, yours are absent. But something gained in the loss is this: character. Professional sports pooh-pooh this as sentimental crap; "Just Win, Baby" is their mantra. But how one handles imminent defeat is critical—the best of teams in baseball will lose many, many games. So do you fall on your sword or give it your best? Del Crandall, manager of the Milwaukee Brewers in June of '72, deserves credit for the quote at the beginning of this article. He didn't use any expletives, he didn't have to. The expletive sentiment was there—he could have referred to "they" as those blankety-blank White Sox and it would have the same effect.

Now if Crandall was a kid playing sandlot ball, he had many ways to escape defeat. Let's count the ways:

1. Feign an injury (the quickest way to bring play, at least your play, to an end).
2. Tell his pals he has to be home in five minutes cuz his folks said so (some mild objections, but kids' protests don't stand a chance against parents).
3. Start a fight (frustration causes you to have *them* fall on *their sword*).
4. Say, "Let's go by _?_'s house." (Fill in the blank with the kid who has the nicest swimming pool).
5. Say, "I'm thirsty. I'm going to A & W, anybody want to come with?" (if he adds, "I'm buying," this is practically fool-proof).

I doubt if any of these thoughts crossed Crandall's mind as he's sitting in the Milwaukee dugout, knowing full well that his 4-0 **lead** in the middle innings will evaporate. Two legends come to mind. Earl Weaver said that in baseball you just can't run out the clock, you have to "throw the damn ball over the plate." And Larry Bird makes reference to fate and the inescapability of things as he crows to his opponent, "I'm going to hit a turn-around jumper in your face and there's nothing you can do about it." Larry Bird's defender, Hector, Del Crandall, and probably the Milwaukee Brewers all try to put up a brave front, but also know what's coming. Al McGuire said that in sports the worst you can do is lose. Maybe he's right, I'm not so sure. At least the Brewers won't have their ankles tied to a Chisox chariot and dragged around the ballpark after their defeat.

So how does this second game play itself out? The momentum shift begins in the home half of the fifth, as leadoff man Pat Kelly (PK) pokes a two-run homer (always a cause for concern when a guy whose home run percentage is 1.8 goes yard). Back-to-back doubles by Carlos May and Bill Melton continue the comeback in the 6th, and then identical scenarios tie and win the game in the 7th and 9th. PK singles, advances to second, and scores on a hit by May. Imagine the torture felt by Crandall—not only to lose a game in which you were up four, but to lose in repetitive fashion with Kelly the main offender. Reminiscent of Bill Murray's dilemma in Groundhog Day. I've learned that early advantage was inconsequential—had Milwaukee been up 5, the Sox would have scored 6; had they been up 8, the Sox would have scored 9; had they been up 20, I would have gone home.

Details matter. And how many baseball people talk about the importance of "adding on" once you have a lead. To wit, a web gem might have made the difference in the game's outcome about an hour or so earlier. In the sixth, with two Brewers on base with one out, and Milwaukee up 4-2, Rick Auerbach lined a ball headed into the left field corner for one or two RBI's. But alas, as Hector's best attack on Achilles was thwarted by the gods, so this best attack was thwarted by Apollo Melton. His robbery kept the game within striking distance.

Pitching matters. Just prior to the walk-off victory, the heart of the Brewer lineup bats in the 9th with the game tied. Mgr. Tanner turns it over to a righty reliever, Cy Acosta. He proceeds to strike out the side—George Scott, Billy Coningliaro, and Dave May. I lean over and tell my family that that was a 'Cy of Relief". They threaten to have me walk home.

Up to this point the season had been magical for the Sox, especially at home. This DH sweep advanced their home record to 24-4. No longer could you label this franchise as hitless wonders. Three hitters surfaced in the top ten (.327 for Dick Allen, .314 for Carlos May, and .299 for Pat Kelly. FYI—Lou Piniella happened to be leading the league at this point). The Sox had 2 of the 3 top RBI men in Allen with 40 (well on his way to the MVP) and May with 30. Tom Bradley, sporting a 7-2 record, enjoyed a spot among the league's pitching leaders. *(Chicago Tribune)*.

These heady times, sparked by the magnificent play of Allen and the ultimate player's manager in Chuck Tanner, aroused Sox fans. The 36,000 fans that showed up for this sweep ballooned season attendance to 140,000 ahead of last year. (Paid attendance was 23,000. How many kids, like me, got free tickets for perfect attendance? Looks like 13 K or so). Good play and the magic of Dick Allen made it fun going to games. Allen was one of the few players who would stop you in your tracks as a fan. Whatever you were doing, it could wait for a few moments as this guy was a thrill waiting to happen. As mentioned in <u>Like Night and Day,</u> Allen was Shaft before there was a Shaft. My favorite memories of his in the '72 season were his blasts to straight-away center field bleachers—home or away. Just incredible power, verified by at least a dozen of his peers in quotes I've read over the years. Several remark how they never saw another ballplayer have quite the season that Dick Allen had in 1972.

The first game, you ask? Perhaps the most unlikely spectacle I have ever seen at Old Comiskey Park. A slugfest. A lopsided slugfest, but still a slugfest. I can't recall the wind ever playing much of a factor on the South side; Wrigley Field—yes, practically every game, but Comiskey Park with its enclosed upper deck, no. I saw seven home runs leave the premises in one game. 7 homers, not in a month, not in a week, but in one game. If some old-timer out there ever saw more, God bless you. Most pleasing, of course, is that the Sox won the home run derby contest by clobbering five.

One of the Brewer clouts came from their own May, Dave May. Years later his son would patrol outfield pastures at Wrigley Field. The other Brewer blast came courtesy of the Boomer, George Scott. A quick Boomer tale. An announcer noticed that Scott wore an interesting set of ornaments around his neck. They looked organic and artsy at the same time. So the announcer inquired about the necklace's origin. Boomer deadpanned that they were the teeth of second basemen that he extracted on his slides into second base to break up double plays. I think the announcer said, "Thank you, George, for sharing."

The Sox lit up Brewer pitching in the opener, especially in the third frame. Back-to-back jobs from Mike Andrews and Dick Allen, and another courtesy of diminutive Luis Alvarado. Allen slugged his second of the game in the 5th, and the barrage mercifully ended with a drive by Ed Herrmann. Remember that this was a franchise that once claimed 71 homers for an *entire season!* Heck, I saw nearly 10% of that total in one afternoon.

Now a hitter with power at Comiskey Park in my childhood meant some-one who could reach the warning track. A home run was impressive, an op-posite field shot, even more so. The Ruthian blasts that made the upper deck gave fans something to talk about for days, given the great distance and the home teams's modest power. But on this day, in game one, with one swing, Dick Allen hit an opposite field upper deck home run. Match that.

GAME 18: BALTIMORE ORIOLES VS. WHITE SOX
WEDNESDAY, JULY 5

Perhaps it was the 4th of July hangover. Maybe it was playing a day game following a night game. Or it could have been the replacement of a bonafide slugger, Bill Melton, with a guy named Hugh Yancy. Young Yancy (21) would go on to play a total of seven big league games, all with the Pale Hose. He reached base with a single and a double in 19 at-bats for a batting average of .105. He played only in the even number years: 1972, '74, '76. And he hails from the locale of the White Sox spring training home for many years, Sarasota, FL. Now you know more about Hugh Yancy than the average person on the street.

But Hugh really knows the reason for the Sox performance this day? I know the recent double-header bombings against Milwaukee is an aberration, but to go from that kind of productivity to a measly five singles is somewhat befuddling. Obviously the opposing pitchers had something to do with the home team's offense. Simply put, Milwaukee didn't have Dave McNally while Baltimore did. This stylish southpaw stymied Sox sluggers so systematically.

As a kid with an Irish heritage, I looked up to three "Mc" pitchers: McDowell, McLain, and McNally. I thought that each possessed a little color to go along with All-Star status. I appreciated McDowell's hummer (his alias, "Sudden Sam"), McLain's eccentrics (organ player, Pepsi consumer, prison time, and 31 wins), and McNally's pure style. Again, why is that lefties can fall out of bed in the morning and look cool? I tried, with little success, to imitate McNally's wind-up and to duplicate McNally's win-loss record. So deliberately would he raise both hands over his left shoulder that his motion served as a hybrid between the full wind-up that is virtually extinct and the no wind-up which is the standard today. He didn't have the Don McMahon "full speed ahead both arms raised to the sky and here it comes" approach, nor did he have the simple rock and throw version that started with relievers and now is ubiquitous among all pitchers. No, McNally had this beautiful delivery halfway between. If you saw him pitch, you'd understand. I don't know how good McNally's "stuff" was—experts never went overboard in praising his velocity, his movement, his off-speed pitches or his command, but he more than got the job done. From '68-'71, McNally won 87 contests and enjoyed four consecutive 20-win game seasons. He led the league in wins with 24 in 1970, and in winning percentage the following year by going 21-5 (.808). Now you could argue that how good would McNally be without the Robinsons backing him up with outstanding defense and offense? Fair question, but I think it cuts both ways: how good would the Robinsons (and all the O's for that matter) be without pitchers like McNally? For several years, a dominant pitcher in the American League with off-the-charts style—that's Dave McNally.

1972 appears to be a tough-luck season for this lefty. His ERA was under 3, and he reached his career high in shutouts with 6. But his win-loss record took a big hit: 13-17. In '72, the three year run of the Orioles in the World Series would end, as another mini-dynasty took its place across the country in Oakland. But on this day Baltimore showed the world, or at least this fan, why it won so many games. McNally blanks Wilbur Wood and the Sox, 1-0. Had it not been for a second inning homer by Brooks Robinson, who knows how long this game would have lasted. Props to Wood--how effective he must have been this day, as he nearly shut down a lineup that had Boog Powell batting seventh!

A closer look at this game reveals how much strategy has changed. In the pre-DH days in the A.L., managers had to make tough calls in the later innings of a close, low scoring game. Namely, do I pinch-hit or let the starter bat. In this case, Manager Earl Weaver lets McNally hit with two Birds on base in a one-run game. He whiffs, but the statement of support and belief in his pitcher is made.

And in the bottom of the 8th, an even bigger decision. The home team loads the bases with three consecutive singles. Even in the pre-pitch count days of '72, a pitching change is probable. Today it would be inevitable. In fact, McNally may not even start the inning. So from my left field perch behind Don Buford, I'm expecting Weaver to make the long walk, take the ball from McNally, pat him on the back side and say good job as he makes a pitching change. Some capable reliever, like Eddie Watt or Grant Jackson, comes to relieve McNally. I wish the things I just described happened. But no, Weaver let McNally pitch his way out of it. Weaver once pointed out that he didn't want starters to be looking to the bullpen for help, because there's no one out there that's better than you, _?_ (fill in the blank with names like McNally, Cuellar, or Palmer).

So what does McNally and the Chisox offense do when faced with a bases loaded, no out situation? Luis Alvarado, batting for Wood, fans. Then lead-off man Walt Williams raps into a 5-4-3 double play. Rally over, inning over, game over. A few outs later, and I trudge back to the park district bus from whence I came, totally frustrated by the turn of events. Wouldn't it have been better to not mount any threat than to have a major tease like this?

GAME 19: HOUSTON ASTROS VS. CHICAGO CUBS
THURSDAY, JULY 13

A baseball mercenary. A term given to free agents on occasion. The hired gun brought into town to shoot down the bad guys from the other team. "It'll cost us," so goes the thinking, "but he'll get the job done."

In a different way I myself was evolving into a mercenary. I do have some spending money thanks to paper routes, but I am a year or so away from getting a driver's license, and public transportation from Hillside to the Chicago ballparks just wasn't feasible. But when things are a priority, like baseball, one figures out ways to get where one needs to go. Seems that there were several groups in the community taking trips to games, so I'd pledge my loyalty to these groups for a couple of hours, they'd take my money, I'd show up for the bus ride, and there you go … a baseball fan mercenary.

Last week it was courtesy of the Thele Park District. Now I didn't live in the park district jurisdiction, but the lady in charge let me hang around with some friends who did. The people there were nice to me, we talked baseball and played Nok-hockey when we needed a break from the sandlot baseball games. My friend Petey and I had some serious Nok-hockey duels. For those not in the know, this high tech game is played with wooden sticks and a wooden puck, and each player takes a turn trying to hit it into the opposing goal. Directly in front of the goal lies a square wooden piece, requiring players to typically shoot bank shots off the side board. But Petey had these trick maneuvers called banana shots, and they represent the high risk-high reward kind of action he lives for. I play a more conservative game, patiently waiting for a mistake, then blasting the puck into the twine. Sometimes the twine would wear out, and the fun would intensify because then the wooden puck would fly across the park should a goal occur. In the dog days of summer, when heat and humidity oppressed, Nok-hockey absorbed many harmless hours.

Eight days ago I acted as a pseudo-member of the Thele Park District as they sponsored the trip that resulted in a White Sox defeat to the hands of Baltimore. This time I pledge membership, for a day, to the Elmhurst YMCA.

Long before the Village People imbued our national consciousness with lyrics and melody, there really was a YMCA. This one not too far from our house had this old gym that smelled like a gym. Just the right fragrant balance between perspiration and lacquer of the gym floor, with a hint of chlorine wafting from the Y's swimming pool. Years later in high school, I'd pony up a few dollars and engage in some pickup games of basketball. This YMCA experience offered no policemen, no feathery Native Americans, and no construction workers with shades, just some folks working up a sweat shooting jump shots and throwing elbows.

These folks sponsored trips to Wrigley Field. I knew absolutely no one going on these trips, but that wouldn't stop me. Watching a ball game has never been just a social affair; in fact, I've often seen it as serious business. Broadcaster Jack Brickhouse may suggest letting the managers do the worrying for you as you try to escape the demands of life, but I soon learned that given the way my two favorite teams play ball, my worries multiplied. So after a couple hours on a bus with strangers, I find myself in the upper deck behind home plate witnessing another masterful pitcher's duel between Fergie Jenkins and Jerry Reuss. Let's go.

After eight sun-drenched innings, we're tied at 2. The bottom of the scoreboard reads:

Vis 7 Hits 6 Cubs.

Reuss struck out 6, Fergie K's 7. Pretty tight and tense, until the last inning. Then Tommy Helms delivers a three run homer and Norm Miller homers with one man on base. Helms and Miller aren't exactly sluggers, but they do provide the 5 run margin of victory for the visitors. The bus ride home, with the traffic, the heat, and the defeat, just wasn't a whole lot of fun.

One last peek at the inside of my scorecard reveals this nugget: the preponderance of good hitters throughout the batting order. How would you like to pitch to names like Jimmy Wynn, Lee May, Bob Watson, and Doug Rader; or Billy Williams, Jim Hickman, Ron Santo, and Jose Cardenal? To prove there were no easy outs, the eighth hole in the batting order was occupied by the aforementioned Helms and Randy Hundley. Even the pitchers could hit—Reuss smacking a double and Jenkins a single.

Glancing at the outside of the scorecard, I notice that pre-game autograph hunting produced some modest results. Two benchwarmers and a coach were kind enough to sign: J.C. Martin and Carmon Fanzone of the Cubs, and Salty Parker of the 'Stros. (I guess the studs from each squad were too busy that day). Taking a closer look at these signatures I shouldn't take for granted their legibility. Pleasing is the word to describe both the penmanship and the momentary interaction to complete the autograph. Many years later, the great Harmon Killebrew initiated a campaign for ballplayers to write their names more legibly. Not exactly on a par with solving world hunger, but still something positive.

GAME 20: CINCINNATI REDS VS. CUBS
TUESDAY, JULY 18

The topic for this next essay is this: Fatherhood in the 1970's. Nothing scientific, mind you, but a compilation of observations. What gets me thinking on this subject is an adult student in my writing class who recently made this remark: "it's possible to give kids not enough attention or too much attention." The first part of her statement we would unquestionably assent to—neglect is bad. The second part is more debatable: is it possible to give kids too much attention? Upon further review and consideration, I think she's on to something. Excessive doting may not be helping youth toward healthy independence—that seemed to be the gist of her position. Balance seems to be the goal with parenting (and with so many other things).

I think fathers had a good handle on this back in my youth. Dads didn't try as hard to bond with children. They were friendly enough, for sure, but I got the sense that they had other things going on in their life, and we as kids understood that. I recall lots of dads smoking cigars, sometimes acknowledging us by name, and keeping their distance. Stands at athletic contests were not filled with dads expecting nor pressuring their sons into an athletic future full of scholarships. Hundreds of dollars were not spent on private lessons, nor were thousands of dollars spent on travelling teams, at least not in my neighborhood. A dad or two would coach the Little League team, but both adults and players knew that kids' preference was to play the game sandlot style without parental involvement or favoritism. Umpiring was not preferred either; if we couldn't come to an agreement on a play, we'd do it over.

So on this particular day I was pleasantly surprised when Petey's dad asked me to go with them to the Cub game. I knew the man, of course, as he was a burly man with thinning gray hair who smoked a cigar. I learned he served in World War 2. He was of French-American descent who married a lovely Filipino lady. One of their children, Petey, was my best friend for a while. He had an older and younger sister who basically ignored us, and we returned the favor. Maybe I saw Petey's dad once or twice at a Pony League game, maybe I didn't. Over the course of several years our conversations commenced and concluded with "Hi." Nothing else needed to be said.

I think fathers knew something then that's out of vogue today: the law of speaking that says as the number of words spoken increases, the value of each word tends to decrease. So as Petey's dad drives us to the ballpark on this mid-summer day's dream, he adjusts the cigar in his mouth and asks this question: "Is Fergie pitching today?" Tantamount to a speech. From the back seat, Petey, this kid named Tim, and I all respond in the affirmative. We may not know our school subjects that well, but we surely knew probable starters. Petey's dad responds with a grunt of satisfaction, and we could easily translate that grunt--the Cubs stood a good chance of winning.

Another novelty—travelling to Wrigley Field via Lake Shore Drive. (The O'Donnells travelled a different way to the ballpark). Glancing to the right I took in the sailboats on the deep blue lake, a tranquil scene. On the other side, the downtown traffic and proximity of sky scrapers kept me wide eyed. Snuggled safely in the back seat with two pals and going to a ballgame, totally trusting that Petey's dad knew where he was going and what he was doing, I couldn't have been a whole lot happier.

But the day got better. The Cubs, with their formidable lineup featuring a Hall-of-Famer batting seventh (Santo), do battle with the Big Red Machine and their three Hall-of-Famers (four if you include Pete Rose). Quick, now, how many teams can you identify with 4 Hall-of-Famers? Baltimore had the Robinsons and Palmer; the Cardinals claimed Brock, Gibson, & Cepeda (Carlton on the Phillies); the Bucs boasted Stargell, Clemente, and Maz; and the A's produced Fingers, Hunter, and Jackson. But with Rose, Joe Morgan, Johnny Bench, and Tony Perez, could any lineup in recent memory match that? Maybe, just maybe the Yankees with Jeter, Ichiro, Rivera, and A Rod. But hold on! We have a last second entry. The Giants of the early 60's could boast **five** Hall-of-Famers. Ready? Cepeda, Marichal, Mays, McCovey, and Perry. (Hats off to you if this was your answer).

The old adage in baseball suggests that Hall-of-Fame pitching will conquer Hall-of-Fame hitting proves true today. The four household names in the Red lineup went 1 for 14 against Fergie. Their entire offense managed but one run. The Cubs scored with a sacrifice fly from Santo plating Cardenal in the 6th. Gary Nolan, arguably the Red ace, kept pace with Fergie with six innings of one run ball. Not nearly as dominating (Nolan yielded six hits and two walks), but just as effective on the scoreboard. Regulation ends with the game tied at 1.

Here's where it gets really good. Fergie retires the first batter then gives up consecutive singles to Ted Uhlaender and Dave Concepcion. Runners at first and second, one out, tie game, 10th inning, a boatload of pitches thrown by your starter on a warm day, and Rose and Morgan due up. Question: would you remove Jenkins? As Weaver left McNally in, Durocher does likewise with Fergie. Many baseball people throughout the years emphasize how Leo Durocher was much more adept at handling vets compared to younger players. He trusted guys who were proven commodities, and that description definitely fits Fergie. This faith in his ace is rewarded with two ground balls to the first baseman. Marvelous performance by Fergie, transcending All-Star stuff to Hall-of-Fame status. And props to the skipper for letting his starter finish what he started. *I don't need no stinkin pitch count.*

The bottom of the 10th doesn't require such a dramatic build-up. Clay Carroll comes in from the Red bullpen to relieve Pedro Borbon who relieved Nolan. Carroll delivers a fast ball to the leadoff batter, Billy Williams. He swings, connects, and the ball reaches the right field catwalk. Ball game. Much obliged, Petey's dad, for a lifelong memory.

GAME 21: CALIFORNIA ANGELS VS. CHICAGO WHITE SOX
WEDNESDAY, AUGUST 2

Okay, we all know that life, sports and baseball mystify. Fact is stranger than fiction, and all that stuff. How and why certain things turn out the way they do befuddles us. A colleague of mine who has Ph.D. in one of the hard sciences, I believe it's physics, once shared this with me—the more scientists know, the more they realize just how much there is that they don't know.

So now here's evidence from the toy department of life, baseball, which supports this perspective. Let's say you have one team that plays two games separated by one month. Both are at home, both are weekday matinee games, both have approximately the same number of fans in attendance, and both feature nearly identical personnel. Now in one game the team yields *18* hits, 10 runs, 5 walks, and commits 2 errors. In the other game, this team surrenders 7 hits, 1 run, 0 walks, and 1 error. What's the probability of the first game ending in defeat and the second game in victory? You probably know where this is going: this team, the White Sox, win the first game and lose the second. How can you put a mathematical formula or any kind of logic around a paradigm like that?

Something else about weekday matinee games from this Chisox era stands out—a bellicose broadcaster belts out his narrative of the game from the deep recesses of the center field bleachers. There's a statue of him on the north side of town, but he began announcing games in Chicago with the White Sox. Shirtless and singing the praises of Falstaff beer, Bill Veeck, and some of the players was Harry Caray. Interesting how Harry had sides: amiable and positive, always, toward the fans and ownership; however, Caray's diatribes toward struggling ballplayers were legendary. Go ask Bill Melton. Other folks who didn't always have a Kumbaya experience with Caray were fellow announcers. Go ask the late Milo Hamilton. But Caray didn't seem too upset about offending people who couldn't hurt him back.

"Here's a guy" who knew where his bread was buttered. His role of baseball ambassador was only surpassed by his strong sense of self-promotion.

This excursion to White Sox Park represented the second outing with the Park District. A warm day with plenty of hits and runs by the home team evolves into a nail-biter in the final frames. The once comfortable four run cushion dwindles to one with the Halos batting in the ninth. High drama here with two out and two on—the tying run at second and the go-ahead run at first. My friend Petey and I stress for two reasons: we want the Sox to win and to win quickly, for we have a Pony League game that night. We're not team-mates during the season, but our two teams happen to being playing each other at 6 PM. The three hour contest has now dragged on beyond 4 o'clock, so we're really hoping that …. A) Terry Forster gets this last out, and … B) rush hour traffic on the Dan Ryan and Eisenhower expressways isn't too bad. Part A is accomplished as Forster gets Leo Cardenas to ground out to Mike Andrews. Part B is accomplished as we make a bee-line for the bus and then a bee-line for our homes once the bus drops us off, and finally a bee-line from our homes to the field. I don't remember if Petey's Braves beat my Dodgers that evening, nor do I care. Today was about having fun, and we had plenty of that.

GAME 21: TEXAS RANGERS VS. CHICAGO WHITE SOX
SATURDAY, AUGUST 5

"Tit for tat." Quite the expression. People live by varying principles to varying degrees, and my folks honored this adage more than most. If somebody does something nice for you, be sure to return the favor. So my parents, in appreciation toward Petey and his dad for taking me to a recent Cubs' game invite Petey to join the O'Donnell family to this contest.

Now how often does both parent and child get to see his/her favorite performer live and in action? Hard to imagine in the music industry that a parent and child would attend such a concert—the Lettermen performing the warm-up act to Black Sabbath, let's say. But baseball's a different kind of animal. On this glorious day, I get the chance to watch my favorite baseball player, Frank Howard, while my old man gets the chance to see his all-time #1, Ted Williams. Granted that Williams is now the skipper and his playing days are long gone, but it still counts. (A tad ironic how in my earliest days of watching the game, both of our favorites shared the same surname, Williams. His being Ted while mine was Billy).

One unfortunate circumstance happened to be the timing of this game in my days of autograph-seeking. That is, I did not seek autographs this day. I did it before and after this game, and had a lot of fun with it, but today I just wasn't into that mode. Too bad, because watching BP about an hour before the game was the best hitter of all-time, and he stood less than twenty feet away. Would he have signed if I asked? Who knows, but I have read countless times how Williams was good to people, especially people who weren't sportswriters.

And that was the highlight of the day: watching Ted Williams watch batting practice. Years later I got some stories from a guy who competed with Williams, Billy Pierce. He had the unenviable task of trying to get Williams out, and with his efforts he earned Williams' admiration. "A tough little lefty," is what Williams would say. And the "best hitter I ever saw" is what Pierce says. I asked Billy once if he had any tales of Ted, and he shared this with me …

"I always knew when Ted was expecting a fast ball. He'd have his head down, put his hand to his batting cap, and adjust it. That's when I knew he was bearing down and gearing up for a fastball, so I'd throw him something off-speed."

I thought it was pretty neat how observation and attention to detail leads to such useful information. And it must have worked, for in his career Pierce held his own against Williams. Bob Feller, the Hall-of-Fame hurler from Cleveland, once told me that he and Ted had a "Mexican stand-off" when facing each other, with neither one owning the other. I'd say that Pierce could make the same statement, perhaps even more so. One source claims that Williams hit .267 off Pierce; some 77 points below his overall lifetime average.

There's an ominous black and white photo from August of '57 that shows Pierce finishing up his warm-up tosses between innings as battery mate Sherman Lollar (#10) is set to receive the ball in mid-flight. In the background amidst the cigar and cigarette haze looms the monstrous scoreboard all lit up with games from both leagues. One of the games shows the Cubs and New York Giants tied in the tenth (the Cubs would go on to lose in 16 innings). The clock reads nearly 10 PM, yet the game is only in the middle frames. In those days the night games didn't start until 8 o'clock, making for some extended evenings. But the focal point of the photo is #9 of the visiting team lurking a few feet away from the batter's box as Pierce completes his preparation. Ted Williams, most anxious to hit, seems to study the pitch the way a doctor studies an X-ray. It did him no good this game, however, as Pierce retired Teddy Ballgame four straight times. In fact, Billy himself got a hit, so I kidded him by saying that on this particular evening, you were a better hitter than the best hitter who ever lived. The Chisox won this game, 4-1, as Pierce recorded one of his twenty victories that night.

Back to 1972 and the game Williams is managing. Once this game started, the fun ceased. The Rangers jumped out to an early 2 run lead, and then put the game on ice with 5 in the 5th. My guy, all 6' 7" of Frank Howard, cracked a run-scoring double and scored in the ambush. Ed Herrmann set off the fireworks by homering in the 4th, the only long ball of the day, but it wasn't nearly enough. Final score: Rangers 11, White Sox 5.

GAME 22: MONTREAL EXPOS VS. CHICAGO CUBS
THURSDAY, AUGUST 10

Another YMCA excursion. Ever notice how groups like these get offers to watch teams like the Astros and Expos rather than the Dodgers or Reds? Probably a matter of supply and demand with regards to ticket availability for group outings. But as summer days dwindle, heck yeah, I'll go see the Cubs/ Sox play whoever, wherever, whenever, and I'll get there however.

Just like you have good days at the office, and good days fishing, one look at the scorecard and you can tell I had a good day for autographs. Could be for a number of reasons: nice weather, get-away day, the last visit by the Montreal club into Chicago, the buffet spread was especially tasty, who really knows? But no less than a dozen signatures scrawled in every direction graced my "official program." FYI: these official programs cost all of 15 cents. The players from Montreal who signed included the following: Hal Breeden, Tom Walker, Ken Singleton, Hector Torres, Ernie McAnally, Mike Torrez, Mike Jorgensen, Carl Morton, Bob Bailey, and Ron Hunt. Which of the above would you treasure the most? I might have to go with Mike Torrez for that infamous gopher ball he served to Bucky Dent in the fall of '78. The most valuable player of the list? I'd probably pick Ken Singleton with Ron Hunt a close second.

I only got two Cub signatures that day, and they weren't even players. But the coaches that were gracious enough to sign included Q.V. Lowe (I'm not making that up) and Ernie Banks. Currently Whitey Lockman was managing the Cubs, and Banks served as one of his coaches. A little known fact is that Ernie is the first black man to manage a major league baseball game after Whitey Lockman was ejected in San Diego on May 8, 1973.

Looking at this list of Expo autographs, and then adding a Ron Fairly, Tim McCarver, and today's pitcher, Bill Stoneman, I'd have to reiterate what was suggested earlier and deem this a veteran and skilled ballclub. And with Gene Mauch as the manager, one would expect this to be a fairly competitive bunch. But as Kurt Russell might say in a hockey movie, "Not tonight."

8-0, Cubs, courtesy of a young kid out of Quincy, IL—Rick Reuschel. This season initiated the 19 year campaign for Reuschel, a quality pitcher. He'd never win any swim suit competition, but he could get batters out. Mike

Schmidt once referred to him as a hamburger. Then when Reuschel went on to record a lot of wins, Schmidt retracted a bit by describing him as "a hamburger who could pitch." In this particular contest, Reuschel scattered eight hits and earned a complete game shutout. Two big innings for the Cubs—3 in the 1st and 5 in the 5th—eliminated any drama in this game. A sense of redemption for the first YMCA Cub game earlier this season.

GAME 23: NEW YORK METS VS. CHICAGO CUBS
FRIDAY, AUGUST 11

I didn't go to this game on the following day, but my brother did and his score-card tells a story, so here goes. (I was jealous, of course, that my uncle would take my kid brother and not me, but I'm almost over it by now).

Milt Pappas, a solid pro for many seasons, pitched for the Cubs in the early 70's. His presence in the rotation made for an effective mix of experience and promising youth. It included the vets of Jenkins, Hands, and Pappas mentoring the young arms of Reuschel, Burt Hooton, and Bill Bonham. In my mind, more than enough talent to win, at least on paper. Kenny Holtzman, very effective but never reaching elite status with the Cubs, departed for Oakland and was an integral part of their championship seasons. In return for Holtzman, the Cubs received a dandy player in Rick Monday.

The second best thing that Pappas did this day was pitch. His line read like this: a measly 4 hits in earning a complete game win against a less-than-intimidating Met offense. The story of the game, however, was Pappas at the plate. He fell a triple short of the cycle, accounting for 2/3 of the Cubs extra base hits. But he drove in 3 more runs than the entire Met offense by knocking in 5. Mind you that this offensive display came against a star pitcher in Jon Matlack. Final score: Cubs 7, Mets 2.

GAME 24: CHICAGO CUBS VS. CHICAGO WHITE SOX
MONDAY, AUGUST 14

"Melton's better than Santo."

"You're crazy."

"I'd rather have Dick Allen than Billy Williams."

"What?! American League is weak."

"Then how come Rick Monday hits homers with the Cubs but not with the A's?"

"Oh, yeah, look at Ken Holtzman---no big deal with the Cubs and now a star in Oakland."

"If you had to win one game, and your life depended on it—Wilbur Wood or Fergie?"

"Are you serious?"

"Wrigley Field's a joke, a bandbox."

"Sox Park is a hole."

"No parking at Wrigley Field."

"No ivy at Comiskey."

"McCuddy's is better than Murphy's."

"Wow, great players you have like Luis Alvarado."

"So, I'd take him over guys like Ken Rudolph, the red-nose back-up."

"You'll never beat Oakland."

"Nice choke job in '69."

And on and on it goes. Some folks may think trash talk was invented in the hip-hop era. Got to know your history: Sox fans and Cub fans have been giving each other crap since there's been baseball in Chicago. This stuff of, "Oh, I'm a Chicagoan and I like both teams," doesn't set well with either fan base. This is baseball, not politics, "So take a side and have fun with it—we won't kill each other, just bust 'em where it hurts a little." That's how baseball fans in Chicago co-existed for so long.

Before the emergence of inter-league play, the Cubs and Sox found time to sneak in an exhibition game during the season. They raised some money for charity, presented something novel for the fans, provided a great opportunity for folks to talk smack, but hardly settled anything. The starters play half the game, maybe. Dick Allen may not show up at all. The 5th or 6th best pitcher in a four man rotation would get the start. On this evening, only three things stood out: Dan McGinn letting a mini-fan touch his Cubbie logo on his uniform, Billy Williams driving a ball off the right field façade in the 4th inning, and Ernie Banks.

All Sox trash talk ends with Ernie, just like Cub fans would be toward Minnie Minoso or Paul Konerko. There's just some people out there who elevate the way we think and act, even if it's just baseball. So Ernie's playing career is over and his coaching career is in mid-season form, whatever that is. Yet, he gets a couple at-bats at the end of this meaningless exhibition game. The place, Sox Park, goes nuts when Ernie's name is announced. You really couldn't tell who was a Sox fan and who was a Cub fan as Ernie strolls to the plate. For a few moments, BS is put to the side as Chicago fans stand as one. A memory. The loudest ovation I ever heard for a strikeout. Aside from Ernie and Minnie, what are some things that Cub fans and Sox fans can agree upon? Here's my list:

- Beer
- Hatred toward New York teams
- Hatred toward the Detroit Red Wings
- Harry Caray
- Appreciation of ballplayers who bust their butt
- Da Bears, Bulls, Blackhawks
- Deep dish pizza and beer
- People in the service
- 16" softball, followed by beer

P.S. To promote unity among Sox & Cub nation, I considered not giving you the score, for that may just divide us baseball brethren, and after all, this is just an exhibition game. But on second thought, no. The Northside JV team prevailed: 3-1.

GAME 25: SAN FRANCISCO GIANTS VS. CHICAGO CUBS
SUNDAY, AUGUST 27

Ever have a premonition of dread, ever feel gloom and doom about to envelop you, ever feel like it's just going to be one of those days? What's that you say? It happens whenever you walk into Wrigley Field?

Well, I told Petey's dad that I was utterly convinced and absolutely certain that the Cubs would lose to the Giants this day. He responded with a perfectly logical question (I hated it when adults did that) that went something like this: "So why are you going?"

I stammered for a few moments, hoping he'd understand not through words but by sentiment that going to the game is what matters the most. For if I went on days that I *knew* the Cubs or Sox were going to win, I'd be stuck at home a lot. As a kid in the early 70's, I was a lot of things, but a home body was not one of them. Better to apply words of wisdom from my mom that fits this scenario, "Nothing ventured, nothing gained."

So Petey and I find our usual place—last row, upper deck, behind home plate. That way if the action of the field is too much or too little to take, I can turn around, look down, and observe what's happening on Clark and Addison Streets. Since we arrived at the ballpark fairly early, I thought I'd swoop down to the first base side and try my luck in procuring a few Giant signatures. I collected four: Jerry Johnson, pitcher; Dave Rader, catcher; Garry Maddox, CF; Damaso Blanco, bench-warmer. It was kind of neat at the Giant dugout to glance upstairs to see if I could spot Petey and our seat location. To my surprise, I could. I suppose that's due to the rows and rows of empty seats around him.

My hunch of bad tidings looked rock solid as the Cubs hit in the 6th, trailing 3 love. The pitcher I tried my best to imitate, Bill Hands, threw well, but a former Cub, Frank Reberger, threw better. Coincidentally, I wrote about Reberger in a previous book of Chicago baseball, Like Night and Day. You might want to check it out (shameless plug).

The big blow from the visitors belongs to Ken Henderson, who was having a career weekend against the Cubs. In the 4th Henderson slugged a ball to right field that ricocheted most erratically, and it wound up as an inside-the-park home run. This takes some doing in the cozy confines of Wrigley Field—one needs not just a fortuitous bounce or two, but plenty of foot speed to blaze a 360 foot counter-clockwise trail. While Jose Cardenal in right and Rick Monday in center were trying to corral the baseball, Henderson turned on the jets and circled the bases, without even a play at home. This gave him a total of five home runs in this three game series, making me wonder if he wasn't really Mike Schmidt incognito.

But the home team roared back the way that cubbies roar, by tallying nine times in the final three innings. Billy Williams hit an outside-the-park home run, as Cub hitters abused the Frisco relief corps of Don McMahon, Sam McDowell (yes, THE Sudden Sam), and Steve Stone (yes, that Steve Stone). I must say it was kind of a neat feeling to depart with a victory when I thought defeat was inevitable; doesn't make up for all the times it went the other way, but it was still nice.

Here are the twelve Giant players who played in this game: Bobby Bonds, Chris Speier, Ken Henderson, Willie McCovey, Dave Rader, Tito Fuentes, Garry Maddox, Dave Kingman (batting eighth?!), and pitchers Reberger, McMahon, McDowell, and Stone. Of these 12 Giants who saw action this day, 2/3 played for either the Cubs or Sox, while three played for both. How many can you identify?

Time's up, here's your answer:

Bonds (Sox & Cubs), Speier (Cubs), Henderson (Sox & Cubs), Rader (Cubs), Kingman (Cubs), Reberger (Cubs), McMahon (Sox), and Stone pony (Sox & Cubs). Howcha do?

SATURDAY, SEPTEMBER 2
PADRES VS. CUBS

I write this with a heavy heart. No, not because a perfect game was lost on out #27. It was because I did NOT go to this game when I had the opportunity.

The old Carol Burnett show had this one character named Eunice. You might remember this skit they did where Eunice would rhetorically ask her husband, "Oh why, oh why, did I marry you?"

Regrets, I've had a few. "Oh why, oh why did I choose a movie over a no-hitter?" It shames me to this day to think that I could have been part of Cubs' history, but I opted to see a movie called <u>KC Bomber</u> at the York Theater in Elmhurst on a Labor Day Saturday. The film stars Raquel Welch as a roller derby diva, and that's all I remember, honest. Some theater trivia ... it was at the same locale that I venture out into a warm July evening air a few summers back after having just watched <u>Chitty-Chitty Bang Bang</u>. Once exiting the fantasy world and entering the real world, I marveled as I looked up at the moon. I think for a moment that as I am walking on York Road, Neil Armstrong is walking on the moon. My inclination is to say small world, but now we have more than a small world to explore.

Back to Pappas as I leave the roller derby queen. "He did WHAT!!!" I exclaimed to my brother. Now I know how it feels to have the winning lotto ticket, but toss it in the junk drawer, only to be pulled out 5 months later. A famous quote is born that day when Pappas understandably barked at the umpire, Bruce Froemming, for calling a borderline pitch a ball to the 27th batter on a 3-2 count. In the aftermath, Froemming boasted that there was only one person who was perfect today, and that was himself. That's one way to get yourself off the Pappas' Christmas card list.

POST-SEASON, 1972

The juxtaposition of more spending money, growing independence, and affordable tickets resulted in plenty of major league baseball games for yours truly in '72. It was a good year to be a Chicago fan. Dick Allen had a year that I don't know if I have ever seen before. It wasn't just the numbers, although those were outstanding. No, it was more about timing, presence, style, drama, excitement, and raw ability. The man simply had a special season culminating with the MVP award.

And on the North Side, Billy Williams also had a season for the ages. He, too, earned MVP honors but finished second in the voting. This time let's look at the numbers: For Williams, .333 BA (led league), 37 HR's, and 122 RBI's. Johnny Bench, the one who did receive the MVP, ended with .270, 40, 125. And in a critical category usually ignored, Williams scored 95 times for his team, compared to Bench's 87.

Some critics saw racism—could two black ballplayers, Allen and Williams, win the MVP during the same season? A no-brainer for me regardless of color, for Williams meant much more to the Cubs than Bench to the Reds. Cincy goes to the World Series with or without Bench; the Cubs go to .500 without Williams (they finished 15 above). Besides, in the near future two black ballplayers would soon win the MVP in the same year on several occasions (Carew & Foster, Rice & Parker, Baylor & Stargell), so why not now?

The less emotionally charged argument about the MVP has to do with team success and not just individual stats. To put it another way, had Bench played for the Cubs and Williams for the Reds, and Cincy ends up in the World Series, I think Williams takes the MVP by a wide margin.

Speaking of the World Series, it lacked nothing in color in '72. The mustachioed A's finally broke through the Oriole juggernaut, and they provided us with ample juicy comparisons. Green and gold vs. red; eccentric Charlie Finley vs. the Big Red Machine; Reggie Jackson, Catfish Hunter, Campy Campaneris, and Vida Blue vs. the household names of Bench, Morgan, Rose, and Perez. The intrigue of this Series cut to each team's identity: for Oakland it was pitching, defense, and timely hitting; for Cincinnati it was bludgeoning the opposition with a relentless offense. The question then centered on these two keys: could Oakland pitching stop or at least slow down the Red hitters, and could the Red pitching, hardly dominant, keep Cincinnati in the game long enough for the bats to take over?

Who would have thought that Gene Tenace becomes Dusty Rhoades, Part 2? By Series end, how could one relatively non-descript ballplayer out-homer the Big Red Machine, 4-3? Incredible, and I wonder what kind of odds you could get on that. Two of the three memories of this Series were Tenace going deep in his first two at bats, and Joe Rudi's brilliant twisting and turning catch against the wall in left field. The A's had the winning formula as well as any team I've ever seen—the ability to pitch, defend, and get just enough offense.

The other memory involves something I've never witnessed before or since. In Oakland, in the late innings of a close game, Johnny Bench steps to the plate. Oakland is set up to walk Bench even though this second best player in the league has two strikes on him. It's at that point when the TV analysist for the game, Tony Kubek, suggests that the audience be aware, because Oakland may feign the intentional walk and try to slip a strike past the batter, Bench. Right on cue, the catcher stands, extends his right arm, and then quickly squats back in his position. The A's pitcher, Rollie Fingers, fires a dart on the black of the outside corner. Bench is totally stunned as the ump rings him up. I have my doubts that I'll ever see that play again.

1973

GAME 26: CHICAGO WHITE SOX VS. MILWAUKEE BREWERS
FRIDAY, JUNE 1

The finishing touches of my biology class this morning meant no more turning green over a graphic video showing how the heart works, no more decapitation of frogs during dissections, and best of all, no more odorous reminders of dead things in large jars. Sophomore year, high school—a very long year indeed. The most angst, most rejection, most cliques and most alienation a person would ever want to have. Enough for a few lifetimes, or at least until school starts up again in the fall. Life as an upper-classman had to be better.

The bright side—surviving this nonsense makes summer that much more fun. Toward the end of this bio. class, a classmate named Jim grabs my attention. Jim, all eighty-nine pounds of him, suffers from Cystic Fibrosis. Whispers about his illness creep among us. You don't need a degree in medicine to know something was wrong, but I never paid that a whole lot of attention. Jim's not the kid you'd feel too sorry for; actually, he's the kind of kid who's more likely to have you feel sorry for yourself. "Spunk" is the first word that I think of when I think of Jim, with "smart-ass" a close second. There were times when I wanted to pound his tiny frame, sickness or no. But I, and probably a few other classmates, took his guff because he was Jim and that was his way. He's really not a bad guy and he really is sick, so we cut him a lot of slack. Besides, he wasn't a wise guy today, because summer vacation was a couple finals away.

"Boomer, are you really seeing the Sox play the Brewers tonite in Milwaukee?" Jim wondered with a hint of envy.

"Yep," was my smug response.

"Wilbur Wood's pitching, should be no problem."

"No doubt."

"Have a good one."

"You too."

Jim would be dead in six years, but not before he thoroughly entertained my roommates and some of his high school classmates at Notre Dame on a couple football weekends. Had he enrolled at the school and if his health allowed, Jim would have made the perfect leprechaun. Feisty, spirited, and a TNCFN attitude (Take No Crap From Nobody). He laughed with gusto and drank beer heartily, never feeling sorry for himself.

The last conversation I had with Jim took place at work. I was lying on the conveyor belt in the basement of the warehouse, with the phone stuck in my ear. I called Jim at the hospital, upon hearing that he wasn't doing so well. Some family member answered, I believe it was his mom, and I held for a while as he labored to the phone. Some time later I hear a "Hello Boomer" on the other end. I knew he was sick, but I didn't expect to be attending his funeral in a few days. His mom wrote me shortly after the funeral, indicating how much my little phone call picked up his spirits. He was exhausted, his mom said, but he took a deep breath and worked his way to the phone. Surprised, I mumbled words mixing appreciation and consolation and went on my way.

Something Jim gave me, and this a real gift, was the establishment of a friendship with a third party who knew us both. This person's name was Don.

About a month later, I'm on the phone again, this time with Don. Somehow the subject of Jim came up.

"He could be a little SOB, couldn't he?" I offered.

"You got that right—at times I wanted to punch his lights out."

"You too?"

"Yeah, and I knew him a lot longer than you did."

This was true as Don and Jim went to grade school together, over on what we'd call the nicer side of the tracks. There's this awkward pause in the conversation, and then it was my turn to take a deep breath as I struggled to say something meaningful. To be vulnerable is risky business, especially guy on guy. Anger and wise cracks? Sure, all the time. But some sincerity and vulnerability?

"You know," I sputtered, "he's in a better place after all that suffering." I gulped. Saying something deep and even religious to a person my own age and not in a religion class was about as common as a Chicago championship. I listened for his reaction.

"Oh yeah." It wasn't the words, it was the sentiment I heard in his voice. A kindred spirit. Someone who "might give the heavens more than just a passing glance." From that moment on—and it's been four decades and counting—Don and I could talk about stuff deeper than sports. Not always easy, mind you, for Don was and is a wise ass himself. But good and gratifying. In his death, Jim initiated a friendship that has stood the test of time. Priceless.

Now back to baseball. Trips to Milwaukee made me, a Chicagoan, feel like a big shot. I couldn't help, for the longest time, to look down my nose at our suburban neighbors to the north. Patronizing words like "quaint" and "folksy" simply roll off my tongue when describing Milwaukee. They might be the brewers of beer, but we're the brewers of big time. I realize now the errors of my ways. Today I appreciate the kindness and courtesy of Wisconsinites, wishing we folks from Chicago weren't such idiots. Chalk up my earlier brashness to youth and stupidity; my recent perceptions to humility and maturity.

This Sox-Brewers game should not have been close. The Sox ran out a solid lineup with names like Kelly, Allen, Melton, May, Reichardt, and Herrmann. Should be more than enough to support their ace, Wood. But baseball, as you know, doesn't always work that way, and the Brewers posted an easy 5-3 victory. Herrmann's gargantuan blast leading off the ninth was about all the excitement the visitors could muster on offense; Bart Johnson escaping a bases-loaded jam was the highlight on defense.

Two pieces of trivia. One will be Short, I promise. When reviewing my scorecard, guess who is identified as the youngest president in baseball. Obviously it will be whoever the president is of the Milwaukee club since this is a Milwaukee program, but can you guess his name? It's Bud Selig, age 38.

The other has to do with Milwaukee's starting pitcher. He had a prominent career in Philly. In fact, he and Jim Bunning carried the load of innings back in the cataclysmic collapse of 1964. From '64 to '68 he posted a mark of 93 wins and 54 losses, with a 20 win season in 1966. He appeared twice in All-Star games during this stretch. Then misfortune struck. He pitched only ten innings in '69, and from that point on his record stood at 20-36. He finished his career, which had a slow beginning, a brilliant middle, and this unfortunate conclusion, at 135-132. Oh, and he was a lefty who started and won this game for the Brewers (and this was the only season he pitched for anyone except the Phillies). His name? Chris Short.

GAME 27: LOS ANGELES DODGERS VS. CHICAGO CUBS
TUESDAY, JUNE 5

Picture this: your final final of sophomore year is finally over. It's late in the AM. You and four friends rush to the train station in downtown Elmhurst. You jump on board for a forty-five minute commute to downtown Chicago. You get a transfer to the Howard line. You sprint to the bleacher ticket window. You dig for a dollar or two or three—highly likely that a couple of friends are broke after train fare and need to mooch off you. You exchange a couple coins with a vendor for a scorecard. A dash to the bleachers in right field. And what's the first thing you see? Fergie Jenkins releases a ball that is never to be seen again. Ron Cey connects and the ball lands in the area outside the ballpark from whence we sprinted. Two Dodgers trot home ahead of Cey, giving the Los Angelers a total of four runs before the Cubs even bat. I busted my butt to see this?!

It's decision time—how serious do I want to take this game? The Dodgers have an insurmountable lead in the *first inning*, I'm with my friends, school's out for summer, and I just bought a scorecard (naturally, the only one of us to make such a purchase). Do I or do I not keep score? How nerdy do I want to be?

Heck with keeping score; I'm in the bleachers where people don't even know their name let alone the score. I defer to my comrades and sit in the bleachers, but I never have enjoyed sitting there. Let me tell you why:

1. Too far from home plate.
2. No way of knowing if ground balls hit to the opposite field will get through or be caught.
3. In fact, no way of knowing right away if balls hit in the opposite field are fair or foul.
4. There is no #4.
5. Things said in the bleachers are witty only if you're completely smashed.
6. Heck, no, I ain't throwin it back. You know the chances of getting a home run ball?

7. Opposing outfielders' performance is directly related to amount of trash talk received.
8. This is the Midwest; show *some* class.
9. Walks around the ballpark are now very limited.
10. If I wanted to be surrounded by drunks, I'd go to Murphy's across the street.

But "when in the bleachers, do as the bums do." So my virgin scorecard makes it home unscathed—a testimony to adolescent peer pressure. Just as well since the Cubs lose big, 10-1. We spend the majority of time harassing Dodger right fielder, Willie Crawford. It works, too, as he hits the snot out of the ball all day long (that was sarcasm).

The only other time that verbal abuse matched what Crawford received from today's audience was at a Triple A game in Portland, OR in 1980. Now how's this for a coincidence—the left fielder on this day for LA happens to be the center fielder who was abused in Portland, Von Joshua. Back in Portland, the hecklers were both drunk and witty, and since there were only four fans in the entire outfield section, their comments could easily be heard by the victim. The verbal arrow that I remember the most was the calculation of Joshua's batting average after he failed to reach base. "You're down to .187, Von" they'd inform him after his most recent ground out. They also reminded him that Class AA ball would soon be calling. I don't know whatever became of those hecklers, but I do know that Joshua went on to become a major league hitting coach.

GAME 28: NEW YORK METS VS. CHICAGO CUBS
FRIDAY, JUNE 29

One of the top five games I've ever seen in person.

I feel responsible for showing a friend named Rico a good time at Wrigley Field. You see this was Rico's first ever major league baseball game. In rapid fire fashion, Rico …

- Hails from Italy
- Speaks Italian at home (his folks no habla ingles)
- Plays soccer and likes Pele'
- Likes Alice Cooper
- Plays basketball
- Eats pasta daily
- Once reached 100 MPH in his Chevy (I have the soiled shorts to prove it)
- Knows and sings enthusiastically the lyrics from "Cisco Kid"
- Makes me laugh, a lot

Save for the speaking Italian at home part, a pretty typical kid in the neighborhood. Probably the biggest difference between us was that I was a Catholic school kid and he was a public.

I thought Rico would like my favorite seats: upper deck grandstand behind home plate. Wrong. Rico had no use for sitting this high—so we shuffled to customer service and made a ticket exchange, hassle free. For an additional $1.75 (not a paltry sum when minimum wage was $1.85), we find our way to the lower deck, about fifteen rows up from the Mets' on-deck circle. Rico was satisfied.

By looking at today's probables, Rico may be in for a treat: Rick Reuschel vs. Tom Seaver. A very good vs. a great; an All-Star vs. a Hall-of-Famer; a hamburger vs. an All-American boy. As you would expect, pitching dominates the game. Reuschel's line (7 2/3 IP, 2 runs, 8 hits, 3 K's) matches Seaver's (7 IP, 2 runs, 6 hits, 5 K's) in a well-played game.

I'm going to put your baseball knowledge in Jeopardy with the topic: Brother Combinations in History for 200. The answer is … "Aviation has the Wrights, fairy tales have the Grimms, and today's contest features these two brothers." The answer is … "Who are Adrian Garrett for the Cubs and Wayne Garrett for the Mets." While Wayne is the more heralded of the two playing by virtue of playing in New York and in a World Series, this day belonged to big brother Adrian. For the season he accumulated 12 hits, 3 homers, and 8 RBI's. I'm proud to say that Rico and I witnessed one from each category as he homered off Seaver immediately following the 7th inning stretch. This gives the home team a short-lived 2-1 advantage. Yo Adrian.

Leading off the 8th for the Metropolitans is pinch-hitter Ken Boswell, and this presents us with good news/bad news. The good news is that Seaver can no longer pitch since Boswell is hitting for him. The bad news is Boswell homers to tie the game at 2. Later in the inning, as the Mets threaten to take the lead, Reuschel is relieved and this now becomes the battle of the bullpens.

New York's leadoff hitter strikes again in the 9th. Picture the center field bleachers of Wrigley Field—the portion above the shrubbery and below the scoreboard. A seat where if you use a strong set of binoculars, you might be able to make out the center fielder. Okay, so that's the place, and now I want to share with you two lines of poetry that goes something like this:

"… Once or twice this side of death
Something happens that stops our breath"

This was one of those times for me. Awe-struck. That's what I was when I followed the path of the ball hit by John Milner. My jaw dropped. I've never seen a ball hit like that in *batting practice*, let alone a game. As the baseball continued to ascend and accelerate, I really thought it might reach the scoreboard. Milner (AKA "The Hammer") did not run right away. I think he was too stunned to move. I can't accuse him of showing up anybody, because I was too stunned to breathe. Although it meant bad news for the Cubs, this moment transcended game, score, inning, etc. Truly a breath-taking, "did that really happen" moment as the enormity of the blast starts to sink in.

The inning concludes with no further damage, so it's the classic, "one run to tie and two runs to win" as we head to the bottom of the ninth.

Years ago, at an Old-Timers game in Geneva, IL, a second-string out-fielder by the name of Gene Hiser makes an appearance. After a brief softball exhibition, I wander up to Hiser and ask if he recalls a certain pinch-hit oc-currence against Tom Seaver in the late innings of a game in Chicago. His face lights up as we share a fond memory. Strangely enough, he was either as wrong as I was about the details or was too polite to correct me.

Truth be told, Hiser did not bat against Seaver with two outs, nobody on base, and the Cubs trailing by one run in the ninth. But that scarcely matters. It is true that Hiser was sent in for a defensive replacement for the earlier hero, Adrian Garrett. Now if you've been following baseball for more than a few years, you know that there are stories upon stories that just can't be made up. Like this, for instance: Gene Hiser in 263 official at-bats spanning a career of five seasons (all with the Cubs) has one more MLB homer than I (and I'm assuming you, dear reader). So on the day my pal Rico attends his first (and possibly only) Cub game, Gene Hiser, all 175 pounds of him, decides to hit the only home run of his career. For the second time in the inning I am numb. Once for the distance, the other for the drama. Hiser's eleventh hour blow to the catwalk extends the game to extras. Not Williams, not Santo, not Monday, not Hundley, but Gene Hiser. Feel the glee.

I think of Rico and wonder how he sees all of this. I wonder if he thinks all games in person are this exciting. I wonder if he's hooked for life, as I was after my first game. I almost lean over and caution him not to expect this at every game, that two home runs of such magnitude are extremely rare. I think this, but don't follow through. Why tarnish the moment?

Now the Mets bat. With two outs and the go-ahead run in scoring posi-tion, the man with a bat in his hands is Milner of course. The one who just struck the ball 500 feet if he hit it a foot has a chance to replicate his Ruthian feat. But this time it comes up snake-eyes, as Cub reliever Dave LaRoche (Adam's dad) fans him.

In the home half, the Cubs take their cuts against Tug McGraw, one of the more celebrated relievers in the game. A single by Kessinger, a walk to *pinch-hitter* Billy Williams (how many times would a Cub fan be happy that Adrian Garrett is playing and Billy Williams isn't), and a walk to Rick Monday load the bases with nobody out. The chances of scoring in this scenario are approximately 17 out of 20. Glenn Beckert, one of the best contact men in recent history, grounds to the shortstop who fires home to record the first out. Then the third place hitter, Jose Cardenal, delivers his third hit of the day, and Rico gets his first win. He's happy, I'm spent, and I'll never forget Adrian Garrett, John Milner, or Gene Hiser.

GAME 29: SAN DIEGO PADRES VS. CHICAGO CUBS
THURSDAY, JULY 19

If you're familiar with <u>Like Night and Day</u>, that classic book about Chicago baseball in the 60's, you may recall that the author at age 6 wondered why the Cubs' uniform is blue. From that era, the Reds and Redbirds have distinctive red colors, the Pirates—like the bad guys in movies—wear black, and the Orioles don a fitting orange and black. So shouldn't a team of bear cubs be decked out in a beige/tan color? But they choose instead a royal blue that remains as central to the franchise as ivy on the wall.

One gander at the Padres' uniform gives notice why the Cubs, in their wisdom, chose blue and not brown. Gross, and I don't mean Greg. Gross as in revolting, hideous, disgusting. Padre is a term for clergy, and I guess players from San Diego wear their garb as a form of penance. The Catholic faith holds that suffering can be redemptive, so here, put this on. You play and live in San Diego, so we'll have to balance off that perk with these costumes. I bet you that concession sales decline when the Padre team comes to town as fans lose their appetite. The only thing that could make the Padre brown look worse in a mingling of yellow to go with the brown, so that's precisely what Ray Kroc and the Padre think tank choose. It's a challenge to detract from the beauty of Wrigley Field, but these uniforms succeed. I'm not sure, but maybe the thinking is that this awful apparel will take the attention away from how poorly the team competes on the field.

All that being said, guess who's winning 4-0 in the 1st inning? This lousy team with a lousier uniform smacks Burt Hooton's knuckle curve around the park, and hard. A triple by Leron Lee and a homer by Cito Gaston (who would later manage Toronto to a couple of world championships) give the visitors a comfortable cushion.

Good Greif is probably what the Padre skipper, Don Zimmer, is hoping for. Bill Greif, the Padre starting pitcher, is bad Greif as the Cubs mount a comeback in the 3rd. A 3-run double and a solo homer by Jose Cardenal (alias "Junior") puts the Cubs ahead. Hooton survives five innings before giving way to a pinch hitter. Far from a quality start, but Hooton gets the "W"—I think I know what he'd rather have. Bill Bonham relieves Hooton and earns a quality save with four innings of one run ball. The Cubs win going away, 12-5. For the record, this marked the only victory the Cubs would enjoy over a 13 game span. On July 10, the Cubs were sitting pretty at 51-38. By July 29 they had gotten a lot homelier, 53-50.

Today's hitting spectacle provided by Junior is complemented by 3 hit games from Randy Hundley and Rick Monday. Arguably the best hitter of this day, however, is Lee from San Diego, who fell a homer shy of hitting for the cycle. A nice win, and even nicer if you happened to be color blind for a few hours.

GAME 30: CLEVELAND INDIANS VS. CHICAGO WHITE SOX
WEDNESDAY, AUGUST 8

Early this morning I remember doing yard work while listening to the haunting vocals of Diana Ross. "Touch Me in the Morning" filled with melancholy stung me as a fitting song. Not so much the actual message of a failed romance but the mood of the piece strikes a nerve since in mid-August the harbinger of another school year looms large.

"We don't have tomorrow but we had yesterday …."

"Yesterday's gone my love, there's only now …"

I wanted to hit the brakes and reset to early June, but there's only now. I pull up a few more weeds amidst the brown grass. But sadness will be put on hold for a few hours as my family and I take in a game tonight … at least that's what I thought.

How bad was this one? Well, look at it this way: should the White Sox bat around and hit a couple of grand slams in the first inning, they'd only be trailing 9-8. That's the optimist speaking. The realist informs us that the Sox go three up and three down in their first ups, so at this rate we'll be looking at a final score of Tribe 81, Sox 0.

Some movie theaters have a policy that if you leave in the first 20 minutes or so of the film, they will refund your money. In the 90's I once made this request to Jim Frey, GM of the Cubs, after witnessing the Cubs get annihilated by the Mets. Frey was decent enough to write back and tell me that while this couldn't be done, he did think the Cubs would play much better ball in the second half of the season. He was wrong.

Since this was a ballgame and not a movie, we had to sit there and take this Indian massacre. When ex-Sox player Walt Williams and future Sox player Oscar Gamble both homer in the first inning, you almost start looking forward to going back to school (not really). So we buck up, hang in there, give it the ol' college try, and wouldn't you know it … by the sixth inning the score read … Indians 12, White Sox 0. John (the Jet) Jeter triples and Carlos May doubles—those are your two hits after 2/3 of the game had been played. We leave this ugliness behind, and this time it's not because of the uniforms. "Touch me in the morning" and tell me this was all a dream.

GAME 31: LOS ANGELES DODGERS VS. CHICAGO CUBS
SUNDAY, AUGUST 19

"I'm going to see two perfect games thrown on the same day!"

My dad, not to be confused with Nostradamus, was on to something. 1/3 of the way through the game, 9 players on both sides have come to the plate, and all 18 hitters have been retired. Tommy John and Rick Reuschel were putting on a clinic and putting crazy thoughts into people's heads as the middle innings approach.

Different styles, different motions, and definitely different physiques but the same results—goose eggs. John would go on to retire 18 Cubs via the ground ball. Not a shock since his out pitch had been a sinking fastball for most of his career, but it was still impressive how his pitches would be hit with regularity, but harmlessly pounded into the turf. (Never owning a blazing fastball, Tommy John quipped that as he was undergoing the famous surgery that now bears his name, he asked the doctor to make his arm like Koufax. When he resumed pitching, he realized he did have a Koufax arm, but it was Mrs. Koufax). At one point in this game he retired eight consecutive batters via grounders, and had a no-hitter going into the 5th. That's when Ron Santo lifted one of John's pitches to the bleachers, giving the Cubs a one run lead. This looked practically insurmountable due to the work of Reuschel. Being more of a power pitcher, Rick struck out the side in both the 3rd and the 7th, finishing the game with 13 K's.

History repeating itself is old news, but it's interesting stuff. Four years ago to the day, Santo blasted a three run homer that proved to be the winning margin. They'd be the only runs the Cubs would score that day, but they're more than enough as Ken Holtzman no-hits the Braves. Would Santo's blast be enough as Reuschel no-hits LA?

The perfect game is lost in the 6th when Reuschel plunks Ron Cey with a pitch. But positive vibes crescendo as Reuschel fans Bill Buckner, Willie Davis, and Joe Ferguson in the 7th. 6 outs to go. Then the man we abused mercilessly earlier this summer comes back to stick it to us. With strong evidence of bad karma, Willie Crawford spoils the no-hitter by singling to lead off the 8th. Applause and cheers all around notwithstanding, Reuschel still needs to protect a precarious one run lead. After yielding another safety to Cey, he wiggles out of the jam and heads into the 9th. 3 outs to go.

It comes down to this: man on first, two out, Cubs lead 1-0. Reuschel vs. Ferguson. Last time, strikeout. This time??? As soon as Ferguson makes contact, Santo hurls his glove to the ground, utterly distraught. He doesn't turn to watch the ball sail out of the field of play. He knows now that the perfect game, no-hitter, and shutout are all gone. Adding to his frustration is the fact that his homer which accounts for the only Cub offense will not be enough. The course of this highly charged and competitive game has dramatically shifted. Santo and the Cubs, either tied or winning for the entire game, now trail with precious little time remaining.

To add insult to injury, the venerable manager of the Dodgers, Walt Alston, who looks like he's 112 years old, officially protests the game over some silly rule. Whatever. With one out and a man at first my hero comes to bat, Billy Leo Williams. I cherish the memory of his ending the Cincinnati game with a homer in the 10th, and hope against hope for a repeat. How about ending this one in regulation?

Instead, he raps the ball hard in the direction of the first baseman. Kudos to Alston for replacing Steve Garvey at first with Bill Buckner. I recall how much trouble Garvey had in throwing the baseball to second base. If he remained in the game, who knows, the ball could be tossed somewhere into the outfield and the Cubs really be in business. As it is, Buckner skillfully completes the twin killing which makes Alston's protest moot.

I look for a glove to throw to the ground. Not finding any, I have to settle for harassing my kid brothers. One out away from a 1-0 victory so cruelly disintegrates into a 2-1 defeat.

POST-SEASON

An excellent Oakland team defends its crown, but it wasn't easy. Just four years earlier, the Miracle Mets took the baseball world by storm by conquering strong teams like the Cubs, Braves, and Orioles. Now it looked like the Mets were going to pull of an even greater upset, having limped to the post-season with a record barely above .500. The NLCS pitted the Mets against the Reds, but that took second billing to Pete Rose vs. Bud Harrelson. Fisticuffs in post-season play? Yes, and I think it distracted the Reds just enough to allow the Mets to squeak by. Harrelson lost the battle to Rose, but the Mets won the war.

The World Series provided an even greater distraction in the conflict between Charlie Finley and Mike Andrews. Long story short, Finley fires Andrews for poor play early in the Series (the almost always dependable A's defense blew Game 2 at home by committing 5 errors, 2 by Andrews). The media salivated over this as the Oakland players rallied behind Andrews, creating a near mutiny. Finley eventually relented as Andrews returns to the A's dugout. After three games in Gotham, the Series shifts to Oakland with the Mets in control, 3 games to 2. Fortunately, the A's hold service at home behind the overall stellar play of Campy Campaneris.

Why fortunately? Because common folk could take the umbrage of *"Amazin Mets"* or *"Miracle Mets"* for only so long. Do you really think the memory of '69 would be such a big deal if it were any other team that pulled this off (the only team that comes to mind is another East Coast club, the Red Sox and their *Impossible Season* of '67). So what would be the aftermath should the Mets score another upset in '73. I shudder to think about it.

Interesting how within a span of eight years that two of the All-time greats left the game after a less-than-glorious performance in the World Series. In 1966 Sandy Koufax's last game is a loss to Baltimore in the second game of the World Series. Koufax was hardly the goat, however, as his mates committed **six** errors in the field. But in '73 the career of Willie Mays, which should have ended sooner, finally comes to a close after some embarrassing play in center field. Mays at 43 hung around a couple seasons too long, watching season batting averages sink to .250 and .211. For what it's worth, I was happy he quit when he did, so that his lifetime batting average would remain a notch above .300 (.302 to be exact. His foil, Mickey Mantle, retired with a batting average just under .300). But if you were a Willie Mays' fan, it had to hurt to watch him leave on these terms. In his own words, it was "Time to say goodbye to baseball."

1974

GAME 32: SAN FRANCISCO GIANTS VS. CHICAGO CUBS THURSDAY, MAY 30

Inflation strikes! Prices soar! Check out the price increase for fine Wrigley Field cuisine:

Item	1973 price	1974 price
Hot dog	40 cents	45 cents
Corned beef sandwich	65 "	70 "
Bratwurst	45 "	50 "
Smoke link	45 "	50 "(worth it)
Italian beef	75 "	80 "
French fries	25 "	30 "
Milk (at a ballgame?)	25 "	30 "
Old Style & Schlitz beer	55 "	60 "
Popcorn	15 "	20 "
Taffy apple	25 "	30 "
This program	15 "	20 "

Surprisingly, several ticket prices stayed the same, and this is when the Cubs were in contention for the postseason. Bleachers and grandstand prices (for kids) stayed at a buck, reserved grandstand remained at $3.00, but the price of a box seat went up by a quarter from $3.75 to an even four dollars.

All doubleheaders started at 12 noon (none of these chintzy day/night deals when the fans are chased out after the first game). No indication of premium, prime, regular rates for ballgames but just one standard price. Inside these Wrigley field programs (now costing you an extra nickel) you had no excuse not to sing the National Anthem as the words were squished right underneath the section of future Cub home games. The scorecards did not allow for much advertising space, no color or glossy photos on the inside, but just enough information to satisfy me.

The left side of the program could have on display a big orange road sign, because the Cubs organization was definitely under construction. Gone were the familiar numbers of 9, 10, 14, 28, and 31. Odder still was to see a player wearing #18, because four time All-Star Glenn Beckert got traded to San Diego for Jerry Morales. Now this number belonged to a promising young 3rd baseman named Bill Madlock. The Cubs made many moves in the off-season: Hundley to Minnesota, Santo to the South Side, Ernie probably assigned to PR work, Hickman to the Cardinals, and Fergie to Texas. Really, the only two holdovers from the 60's club were Kessinger and Williams. I wonder how these two handled the wholesale changes, with both knowing that the business of the game dictates personnel moves, but seeing their teammates for a decade or so sent somewhere else must have had some impact. I'm guessing they handled this as they handled everything else in their Cub tenure—professionally.

This particular game toward the end of my junior year in high school satisfies the home crowd. An enigma for several seasons, Bill Bonham, gets dinged up for 11 hits, but allows only 3 runs in a complete game victory. The Cub offense is much more efficient—two doubles and two runs scored by Williams, and a pair of RBI's from Rick Monday and Jerry Morales. A former Chisox favorite of mine, Tom Bradley, started for the Giants and had a no decision.

I had the good fortune of crossing paths with Bradley some thirty years later and enjoyed a casual chat with him prior to a minor league baseball game. At this point in his career he served as a pitching coach. Bradley still wore glasses, which was his most distinguishing feature, but a couple other things changed. Girth, mainly, but also a demeanor of jocularity. I remember watching an intense and hard throwing competitor whenever he pitched in the 70's. He performed at a high level for a number of seasons, among league leaders in strikeouts for a season or two. As a member of the Sox pitching staff, he toiled as the important #2 starter behind Wilbur Wood.

Now this heavier version of Bradley talked freely about several things, most notably pitching. He spoke with ease and candor; he spoke as one willing to share knowledge freely with no need to impress; he spoke as one who had success at the highest level of his profession; he spoke with humililty. In the few minutes I sensed that I could go ahead and pick his brain, and an attitude of ..."help yourself to anything that might help you or the kids you're trying to teach." So I did. Change up grips, fastball counts, and tough outs in the AL kept the conversation flowing. No great revelations, but it felt good to know that what I have been teaching high school players are things he teaches to young professionals.

Back to 1974. On this afternoon Bradley pitched well, giving his team a chance to win. He left the game in the 8th with the score tied at 3. The Cubs push two across against a reliever named Elias Sosa, the man who gave up the third and final home run to Reggie Jackson in Game 6 of the 1977 World Series. Bonham did a fine job of keeping Barry Bonds' dad, Bobby, off base, as he finished strong by retiring the last six batters he faced. Good game to start the summer.

GAMES 33 & 34: MONTREAL EXPOS VS. CHICAGO CUBS
WEDNESDAY, JULY 31

"The best thing in life is winning a major league baseball game. The second best thing in life is losing a major league baseball game" . . . . . Chuck Tanner

Chuck put together a fine managerial career. The way he handled Dick Allen in the White Sox exciting season of '72 was exemplary. On the national front, he guided the Pittsburgh Pirates to a World Championship in 1979 behind the musical inspiration of Sister Sledge's "We Are Family." In that Series, he resurrected the Bucs after they fell behind, 3 games to 1. But with all due respect to Chuck and his impressive accomplishments, I think the second part of his quote above is nonsense. What if you're rooting in earnest for a team on a particular day and you are told that there is 100% chance that your team will lose. Would you still go?

Here's my answer: No. I'll go watch KC Bomber for the second time before I knowingly add pain to my life that does not serve some greater good. Going to a baseball game is an investment on many fronts, and I don't want to invest in a guaranteed losing proposition. Speaking from the experience of watching a Chicago team lose over 200 times, I know this about myself—losing does not put me in a good place. I'm no fun to be with, I don't like life for the next few hours, and why fake it? I'll get over it, usually sooner than later, but Mr. Tanner, losing is far from the second best experience.

I have a friend, JD, who is a fan of Notre Dame football. Imagine a crisp autumn day, a light jacket kind of day. Fall leaves refulgent, clear skies free of humidity, aromas of barbeques, and add a few more of your favorite sensory experiences. You're in the throes of all these pleasures as you exit the football stadium. The Fighting Irish just lost. Someone comes up to JD and says, "Hey, it's still a nice day." How will he respond? Something along these lines, "No, it's not a nice day. Notre Dame just lost." Now that's what I'm talking about. We'll be okay eventually, but right now we're just not happy. Sorry Chuck.

Now to the games. A fan knows it's a long day when Mike Jorgensen by himself drives in more runs in one game than the entire Cub team does in two games. Mike Jorgensen. Jack Brickhouse once said of him something along these lines, "Mike Jorgensen has ten home runs this year, and 12 have come against the Cubs."

Question: Statistically speaking, in baseball, does the team that scores first usually win?

Answer: Yes.

Translate: We're in trouble, again. In both games, the Expos score before the Cubs come to bat. Imagine watching six hours of baseball and the team you're rooting for is never ahead, and save for a few pitches, is not even tied. That stinks. The national anthem before game one and the snacks before game two are as close as you're going to get to being ahead. Mr. Tanner, I rest my case.

One day in my writing class a student came up to me and asked if I ever heard of Carmen Fanzone. Of course, I replied. She went on to tell me that she once dated him. We went on to talk about his real claim to fame: his ability to play the trumpet. As a trumpet player, he was outstanding; as a baseball player, he was an outstanding trumpet player. But Carm did provide us with some false hope and a couple of runs as he knocked out a meaningless home run with two outs in the ninth. This made the score a little less lopsided, 7-4 Expos. As a reward for this feat, Fanzone got the start in game 2 and goes 0 for 2 with a walk. But in fairness to Carm, nobody did well in that second game, either. Kessinger leads off with a single, and then twenty-three outs later, the Cubs explode with their second hit, a single, courtesy of the pinch-hitting prowess of George Mitterwald. Here's a stat for stat freaks like me: in these two games, the pinch hitters for the Cubs went 2 for 3. The Cub starters that day went 6 for 56. Maybe we started the wrong guys.

Or maybe the pitching wizardry of 21 year old Dennis Blair was too tough. If you know anyone related to Dennis, you could tell them that he threw exactly one shutout in his entire career, and I saw it. I looked him up and discovered that he went from having a good year (11-7), to having a bad year (8-15), to being banished to the Padres (0-1), to being out of baseball. So much for the Blair Pitch Project. But on this warm summer afternoon, in the nightcap of a doubleheader, Dennis Blair was nearly unhittable. He stymied quality hitters such as Madlock, Monday, and Williams. Tip of the red, blue, and white cap to you, Mr. Blair. If I was old enough I'd offer to buy you a Molson's and drown my tears in it.

GAME 35: SAN DIEGO PADRES VS. CHICAGO CUBS
SATURDAY, AUGUST 17

My brother and Boog Powell were born this day. They're both big, and both like baseball. Today Boog is a leg up—he didn't have to watch the Cubs get humbled by the lousy Padres.

To give credit where it's due, the heart of the Padres' lineup came at you with two Hall-of-Famers. The good news for the Cubs is that one of them was just starting out and the other is winding down. Both are years away from peak performance. Dave Winfield and Willie McCovey, or Winny and Stretch. Today they combined for two walks, two singles, a double, and a game-deciding home run.

To give criticism where it's due, the Cubs mismanaged this game. Experts maintain that managers decide the outcome in only a handful of games throughout the season. Others say that managers lose more games than they win. Possibly. This game lends credence to both theories. In the late innings of a close game, the Cubs grab the lead on a bases loaded walk to Billy Williams. In the next half inning, a questionable non-decision decides the game. All you second guessers, stay with me. All those who can't stand second guessing, jump to the next game. Okay, with one out, McCovey walks. Not a bad idea to pitch around Big Mac. Now Winfield bats. So far today he has walked, singled, and singled. I'm guessing that he's seeing the ball pretty good. Following him in the lineup are hitters like Derrel Thomas (a name good in the NFL but not in MLB), Fred Kendall (best known for being the father of catcher Jason), and Dave W. Roberts (he hit .167 in '74). Now what would you do? How about pitching around Winfield and going after Moe, Larry and Curly? But the Cubs being the Cubs pitch to Winfield, he clubs it over the outfield fence and onto the catwalk. Ballgame, Padres. Thomas, Kendall, and Roberts are all retired after this home run, of course.

GAME 36: LOS ANGELES DODGERS VS. CHICAGO CUBS
WEDNESDAY, AUGUST 21

What's truer: Trends or Law of Averages? Let me explain. When there are multiple outcomes to an event, but the same outcome keeps occurring—will the next outcome likely be different because the Law of Averages kicks in? Or do events obey things like momentum and trends and have similar, if not identical, outcomes?

To illustrate, I've noticed some tendencies start to emerge over the past few seasons. When I watch the Cubs play the Dodgers, the Cubs lose. And when I watch Bill Bonham pitch for the Cubs, the Cubs lose. It got to the point where our family started referring to the pitcher as "Bill Bomb-him." From Sister Agatha in 8th grade math class we learn that two negatives, when multiplied, creates a positive. Using that logic, if I take these two negative trend-setters, Dodgers owning Cubs and hitters owning Bonham, shouldn't there be a positive, "let's go home happy" outcome? Makes sense right?

We're sitting pretty all the way until the third hitter of the game. Then two walks and Bonham gets bombed. To be precise, a three run bomb by Willie Crawford (I think he's *still* mad at us for the way we trash-talked him last year) pretty much ices the game in the first inning. I'm ready to leave.

Final, 7-5 Dodgers. Why am I such a chump? When you have a guy like Jim Tyrone batting sixth, I only have two questions:

1. Who hit 7th and 8th?
2. Did you really think the Law of Averages would catch up to a World Series contender facing such a feeble offense and mediocre pitching?

Now I get it. When you *add* two negatives together, you get a bigger negative.

GAME 37: ST. LOUIS CARDINALS VS. CHICAGO CUBS
SATURDAY, SEPTEMBER 28

Decisions, decisions. ND football or Chicago Cub baseball? My dad scored some tickets to see the Fighting Irish play Pur-don't University from West Laughiette, IN. I also had the opportunity to see the Cubs battle the Cards in the next-to-last game of the year. Let's see … Cubs in a meaningless, play-out-the-string game or the Defending National Champs of college football seeking to repeat? The value of the football ticket is probably quadruple what the other ticket is worth. After a few moments of deliberation, I'm off to Wrigley Field and my dad wonders about me.

Did you ever read the piece by John Updike entitled, "Hub Fans Bid Kid Adieu"? It's a masterpiece, and if you're not doing anything terribly urgent right now, I'd encourage you to Google it up and take a few minutes to read it. Go ahead, I'll wait.

(Here's where I put everything on hold and play some elevator music).

Still waiting.

Still waiting.

Almost done?

15 minutes later …

There, now, wasn't that good? I figure if you're going to take the time to read about a skill, it's wise to read about the best from the best. In hitting that would be Ted Williams, and in writing you could make a strong case for John Updike.

Now I'm not going to say Billy Williams, who can initial HOF after his name, rivals Ted as a hitter, because he doesn't. And about the only things that Updike and I have in common would be our first name and we have both worked at an A & P. But you know what, for a few minutes I feel there's a genuine connection here.

Next question: what's the greatest change that's happened in baseball over the past century? That's unfair, why don't I just ask what's the meaning of life? But still, what's happened in baseball that's created the biggest change? While you argue among yourselves, I'm going to throw this out there: the mobility of players. A century ago, a player was associated with one team, and so when you thought of a team, you thought of certain players. It's something that even as late as the 60's you could count on. Look up all-time record leaders, and you'll notice how players from the first half of the 20th century are listed with one team.

So Ted and Billy Williams shared a common bond of a one team player, at least until 1974. I had a vague sense that when Billy played these last couple of games vs. St. Louis, this could be the last time I see him in Cubbie blue. Why wouldn't he follow the path out of Chicago already blazed by Santo, Jenkins, Beckert, Hundley, Holtzman, etc.? So I'm thinking that I may be witnessing something special as he circles the bases in the 4th inning after he drives a Lynn McGlothlen pitch out of the park. No, it wouldn't be his last at bat with these little bears, and they still had a game to play tomorrow. But I felt pretty sure that this would be his last home run as a Chicago Cub.

This was one of the few times when the final score was anti-climactic. St. Louis still led, 3-1, after Williams' homer. The Cubs rally late to beat up the Birds, 8-3. Bill Madlock delivered the blow of the game by tripling with the bases loaded.

Studying the rosters of the game and one can see that 1974 was a time of transition. It almost had a "tweener" feel to it, with some players in the twi-light of their careers while other still a few years away from their prime. On the Cubs you had Williams and Don Kessinger. On St. Louis, you had folks like Lou Brock, Joe Torre, Sonny Siebert, Ron Hunt, Claude Osteen, and of course, Bob Gibson. In fact, Gibson reported that he knew his career in baseball was over after an encounter with a Cub player who played today. One day (not today) Pete LaCock took Gibby deep and that was it. He said that's the moment when he knew it was time to quit.

Sprinkled throughout the September call-ups for the Cardinals were some future stars. Jose Cruz—a splendid player with the Astros down the road—served as nothing more than a role player with this team. How frustrating for someone with his talent to look up and see the starting outfield of Brock, Bake McBride, and Reggie Smith. Good luck. Another name really jumped out at me: 18 K. Hernandez 1B. I knew Hernandez starred with the Cards, and his clutch hit in the '82 Series against the Brewers still pains me to this day. But I had no clue that he surfaced in '74. Pretty cool stuff for baseball addicts.

When the O'Donnell family reconvened at the end of this sports day, I found myself in the role of consoler. The chances of the Cubs winning and ND losing on the same day in the '70's were pretty small. This era saw ND annually compete for the national championship and the Cubs were … the Cubs. So I gently approach my ol man after Purdue defeated the Irish and Ara Parseghian (his last year as head coach) and QB Tommy Clements, and encouraged him to "stick with the Cubs." Not that funny today, and even less so back then to an avid ND fan and White Sox fan. I didn't say a whole lot more.

A special day, though, as one Cub fan bids Williams adieu.

POST-SEASON 1974

Teams have a way of growing on you. Like the Oakland Athletics. In 1972 I did not care for them at all and wanted the White Sox, then the Tigers, and finally the Reds to conquer them. They all succumbed to this group of brash and hairy players running around in softball uniforms. Their fan base underwhelmed me--those late games in Oakland drew crowds the size of WNBA games. The massive Oakland Colliseum reminded me of the mausoleum where Cleveland played in the 70's. The Indians could have a crowd of 30 K and the place is still mostly empty. Should such an indifferent fan base deserve a championship? But that season the A's edged out Dick Allen and his epic performance, the Tigers and their gritty veterans, and the early machine days of those Big Reds. So okay, we'll give you that one.

1973 saw the Mike Andrews debacle overshadow baseball. The Mets went from Amazin' in '69 to mediocre in '73, yet stretched the Series to seven games. Thank goodness history did not repeat for New York; for me it was a case of wanting the Mets to lose more than pulling for the A's to win.

Now in '74 I'm all in. As long as I have a memory I shall relish this Series and all the tidbits associated with it. Like working at Pizza Hut in the back room and listening to the games on the radio. I multi-tasked years before it became popular as I washed dishes while shaking my head in disgust as designated runner Herb Washington gets picked off first base. Finley, not afraid to try things, employed Washington as a late inning runner—and that was his entire reason for being on the roster. Why not, Finley reasoned, have a running specialist since we already have them in hitting, pitching, and fielding? Later in this game a blend of disappointment and appreciation takes over as Joe Ferguson in medium deep right fires a strike to the catcher to nail a tagging baserunner. This is not an exaggeration—this throw was more in the strike zone from 260 plus feet away than pitchers who throw from 60' 6".

With plays such as these, the Dodgers tie the Series at one game apiece, as the action moves northward to Oakland.

A Chicago sportswriter who I did not like smugly assured his audience that this Series would not be returning back to LA, for the Dodgers would sweep the next three games in Oakland. Now I have no problem with predictions, and I'm proud to say that I can be wrong as well as anybody when it comes to calling winners. To wit, I got lucky with the NCAA Men's Basketball Tournament in my senior year in college, so good that it boosted my grade half a letter in one of my classes. But since that time I've been in the throes of a skid of nearly 50 years—approaching Cub numbers in futility. So go ahead and be wrong, that's all right. But it's the guys that are so cocksure of themselves that just give me extra incentive as a fan to hope and cheer harder so that they eat every letter and punctuation mark of their column.

It's now Game 5 and Oakland leads the Series, 3 games to 1. Two key plays reside in memory for light years to come. Here they are in no particular order:

1. With the score tied in the late innings, Dodger relief ace Mike Marshall faces Joe Rudi, who for my money happens to be Oakland's top clutch performer (that's right, all you Reggie fans, I said Oakland's top clutch performer. Reggie is probably third with Campy second). Now there's a disturbance of some sort on the field causing a significant delay before play resumes. Normally, the pitcher tosses to the catcher to keep his arm warm and loose. But the cerebral Marshall (Ph.D., I believe) eschews any throws and simply waits until it's time to pitch. So finally Marshall hurls the sphere toward the plate, and Joe Rudi does not miss a stitch. A's now lead, 3-2.

2. Bill Buckner. ("Billy Buck," says a miked-up Tommy Lasorda coaching at third, "loves to play the game"). Now 90% of the free world knows Buckner's infamous claim to fame when it comes to World Series competition. But I wonder how many know that he was on the wrong side of another famous play a dozen years earlier? Here's how it happened: Billy Buck strokes a gapper to deep right center. He's not as gimpy as he would later be with the Cubs, so Buckner heads for third after a boot by Bill North. A perfect toss from Reggie Jackson to second baseman Dick Green is in and out of Green's hands in a nano second. The pinpoint relay to A's third baseman, Sal Bando, arrives a half a heartbeat before Buckner. Slide, tag, out. Game, series, three-peat. The most joyous celebration on the field might have come from

relief ace, Rollie Fingers. You could hear him say repeatedly, "What a play, what a play!" Here's an over-the-top statement that I'll offer: this play to retire Buckner is one of the finest executed plays I've ever seen in a big game. For if any one of the three (outfielder, relay man, third baseman) was a split second slower in their execution, Buckner is safe at third, and odds are that he scores the tying run. They turn a hit, followed by an error, into a picturesque out. But this play, a joy to watch and even fun to re-live, epitomizes why Oakland won back in the early 70's.

Were the Oakland A's in the early 1970's a baseball dynasty? Yeah, I think so. Not so much if you look at longevity or dominating talent, but more in the way they played the game. They'll never be a threat to the '27 Yankees place in history, but they deserve to be mentioned with the best teams ever assembled. Consider two final thoughts about Oakland as we close the book on the first half of the decade ...

- In this '74 World Series, Oakland held the Dodgers to 11 runs over 5 games, winning 3 games by a margin of 3-2. Far from dominating, but excelling in what matters the most: pitching, defense, and timely hitting.
- In a five game Series, the A's used a total of *five* pitchers. Heck, I think I've seen some post-season games where managers will use five pitchers in an inning. I bet you can name all 5 Oakland pitchers for 2 made the Hall-of-Fame, a third won an MVP, and the other two simply outstanding. Here they are: Rollie Fingers, Catfish Hunter, Vida Blue, Kenny Holtzman, and Blue Moon Odom. The game plan is simple—with pitching like this, get three runs and get a victory.

I suppose I can't give that cocky Chicago sportswriter too much grief because he was half-right ... The Series never did make it back to LA (proved too much for the man).

1975

(Note to reader: If you don't want to read memoirs from life outside of baseball, jump ahead to the next game in April).

Senior year, high school. Spring time brought an air of invincibility among students. The ones who **really** wanted us to graduate were teachers and administrators. A senior, once accepted at a college or university, cared even less about studies. There was this sense of … "I'm a second semester senior, teach, what are you going to do, flunk me?" … knowing that it just would not be worth the hassle. An attitude of "let's just get through this" permeated the building. As my friend Zorb said, "I actually look forward to going to school." And this came from someone who spent more time in the dean's office than in the classroom. The TO DO List shrunk to two imperatives: 1. Have fun 2. Stay out of trouble. I'd say we never dipped below .500 with these objectives.

Outside the class, sports kept us somewhat in line. If you got into too much trouble, you couldn't play and the vast majority of kids know that senior year is their last serious go round in playing for a school. Our basketball team faced a special challenge: we had exactly zero starters returning from the previous year. We also entered the season with a new coach (the old coach wasn't dumb—he could see a train wreck coming round the bend). After starting the year 0-4, euphoria is the word to describe our first win. From that point on we competed well—finishing right at .500. We upset a couple of teams better than us, beating a team in the regionals that had defeated us twice during the regular season. Probably my second happiest memory. The downer was losing several games in the final seconds in which we held the lead. Some "fans" said we were experts at snatching defeat from the jaws of victory. I learned that knowing how to win is as important as anything else, and this knowledge comes via experience, something we lacked.

The baseball season in spring, as virtually every high school baseball season I've ever seen, needs but two words—cold and wet. I've been a one man crusade in trying to switch high school baseball from spring to autumn. Alas, no takers. I argue that the seven or eight weeks of September/October will allow for many more playable and pleasant days of baseball weather. I even suggested switching boys' soccer with baseball, because soccer can be played in more inclement conditions. Again, I feel like I'm talking to the wall. Usually the counter-arguments center around having baseball and football in the same season. So we're stuck with a handful of games played in decent conditions. Notwithstanding the weather, our season was okay—not a tremendous amount of talent but we managed to win more than lose (that is, when we got a chance to play).

Other activities winding down the high school experience include work--making pizza at Pizza Hut with and for my friends--and going to prom. This was big—downtown Chicago, with the theme song a happy tune called "Dancing in the Moonlight." And of course every prom must have slowing dancing to "Color My World."

With diplomas in hand, the summer season brings us songs on the radio that were played endlessly. "Old Days" by Chicago, "I'm Not in Love" by 10 CC, and leading the way was "Love Will Keep Us Together," by Captain and Tennille. Give me a nickel for every time I heard this song and I would not have to work, at least for a summer. Speaking of work, this was the time for my first real forty hour per week job. My dad landed me a spot doing warehouse work, at a site just blocks from the old Chicago Stadium. This was my first taste of the real world, with men, not kids, who had to provide for families and take work seriously. While they're cussing, laughing, and guzzling coffee, I wondered: "what am I doing here?" My first impression was ... How can people do this all year round? My second impression was ... Do *I* really have to do this? My third impression was ... I'm going to college so I can do something besides warehouse work as an adult. I'm thinking that this was the real reason why my dad wanted me to work there: get an education so you can do what you want to do and not what you have to do.

I tell you, this work was no fun. The people, yes; the work, no. Up early to ride the morning train with non-communicative commuter zombies. I think I did see a couple customers snack on human flesh when they thought no one was watching. They never, and I mean never, exchanged even the simplest pleasantries. I remember this one young lady who rode the train and wore a nice dress every weekday for four summers. Not once did I see her smile.

But we had something to look forward to after the first full day of work: a concert featuring the Beach Boys and Chicago at the old Chicago Stadium. My first real concert with these two iconic groups performing all their hits. A lasting memory came at the end of the show—Chicago's encore was a song by the Rolling Stones, "Jumpin Jack Flash." I didn't know groups did that, playing songs that weren't theirs. I thought that was pretty cool. The other memory wasn't as pleasant—getting lost, again. Leaving the Chicago Stadium parking lot can rattle even the experienced driver, and I got turned around in a hurry. Rather than taking the Eisenhower expressway westward, I ended up northbound on the Edens expressway. After a while on this wayward route I pull into a forlorn bowling alley in what seemed to be central Wisconsin. I got my bearings straight and made it home without further incident.

Thus ended my first day of work with getting lost *twice* (once getting off at the wrong stop on the train trip home and the aforementioned misadventure on the expressway) and seeing two Hall-of-Fame musical groups. Can't say I've had many days like that one.

But I wasn't the only one lost this summer. The Chicago National League ballclub seemed to be scrambling to find some identity with their changing of the guard now complete. An impotent lineup and a mediocre pitching staff would plague this team for years to come.

The Sox pitching staff resembled a wedding dress—something old and something new and something blue. The old were the starters: Wilbur Wood (a twenty game loser), Jim Kaat (a twenty game winner), and Claude Osteen (7-16). The new were flamethrowing kids in the bullpen: Terry Forster and Rich Gossage. The blue were the losses that piled up that year (86) and a drop in the standings to 5th place.

Dick Allen left for good after several false retirements. The offense still had punch to it with a young keystone combo in Jorge Orta and Bucky Dent. Carlos May and Pat Kelly continued to produce as capable hitters, and middle-of-the-order guys in Bill Melton and Ken Henderson were dependable. But the trivia question from this team that would stump a lot of die-hard Sox fans is this: Can you name the hitter who led the '75 team in home runs? The answer is Deron Johnson, a grizzled veteran who did not play the full season but still managed to slug 18 homers for Chicago before being traded to the Red Sox.

I'd be remiss if I didn't give some attention to the feel good story of "Local Boy Makes Good." Lee "Skip" Pitlock, who hails from Hillside, IL, made us all proud as he pitched for the White Sox in '74 and '75. I remember meeting him as an alum of the same grade school and high school that I attended. In fact he grew up in a simple home right across the street from our grade school, St. Domitilla. I never did see him play as a kid growing up in the neighborhood because he had ten years on me, but I do recall watching his younger brother knock the stuffing out of the ball in Pony League. Skip Pitlock pitched for the Giants in '70, and then didn't resurface in the majors until four years later. His numbers weren't remarkable, 8-8 as a starter and a reliever, but just to have someone compete at the major league level from your small town excited many of us.

GAME 38: MONTREAL EXPOS VS. CHICAGO CUBS
SUNDAY, APRIL 21

Q: How do you know when a game you've attended is dull?

A: When the strongest memory you have of the experience is listening to "Aqua Lung" by Jethro Tull on the ride to and from the ballpark.

Four teammates playing ball in high school pile into a red stick-shift foreign-made car of some sort. Make? Model? Year? Don't know and don't really care. But the driver and teammate, Kris, has a state-of-the-art stereo system. By now 8 track tapes were already on the way out as cassette tapes emerge. The rule when it came to car music to was this, "When you got the keys you do as you please." So I was held hostage as we listened to such beautiful lyrics as "… snot running down his nose …" several times on this journey. For every "Bungle in the Jungle" and "Living in the Past" song that I enjoyed by this group, there were 5-6 that I could barely stand. But I told myself to man up and bear it—I'm with teammates and going to a Cub game.

Once inside we sat in the deep right field grandstands, the same location where I watched Kenny Holtzman toss his no-hitter six years earlier. I wondered if today's starter, Steve Stone, could match Holtzman's feat. Conditions were lousy for hitting and the Montreal lineup was weak, so I harbored hope. Stone did make short work of the Expos; no no-hitter but a dominating shut-out. The Cubs got to a young Steve Rogers and the no frills, no thrill game ended up 6-0.

On the way to the car, one of my friends observed that this hardly seemed like a Cub game. I knew right away what he meant—a bland and non-entertaining ballgame is not what people come to expect at Wrigley Field; it's a place where weird things happen. But not today, so it's back to more flute music on the way home. Things could be worse—I might be forced to listen to Ian and the boys after a Cub loss … but I'd rather not think about that.

GAME 39: DETROIT TIGERS VS. CHICAGO WHITE SOX
FRIDAY, MAY 23

The Tigers, like the Cubs, engage in a retooling, if not rebuilding, project. Gone were the household names of McAuliffe, Kaline, Cash, and Northrup. Recognizables still there from the glory days include folks like Stanley, Freehan, Horton, and Lolich. A dynamic and colorful character spiced up the Tiger lineup, and that would be Ron LeFlore. An interesting blend, but could the Major, new Tiger manager Ralph Houk, win with all these changes?

It looked grim for the visitors, as the Sox led 9-1 after five innings. A three run blast by the venerable Deron Johnson, who seemed old a dozen years ago when he starred with the Reds, propels the Sox to an imminent slaughter.

But wait. Some 13 Tigers bat in the 7th inning. I hate it when that happens. Do you have any idea how such outbursts wreak havoc on a scorecard? And while I'm complaining, just how does a team manage just one run on three hits in six innings, then collect seven runs on eight hits in one inning? Crazy game. To add to the bizarre series of events, a batted ball leaves the premises by the most unlikely source, Gene Michael, AKA "Stick". One home run and seven singles (five in succession) later, and we have a ballgame.

Limping into the 8th inning, the Sox cling to a one run lead. After the Detroit bullpen issues that dreaded leadoff walk to Johnson, the Sox earn an insurance run, and hold off Detroit in the ninth to escape with a 10-8 victory.

GAME 40: NEW YORK YANKEEES VS. WHITE SOX
SATURDAY, JUNE 6

Old-timers game at Comiskey the following day, June 7. Yankees vs. White Sox or Goliath vs. David. Broaching the subject with Bill Pierce, the pressure on Chisox pitchers to keep their team in games during the 50's & early 60's must have been tremendous. Check out some of the names from the White Sox "old-timer" roster: Al Weis, J.C. Martin, and Dave Nicholson. The best position player, Luke Appling, seemed to be 96 years young. Nellie Fox and Luis Aparicio showed up, but how much Go-Go did they have Left-Left? I suggested to Pierce that he'd have to pitch a shutout to earn a tie, and he didn't disagree. Now consider who the Yanks had playing for them: Moose Skowron (traitor—I saw him play for the White Sox in the 60's), Joe Pepitone, Elston Howard, Bobby Richardson, Gene Woodling, Tommy Henrich, and Enos Slaughter. Speaking of Enos, I looked at these two lineups and wondered if the Slaughter rule would be in effect?

But as most old-timers "games" turn out, this wasn't competitive at all. These old folks yucked it up, would occasionally provide an "OOHH" or "AAHH" by making a decent play, but mostly tried to avoid pulling their groins.

Now the night before, the Yankees, who always seemed to be way ahead of the competition financially, proved to be shrewd business people yet again by investing in Bonds. Bobby homered, singled, and homered in his first three at bats, making the score Bonds 3, White Sox 2 by the 5th inning. His mates contributed late as the Yanks won decisively, 6-3.

Keeping the game from getting out-of-hand was a folk hero/matinee idol. I had a friend named Stephan in grade school and high school who put together "The Legend of Bucky Dent." More about that later. Suffice it to say that the real legend came to into existence in Savannah, GA in 1951. His birth name was Russell Earl O'Dey, but fortunately he became known as Bucky Dent. "The Legend of Russ O'Dey" just doesn't strike the same chord.

Country bumpkin or no, this capable little player bothers the Yanks this evening with a two-run double in the 2nd and scoring himself in the 7th.

Perhaps such prowess impresses the Yankee brass so much that they snatch him away a couple years later. He'd even manage the Pinstripes later in his career. Ultimately his transfer from Chicago to New York would put a serious dent into the hearts of both Sox faithful—the Red and the White--but that was down the road a bit.

GAME 41: KANSAS CITY ROYALS VS. CHICAGO WHITE SOX
FRIDAY, JUNE 27

This game features a couple of "tweener" teams—a team that was good and is now in decline versus a team that will be good but isn't there yet. So although this particular game was fairly meaningless because neither club would threaten the A's this year, this still proved to be a pleasant evening.

Several memories and reflections:

- My first up close and eyewitness encounter with George Brett.
- The twi-light days of Harmon Killebrew. Seeing him in a Royal uniform caused me to do a double take. Would Lee ever fight for the Yankees (take your pick—Robert E. or Bill)? So how could the Killer be anything but a Twin? Nevertheless, I comforted myself by thinking that as one all-time great (Killebrew) leaves the arena another (Brett) will take his place. As <u>Blood, Sweat and Tears</u> might say, "there'll be one player born in this world to carry on."
- More on Killebrew and his retirement. The Killer knew his time was up when as he was signing autographs with the Royals he overheard a conversation that went something like this: "Who's he?" (meaning Killebrew). Someone responds, "Oh, he's someone that used to be good."
- Another excellent player on the cusp of Hall-of-Fame status was wrapping up his career: Vada Pinson. I had seen him when he starred with the Reds more than a decade ago, and now caught him in his swan song season. Remarkable that he was pushing forty and batting leadoff tonight. Definitely one of the best players not in the Hall-of-Fame. How do you keep a guy out who has 2757 career hits? Perhaps the Hall should have an "honorable mention" wing for such players.

The hero for KC tonight would not be Brett, Killebrew, or Pinson. No, the star of the show looked to be another fine hitter, Hal McRae. His single in the fifth opened the scoring and his two-run triple in the 7th gave the visitors a substantial 3-0 lead. The Sox looked snake-bitten from the get-go as a double, single, and single by the first three hitters (Pat Kelly, Jorge Orta, and Carlos May) produced zero runs. That's hard to do. Kelly gunned down trying to stretch a double into a triple brought that on. From that disappointment the Sox offense went into hibernation until the 8th. That's when May makes it a game with a two out, two run triple plating Kelly and Orta. But May himself doesn't score, so the Sox need one to tie and two to win heading into the ninth.

Walk off, a term used extensively by ESPN sorts, wasn't used in the 70's. But that's precisely what home team fans root for, hope for, dream for, etc. to satisfy their emotional investment over the past 150 minutes or so. As true in 2016 AD as 1975 AD or 1975 BC.

Credit due here to Chuck Tanner, White Sox skipper, for having the guts to run when it's game time. Bee Bee Richard, a utility shortstop with a potent arm and quick feet, runs for Ken Henderson after he leads off with a single. Richard's claim to fame, at least in my memory, could be this: tagging up and scoring on a fly ball to center field. Happens all the time, you say? How many times have you seen someone tag up and score from *2nd base?* So tonight Richard scampers to third on a one out single by Bob Coluccio. Now here is where three things can happen that can decide the outcome of the ballgame. The next hitter, our friend Bucky Dent, can hit a sacrifice fly and Richard can tag and score from third base to tie the game. Or Dent can drive an extra base hit and give the Sox the victory. Or Dent can ground into a double play and the Royals win the game. Tanner puts pressure on KC's defense by having Coluccio swipe second—a bad throw or any hesitation and Richard scoots home with the tying run. There's no such luck as Coluccio makes second and Richard stays at third. But now a ground ball will not end the game. Dent delivers a fly ball deep enough to left fielder McRae to drive home Richard with the tying run. The strategic floodgates open for both sides. The 9th place hitter for the Sox is a good one, catcher Brian Downing. He receives an intentional walk to set up a force play at any base. Then the timeless manager for the Royals, Jack McKeon, brings in a lefty, Steve Mingori, to face Chicago's lefty leadoff hitter, Pat Kelly. Now Kelly has two doubles in four at-bats and just scored the previous inning. Would you pinch-hit for him? Here are your possible substitutions: Bill Stein, Pete Varney, Jim Essian, Nyls Nyman (another lefty), and Buddy Bradford. You could use a pitcher to pinch-hit, but Gary Peters has been out of baseball now for three years. Besides, he's a lefty.

Okay, so those are your options, what would you do? I'll give you a few moments to think about it ....

Here's what Tanner does: he has Stein hit for Kelly to play the righty-lefty percentage. Stein taps one in the infield. Tony Solaita, the Royal first baseman from Samoa, fields the ball and tosses it to Mingori covering first. Mingori misses the ball and the speedy Coluccio scores the winning run from second base. An unlikely victory: shutout and down by three with six outs to go, the Sox score four times with one out to spare to win in regulation. We have a happy start to the weekend.

GAMES 41 & 42: PITTSBURGH PIRATES VS. CHICAGO CUBS
FRIDAY, JULY 4

Let's start with how the day ends. With one out, Andy Thornton, a righty pull power hitter for the Cubs, lines the ball hard down the right field line. You know how announcers say that if so & so hits it to such & such a place, he could run forever? I hear this about once per broadcast. Well, this was one of those times. By the time the right fielder, Bill Robinson, picks up the ball, Thornton chugs into third with a stand-up triple. Since the game is tied in the bottom of the 11th and since we're moving toward the bottom of the lineup, Pirate manager elects to walk the next two batters. So the bases are loaded (as are a lot of the fans at the end of six hours of baseball), one out, game tied at one, and Jose Cardenal facing the Pirate southpaw *starter,* Jerry Reuss. Now no fair second guessing Murtaugh on pulling the pitcher until you've got the facts straight: 6 games in a span of 4 days (double headers on Friday and Sunday). It doesn't look like rain any time soon. And then consider that this rally marks only the fourth time in 11 innings that the Cubs had a runner in scoring position. Okay, now what would you do if you're Murtaugh? (As someone once said, there are two things that every man in the United States think they can do better than anyone else: cook a steak and manage a baseball team. I plead not guilty and guilty, respectively). To end the drama—Cardenal singles to right and the results of the day look like this: Chicago 6-2, Pittsburgh 1-1 (call me crazy, but I love writing down the results of a double-header, especially if it's a Chicago sweep).

You read correctly, the famous Lumber Company with sluggers galore held to two runs over 20 innings. In large part this was due to a rock solid performance by Steve Stone in the opener, and southpaw starter Geoff Zahn in the nightcap. And who knew Knowles out of the bullpen would get the win with a perfect 11th?

Both games, in fact, were well pitched by both teams. The Cubs did not break open the first game until they plated four in the 8th. So most of the time watching this game was spent squirming and longing for breathing room.

In a few paragraphs we'll take a closer look as to why the Bucs ineptitude on offense against Cub pitching is so remarkable. But what I remember the most from that afternoon are the intermittent concerns and anxieties from my friend, Rob. You see, Rob, a typical Cub fan, has this loyalty to Cub players, present and past that borders on the irrational. In Game 2, the regular Pirate second baseman, Rennie Stennett, has the day off as his proxy, Paul Popovich, figures to have some decent looks at the lefty Zahn since Popo is a switch-hitter. Now Popovich generated about as much love as a utility guy can ever expect to have during the Cubs' hey-hey days. Signs and banners praising this guy decorated Wrigley Field; simple things like, "Pop a pitch, Popovich!" supported Paul should he make a rare plate appearance.

So my pal Rob, quite aware of Popovich's anemic numbers (there's a reason why some guys are utility guys) fears that with every out that Popo makes, his demotion to Triple A becomes more and more certain. After grounding out twice and flying out once in the nightcap, Rob leans over to me and predicts that someone has already packed his bags in the clubhouse. One more out and his fate is sealed. Much to the delight of Rob and maybe the Popovich family, Paul's departure may have earned a reprieve as he strokes a one-out single in the 10th. It got to the point that Rob wanted Popo to outperform the Cubs. Truth be told, I was hoping too that Popo would do well, but in a losing effort. Reprieve and relief as Popo doesn't go oh-fer and the Cubs win twice. But is it enough for Popo to keep his job?

GAMES 43 & 44: PITTSBURGH PIRATES VS. CHICAGO CUBS
SUNDAY, JULY 6

Guess who's batting eighth for the Pirates in Game 2 two days later? That's right, Paul Popovich. The Pittsburgh front office did not send him packing after all, so Rob can rest easy. Nevertheless, this would turn out to be Popo's last go-round in the majors, as the soon-to-be 35-year-old was playing in his final season in '75.

Now back to normalcy, unfortunately. Before the Cub defense recorded their sixth out in the first game, the Pirates scored more runs on Sunday than they did in the two games on Friday. I ask you: how can one team totally handcuffed by another team's pitching just forty-eight hours later explode for *eighteen* runs? Do the math and you'll see that the Bucs went from averaging one run per ten innings to two runs **every** inning! In fact the Pirates nearly accomplished something this day that teams could only equal but not surpass—score in every inning. A 3 up 3 down ninth spoiled that bit of fun/embarrassment. Was it 1) exhaustion from running the bases, 2) saving themselves for Game 2, or 3) Cub pitchers finally figuring out how to get these guys out? My guess is either #1 or #2.

This was your more typical Cub-Pirate game of the 70's. Six homers and thirty runs. Even though the home teams manages a dozen runs, they fall a half dozen shy. Ten pitchers called into duty in a sloppy affair that looked like extended batting practice—that's really what this day was about.

That, and two other things. One of them happened to be my first date at a Cub game. It wasn't romantic—much more activity in the bullpen than in the stands. Pretty embarrassing, actually, to bring a date to a major league game only to watch little league performances. But there was some good news. The second game of the doubleheader got rained out. (I wonder if Murtaugh now regrets not pulling Reuss two days before. My guess is that it never crossed his mind). We now have an excuse to do something more fun than watch Buccos running the bases.

Actually, taking two out of three from Pittsburgh is more than what a Cub fan could hope for. In '75, the Cubs have no young promising pitchers and mediocre veteran arms at best. No speed, and save an occasional blast from

Monday or Thornton, no real power threats. A budding hitting machine in Bill Madlock (he did lead the league with a .354 average), but not enough help around him. Not when batters like Pete LaCock and Jerry Morales batted in the middle of the lineup, and you're going up against 3-4 hitters like Al Oliver and Willie Stargell. The pitching had one legitimate star, Rick Reuschel. Outside of Madlock, Monday, and Reuschel, I doubt if you could find many players who would start on other teams. This was not the golden era for the Cubs, so Cub victories were not taken for granted.

ALAN

Alan worked with me at the warehouse for four summers and four Christmas breaks. We both got our jobs via nepotism; our dads worked in management positions with a company that did a lot of business with the warehouse. My dad would contact the owner, Bill, several times a day and would even pay a personal visit once or twice a summer. I learned early that "it's not what you know but who you know" because I was pretty bankrupt when it came to warehouse IQ and skills. Yet I never felt shame for not getting this job on my own merits, and I doubt that Alan did either. The subject never came up, and we kept going back there for work.

Al was a year ahead of me in school, and light years ahead of me in partying. He talked of romantic adventures with his girl friend to pass time as we loaded and unloaded boxes from trucks. His descriptions were pretty tame by today's standards, and I listened half out of curiosity and half out of politeness.

Al and I did share a passion, a topic that would entertain us for hours on Monday AM's. We would rehash, mimic, and even act out the previous night's episode of Monty Python's Flying Circus. For one half hour on Sunday evenings, my sides pained me from violent laughter. "The Twit Race", "The Llama Song", "The Lumberjack Song", "the SPAM skit", the soccer game with pirates, the animations, and practically everything else they did knocked me out; re-creating the show the following day proved to be as much fun. A word, just a word, from the night before and we'd convulse with laughter. Older folks at work, which included everyone but us, either didn't watch it or find it as funny as we did, but we were okay with that. Actually it made it better to see the bemused looks on others as we repeated lines from the program.

Our mutual interest in Monty Python more than made up for any differences between us. He played hockey; I played baseball. He got high, I drank Old Style. He had long hair parted down the middle, mine was short. He was soft-spoken, I could be outspoken. He drove his own car, an Audi, to work; I took the train. He liked Little Feet and Zeppelin; I listened to Chicago and Earth, Wind, and Fire. He would sometimes go to concerts on weekends, I went to ballgames. He bought lunch, I brown bagged it. He was an efficient worker, I frequently spaced out. He made me laugh a lot, and I tried to return the favor. During the four years of college breaks, the mundane and monotonous warehouse work seldom got the best of me because of Al.

GAME 44: CINCINNATI REDS VS. CHICAGO CUBS
SATURDAY, JUNE 14

If you've played enough pick-up basketball games over the years, you're likely familiar with the term, "**MISMATCH**." What you're likely to see when you hear this word is a man of decent size with decent skills being defended by a player of inferior stature and athleticism. "Mismatch." And if the ball makes its way to the more talented player, and should he score, the next thing you're likely to hear as the teams run to the other side of the court is "**That's all day, baby, all day!**" How I hate it when the guy I'm guarding says that, but it generally motivates me to play better.

Mismatch. How many times after filling out a scorecard in the 70's does the concept of mismatch enter my consciousness? Remember that scene in the movie A Christmas Story, where Ralphie frantically ducks into the bathroom for a few moments of solitude as he deciphers a radio message via a ring he got in the mail? Then remember how disappointed and disgusted Ralphie turns when he realizes that the message is nothing more than a commercial? That's me ... I'm so excited to be at the ballpark as I joyfully jot down the names of the starting lineups in the appropriate spaces. Then, when Mr. Piper finishes his announcements, I step back to take a look at the entire finished product of the team's personnel. Bam! Mismatch. It's not a lousy commercial but a lousy mismatch.

Once again, what was I thinking? Did I really think that today's the day when this "little blue bicycle" vanquishes the "Big Red Machine"? The Cubs are going to catch lighting in a bottle and play a flawless game and knock off baseball's best team, right? Compare the first five hitters in each lineup. Reds: Rose, Griffey (Senior), Morgan, Bench, Perez vs. Cubs: Kessinger, LaCock, Madlock, Monday, Morales. And if that's not lopsided enough, how about a future 50 homer guy batting 8th—George Foster. If you listen carefully you can hear Mgr. Sparky Anderson crow, "All day, baby, all day!"

The game was not as close as the 4-1 score in the 7th would indicate. The only extra base hit for the Cubs came courtesy of Steve Stone, starter (a three-peat in alliteration). The score doesn't always reflect dominance in sports. Football has its "time of possession" and hockey has its "shots on goal."

Baseball has batters who reached and runners stranded. Through 6 innings the Cubs sent 23 men to the plate, or five over the minimum. The Reds send 32 men to the plate in that same time period, or 14 over the minimum. This one's so one-sided that I stopped keeping score in the 7th, a rarity. Johnny Bench finished the day going 3 for 3 against Stone and 2 for 2 against Bob Locker. That's all day, baby. Final score: Reds 11, Cubs 3. Mismatch.

GAMES 45 & 46: MILWAUKEE BREWERS VS. CHICAGO WHITE SOX SUNDAY, JULY 20

A family affair, not referring to Sly & the Family Stone or Buffy and Jody and Mr. French, but the O'Donnell clan. Pack up the car, grab a big bucket of fried chicken from *Church's,* and head to the ballpark for a doubleheader. My, my— hot fun in the summer time. All that's missing is some lemon meringue pie and a few tunes from Petula Clark—stuff the whole family can enjoy. Maybe that's waiting for us on the way home.

What we got at the game was a genuine feast with a slew of early White Sox runs: 7-2 at the end of 2. Fried chicken and RBI's, a lovely combo. And a side order of cole slaw and Hall-of-Famers. Can you guess who batted 2nd, 4th, and 9th for the "Crew" in this first game? I'll start with the 9th place hitter— who happened to be a character extraordinaire. Gorman Thomas. Now the name itself should tip us off—doesn't it seem backwards to you? Shouldn't it be Thomas Gorman? How many grade school teachers made that mistake the first day of school? Anyway, this Thomas guy's performance in baseball often resembled a roller coaster ride. It was once said of him that in every game, he'd either hit a homer, strike out, or make a great play in center field. (If memory serves, I think it was Thomas himself who said this). Well, guess what? In the second Thomas homers and in the fifth he whiffs. I notice he had four put-outs for the day in center field, but I can't testify if any were spectacular.

Now to other noteworthy members in the Brew Crew order: one Hall-of-Famer in the embryonic stages played shortstop. His name is Robin Yount. (Another quirky name. Aside from Batman's sidekick, I always associated Robin as a name for birds or girls). He squeezed in the lineup between two solid pros: Don Money and George Scott (AKA the Boomer—and I really like that nickname).

Allow me to digress with a quick tale about Don Money (don't worry; the game's a blowout so you're not missing much). One day I snuck into Money's clubhouse as he managed a Class A team in the 90's. Now you should know that he's the kind of guy who had no big time attitude whatsoever—you could shoot the breeze with him as easily as you could with your best high school buddy. He had stories about lots of players, past and present, and they were entertaining without the dirty gossip. So let's fast forward a few years. My youngest son wanders the field prior to a Class A minor league game. The home team has this weekend ritual of letting kids get autographs from the minor league players—players they wouldn't know if their allowance depended on it. So my kid meanders from the home side to the visitors dugout where Money *still* happens to be the manager (he must really love this game, methinks). So I introduce my son to Skipper Money, and he acts as though my kid isn't some snot-nosed irritant but just a ginger with freckles worthy of some attention. After the lame introductions, Money smirks at my kid's shirt laden with autographs from both teams. He decides to add his name to the mix. So Money takes his marker, pulls down the kid's shirt a little, and scrawls his name on my kid's neck. The three of us grin at the moment, and then my kid and I skedaddle before the minor league players come along and take over the premises. They probably wouldn't get what just happened. And these are the players that Money has to mold into becoming millionaires some day. Tough job but someone's got to do it. In fairness, players at Class A ball interact well with the fans—courteous, accommodating, and never acting like they're doing you a big favor by acknowledging your existence. Should they arrive at the major league level—well, that's a different story for some. But the bottom line for me that day—Don Money made a memory by signing my kid's neck.

Enough with the tangents, who's the Hall-of-Famer hitting clean-up? The player whose name comes first in alphabetical order in your *Baseball Encyclopedia*. The guy who hit more steroid-free home runs than any other person, Henry Aaron. (And now it's time for one of my favorite baseball trivia questions ... What do Babe Ruth, Hank Aaron, and Willie Mays have in common? HINT: It has something to do with cities, but nothing to do with baseball statistics. I'll give you some time to think about it; the answer will come at the end of the Game 2 synopsis).

Aside from the Thomas' blast, my favorite knuckle-baller—Wilbur Wood—stymies Yount, Aaron, and the rest of the Milwaukee lineup in a 10-2 laugher. The offensive star of the game goes to Ken Henderson of the Chisox for his four safeties and three ribbies.

GAME 2

How do you know that you're off to a bad start? Here's one way … by the time your team bats for the first time, you're already on your second pitcher. Claude Osteen, the esteemed lefty who twice was a 20 game winner for the Dodgers, is wrapping up his career on the South Side. The Brewers rejoice that he hasn't called it quits yet as they're a homer shy of hitting for the cycle in the first inning. The aforementioned Aaron leads the way as he triples home a run and moments later scores on a Charlie Moore single. Well, the first game was fun and the chicken was tasty, so I'll take 2 out of 3, at least that's what I'm thinking. The Sox dug a huge hole …

… but hit their way out of it. Between the 2nd and 7th innings, the White Hot offense smacks around four Brewer pitchers to the tune of 10 runs. Not bad—20 runs scored in 16 innings. Bill Stein delivers the biggest blow—a three run blast in the fourth—and Bill Melton adds a solo drive in the 6th. (Pardon me for yet another diversion, but I have to ask: what's the first thing you think of when you hear the name Bill Stein? For me, it's a frosty mug with a lot of foam. I can't think of his name and not get a little thirsty). The Boomer on the Brewers homers in the 9th, but it's way too little. Final scores: Chicago 10-10, Milwaukee 2-5.

I had to do some digging around, but my eyes bulged when I discovered who the winning pitcher was for this game. After Osteen makes his early departure, a long reliever by the name of Danny Osborn holds the Brew Crew in check for six innings and earns the victory. In his only year in the majors, Osborn finished with a perfect 3-0 mark out of the bullpen. Now take a guess what Danny's nickname is. It's Ozzy. I'm not making that up. Crazy, but that's how it goes.

Now back to that trivia. Aaron, Mays, and Ruth all ended their careers in the same city where they started, but with different teams. And you could also add this—they're best known for their play in another city in-between. Aaron began with the Milwaukee Braves and ended with the Milwaukee Brewers (probably best known for his time in Atlanta where he passed up the Babe).

Mays started with the New York Giants and ended with the NY Mets (but spent most of his time in San Francisco). And the curse of the Bambino originates with the Boston Red Sox but his career closes with the Boston Braves (with the NY Yankees in-between, of course).

GAME 47: ST. LOUIS CARDINALS VS. CHICAGO CUBS
SUNDAY, AUGUST 3

Cubbie blue vs. Cardinal red. Big city on the lake vs. large town on the river. Skyscrapers vs. the Arch. Studs Lonigan vs. Samuel Clemens. Old Style vs. Budweiser. Wrigley Field vs. whatever they got.

There are many ways to metaphor this rivalry. THE rivalry in MLB, so we're told and told and told, is the Yankees vs. Red Sox. Just a tad of East Coast bias, maybe? We also have Giants vs. Dodgers on the Left Coast, and this Cub vs. Card matchup in the heartland. I sensed that the White Sox and Yankees had something special in the early 60's, but it waned as time passed. I wonder in the next few decades what other rivalries might emerge to help generate interest and sell the product. Could we hear announcers say that we should "throw out the records whenever the Diamondbacks and Padres get together?" Or "no matter where they are in the standings, whenever the Astros and Mariners play it's a war"?

Isn't it true that these rivalries are more fiction than fact? Proximity, longevity, and familiarity breed contempt, but are the animosities anywhere near the degree that the baseball culture suggests? In a moment of refreshing candor, a commentator once likened the rivalry between the Red Sox and Yankees to the rivalry that exists between a hammer and a nail. A quick check of the post-season dominance by NY validates this statement and should lessen the hype.

For the Cub/Cardinal feud, I'd say it's more like Wile E. Coyote vs. the Road Runner. (You don't know how much this last statement hurt). But feelings aside, here's what you do: add up all the world championships that the two teams have claimed over the past century, subtract the number of championships the Cubs have won, and you're left with the number of championships that the Cardinals have won. (I now feel like biting something. Preferably something red and birdy). But here's a bone for us Cubby fans to savor: after the NLDS series of 2015, the Cubs are undefeated in all the post-season matchups with the Cardinals. And the reverse is just as sweet—St. Louis has lost to the Chicago Cubs in every single post-season series that they played against them up to 2016.

World championships: big edge to St. Louis. Head-to-head, however, is another story. My personal history testifies to this truth—these games are close and the records are close. Throughout my five decades of watching Cub games in person, I've seen the Cubs dominate a few clubs (Giants, Astros, and Padres) and get dominated by a few others (Phillies, Dodgers, and Reds). Most hover around the break-even point, including St. Louis. To be more precise, in all the Cub-Cardinal games I've seen in person, the record stands at 14-13, Cubs. It does seem that no matter how much the Cubs struggle, they do compete well against the Dead Birds.

In sum, those roadrunners on the Cardinal roster—the Brocks, the Smiths (Ozzie, Reggie, Lonnie), the Colemans, the McBrides, the Pendletons—seem to fly around the bases and the outfield pastures. Meanwhile the Coyote Cubs keep trying, but keep getting nailed by the ACME anvil when it comes to the big prize. But mano-on-mano the Coyote holds his own.

Unfortunately the birds ruled this day. The coyote on the mound, Rick Reuschel, kept St. Louis at bay for most of the game: 2 earned runs through 8 innings of work. A couple Redbirds who spent most of their careers in Dodger Blue—Ron Fairly and Willie Davis—did the damage. Fairly doubles and scores in the 4th, while Davis triples in a run in the 8th (I thought I heard him say "Beep, beep" rounding second). Meanwhile the Cubs impotent lineup withers in the desert sun flailing away against Bob Forsch. Three singles and one double scattered over nine frames. Just not good enough, but what does one expect when your team has Pete LaCock batting third? Final score: Roadrunners 4, Coyotes nil.

LEN

Upstairs, keeping to himself, works Len. You'd see a silent man about 5'6" in height, 155 pounds in weight, dark-rimmed glasses, and hair that is grey, white, uncombed, and voluminous. Heads of hair sometimes have minds of their own. It's like the master concluded a long time ago that hair maintenance is not a battle worth fighting, so have your way with my head and just leave me alone. Picture Einstein's hair matted down with a bit more pepper and you'd be approaching the Len look.

Len was an artist, and a genius, and eccentric. I've seen more than a few folks take on eccentricity because they fancied themselves as artistic geniuses, but it was never an act with Len. He was who he was and did not give a gram of a rat's buttocks if someone objected. He was too old, too focused, and too comfortable in his skin to be swayed.

Work to Len was like breathing to you and me. How many people have you come across that needed cajoling into taking a break? When the clock struck 10, more often than not one of us had to remind Len that it was time to cease his project and join us downstairs for a few minutes. The same thing would happen two hours later ...

"Len, time for lunch."

"Oh, is it time?" (He'd have this startled expression and caught off-guard with this novel concept of lunch. After seventy-some years of lunches, you think he'd be ready for it once in a while. But no, his reaction to lunch-time is just like a grade schooler's reaction to the fire alarm). Len responded in this soft and raspy voice sounding like he constantly needed to clear his throat.

"Yeah, Len, it's time. Where are we going today?"

"The usual, I guess."

"The usual" meant a hot dog stand that served Italian beef, Polish, and fries that soaked the wrapper and the bag with grease. Being a brown-bagger from home, I usually took a pass on this fine dining. But every so often, when I had a spare quarter and the appetite, I'd indulge in a gravy sandwich. A stale piece of Italian bread, drenched in Italian beef gravy to make it less stale. Good and good for you.

After eating I often broke out the "Ask Ann Landers" section of the <u>Chicago Sun-Times</u> and read aloud the questions with her corresponding advice. (The sports section was inhaled at the first break). It was often good for a laugh or two, and we thought that the advice we proffered would work much better than Ann's. (Too bad most of it couldn't be repeated in mixed company).

Speaking of newspapers, Len would read his but we couldn't. That's because it was written in Polish. For this he caught crap from some of the co-workers—who were always scheming how to give crap to other co-workers, especially Len. "Go ahead and read your Polish communist paper, Len," was maybe the kindest remark that was said. Len would smile at the friendly insult and keep reading.

At one o'clock, or thereabouts, Len climbs the stairs to resume his masterful work. Most of the people throughout the day were working stiffs—truck drivers, warehouse workers, the UPS guy, and window trimmers—but Len was different. He revered what he was doing; this was not just a job for Len, and he was not just a guy putting in his time. He not only had the hair for what he did, but the imagination, the creativity, the patience, and the talent.

On a bi-weekly basis I'd push a broom by his working quarters to keep his sacrosanct area workable. On a monthly basis I'd stroll by his enormous table and ask Len what he was working on. I was mildly curious and interested, but I also knew that this simple inquiry would eat up fifteen minutes of the day. In random fashion, Len would offer stories of setting up stages decades ago that served Mayor Daley (the dad, not the son) and the debutante ball. The twinkling look in Len's eyes accompanied his description as how these young ladies looked and how they'd grace the sets that he constructed. Then he might reminisce about crimes he witnessed first hand courtesy of Chicago's infamous mobsters. I recall his description of one local retail owner reaching into the pocket of a fatally wounded hoodlum claiming that "this guy owes me money" and he helped himself to some of the cash from the dying man's wallet. Then there was the subject of stained glass windows. Stained glass windows. My weaknesses at this time in my life were the two strike curveballs and accounting class, not necessarily in that order. Len's weakness: stained glass windows.

I learned from warehouse colleagues to be sure that my insurance policy is in good hands before riding in a car that's driven by Len. Rules of the road? Len wouldn't allow such trivia to get in the way of the constant look-out for potential art ideas that came to him via stained glass windows. Survivors from Len's driving adventures warned me that should a stained glass window appear on some architecture, most likely a church, Len would get lost in its beauty for several blocks before and after spotting it. Intersections and oncoming traffic should not interfere with inspirational art.

The most binding element in this warehouse, even more so than Monty Python, break times, and Ann Landers, was baseball. I made the mistake of assuming Len's indifference to the sport because of his artistic passion. I mean how much baseball can a guy know if he's that much in to the artsy stuff? Thank goodness elderly possess the poise and wisdom to keep the cockiness of youth in its place. Thank goodness I had Len. I approached him condescendingly one day informing him of the Sox defeat from the previous night, assuming he's oblivious to this important piece of news. Len looks up, adjusts his glasses, and in that raspy voice tells me that not only did he know the outcome, but told me in no uncertain terms why they lost the game and who from the ballclub needs to be traded. To keep me in my place he'd even tossed in an eye witness story about Babe Ruth and how he carried himself compared to today's ballplayers. I learned lessons that day on baseball and humility. I turned and finished my sweeping.

GAME 48: BOSTON RED SOX VS. CHICAGO WHITE SOX
SATURDAY, AUGUST 16

"What is this game, this BAZE-BOL? How you play?"

Jackson, a clown I've known from 4th grade, walks from the car to White Sox Park. A handful of us who went to grade school and high school together take in a game as we're days away from scattering to colleges throughout the Midwest. This Jackson, who has lived his life in the western suburbs, has *never* been to a baseball game in his 18 years. Hard to imagine, especially since a few of his friends are addicted to the sport.

"You must explain this BAZE-BOL to me," he requests in an exaggerated Eastern European dialect. "How they play? Is it like FUT-BOL?"

Naturally I remember the first game I saw in person but I also recall the first games that a few of my friends saw. Now that I think about it, I may have been part of the reason they went—constantly bugging them and talking about the game—so maybe they went just to shut me up. Regardless, Jackson's attendance sparks my interest, I'm interested in hearing his reactions to my addiction. He's a nut case, but that hardly distinguishes him from the people I hang with.

Take Stephan, for instance. He's another guy who makes the trip and he's into numbers and would pass as a baseball junkie. Scouring quirky stuff, like bizarre names, is what he does. (Speaking of quirky, during study hall he'd pass the time by slamming shut a fat text book, seeing how many times he could do it before the moderator told him to stop. His record, I believe, was in the twenties. Funny how I have a different take on this now that I'm a teacher vs. then as an irresponsible kid). His efforts of examining minutiae would occasionally pay dividends, as it did with his creation of a legend, "The Legend of Bucky Dent."

In the early days of high school, Stephan discovered that in the bushes of the White Sox organization was an infielder named Bucky Dent. Stephan's eyes bulge and his mind explodes. One look at that name and Stephan had years of fertile material. I'll do my best to present the story as Stephan would .....

One day, Bucky's family takes a trip up north to watch their Bucky play ball. Come to think of it, every trip for this family to watch Bucky play had to be north. Anyway, as the Dent clan motors up the highway in a vehicle resembling the Clampetts, they stop every so often to hunt and fish and camp, sometimes roasting the road kill. Feasting on squirrel and moonshine, they wonder if northerners can fix victuals for Bucky as well as Ma. And as they converse they hope that Bucky isn't duped by these big city slickers, seeing as how book learnin for the Dents hits the wall around third grade.

After several days of travel, the Dents make it to White Sox Park. They're comforted to know that Bucky's team plays on the South Side and that players on the team are called Southsiders. Inside the stadium, Becky Dent, Bucky's sister, exclaims: "Golly, Ma, Bucky has shoes on and 'taint even Sunday!"

Once the game begins the Dents decide to head to the concourse to find what kind of supplies they can buy for lunch. Nothing but peanuts appeal to their taste, so after purchasing ten bags, they hear on the PA, "Now batting, Number 30, Bucky Dent." The family rushes back to their seats just in time to see for the first time ever, a pitch thrown to Bucky.

Ma Dent is alarmed, "Land sakes, Verle, someone's chuckin' somethin at our Bucky! Wonder if Bucky sassed him before the game and now he's getting back at him. Taint seem fair, that one guy has a ball and Bucky just a club. Becky, you run down and fetch Bucky's shotgun from the truck. This needs to be a fair fight. This oughta —"

"Wait a minute, Ma," interrupts Verle, Bucky's father. "The chucker missed Bucky and hit the guy squattin behind him wearing all that body armor. Bucky's not even mad. Let's hold off on that shotgun."

Bucky hits the next offering from Roger Moret and pops the ball up to the second baseman.

"Mercy!" Ma exclaims. "Did you see that? Our Bucky protected himself by hitting that ball before it hit him. Then he takes off like a deer, not to the hurler nor to the guy who's fittin to grab it, but runnin like the wind on that line that leads straight to one of those pillows on the field. My, my. I ain't never seen Bucky run so fast since that bear chased him in the woods back when he was six."

"Ma," Becky asks, "how come Bucky's team called the White Sox wear lots of red, whilst that there team called the Red Sox barely have any red on their outfits?"

"Remember child we's in the north. People may be book smart, but not too sensible. Why, look at all these people payin good money to watch other people play and have fun. Don't worry, baby. Maybe Bucky will learn 'em some common sense."

So for Stephan, a dream comes true. Bucky Dent, who he's followed since he was knee high to a grasshopper, makes it to the big leagues, and makes it big. And right here in Chicago. And we're now going to watch him play short-stop and bat second. Stephan and the Dents couldn't be any prouder.

That's where the fun ended, mostly. The Bosox leadoff man scores and I got this theory that when this happens, the visitors don't do a whole lot more scoring. That part of my theory holds true. Unfortunately the Chisox score even less. The highlight of the day takes place when our Bucky singles to lead off the seventh. The home team has just their second hit of the day, but the good news is that they only trail by 2. The next player raps into a double play. Hope evaporates. Another fan favorite, Wilbur Wood, baffles Boston's World Series lineup (household names like Yaz, Fisk, Lynn, Evans, and even Cecil Cooper before he departs for Milwaukee) and holds them to 2 runs through 8. But the Dead Sox blow it open with a 3 run 8th as Moret and Jim Willoughby shut out the White Sox.

Roger Moret's dominance of the Sox typified the success he enjoyed over the rest of the league that season as he finishes with a sterling mark of 14-3. In '73 his record was 13-2. Still, overshadowing his success on the mound was an incident that occurred in the locker room. One day before a game Red Sox personnel discover Moret to be in a catatonic state, totally frozen and un-responsive for over an hour. Fortunately he recovered and moved on to pitch with Atlanta and Texas, never coming close to approaching his gaudy numbers from before. But just to recover from this condition and compete again at the major league level was inspiring. Reminiscent of another recovery by a Boston player, Jimmy Piersall, as seen in the fim, *Fear Strikes Out.*

POST-SEASON 1975

Just as 1776 can't be mentioned without thinking of some kind of declaration, 1975 can't be mentioned without thinking of the World Series. Okay, that's a stretch, but *Sports Illustrated* did get it right when the Fall Classic celebration graced its cover with these words, "A Series to Shout About." Weeks preceding the World Series, SI raised the question, "Four in a Row?" as a Reggie Jackson dons the cover. I was hoping for the Oakland A's to quadpeat, and the main reason had to do with a National League acquisition, Billy Williams. Here's a guy who never sniffed the postseason with the Cubs, and now he's on the verge of playing in the World Series. He was traded very late in his career to a legitimate contender that seemed to take winning in stride, unlike Chicago. What Williams went through was similar to the Mark Grace experience with the Arizona Diamondbacks some 26 years later. Unlike Gracie, Billy would never make it to baseball's championship round, since Boston dethroned Finley's team.

Like the Mets of '69, what could possibly be added to the epic match between the Reds and Red Sox? Such a phenomena affected even the cold world of academia, as my English professor cut us some slack with the assignments since we glued ourselves to televisions and couldn't quite make it to the library. How could we possibly study drama in our anthology while there was so much drama in Boston and Cincinnati?

My English teacher would be proud to know that I did acknowledge some irony as the final scenes at the Fens were being played out. As soon as Joe Morgan blooped a single to center that scored Pete Rose with two outs in the ninth in Game 7, I leaned over to my roommate and said that with all the drama, heroes, and controversies (think Bernie Carbo, Ed Armbrister, and of course, Carlton Fisk) that this Series ends on a dinky little hit.

And it did.

1976

GREG

To what shall I compare thee?
To children playing, full of glee?
To eagles soaring, brave and free?
To placid lakes and serenity?

Nay, thou dost betray poetic verse
As thy tongue contains ev'ry curse,
Speak ye long or speak ye terse
Decorum never, profanity first!

Greg was Len's partner, as much as Len could have a partner. These two vets had separate tables, separate styles, separate skills, separate everything, which made them the perfect odd couple.

When it comes to vulgarity, truck drivers, sailors, and Joe Pesci have nothing on Greg. Think of the famous Lee Elia tirade; I got treated to that kind of performance on a daily basis. But whereas Elia's erupted after reaching a breaking point of frustration (in *early spring*, mind you), Greg's torrent of blue words came naturally and unforced. A sentence—heck, a phrase—from Greg without a couple of curse words sounded awkward. Yet in the presence of ladies, and not too many ladies frequented the bowels of the warehouse where we worked, Greg morphed into an elderly Eddie Haskell from Leave It To Beaver. He would flirt, smile more and curse less.

The tone and content of Greg's words to Len would constitute verbal abuse in today's world. Back then and between them they were terms of endearment. From Greg's table he would curse a blue streak at Len for something he did or did not do, and Len would smile. He wouldn't even bother to look up; he'd just smile and continue his work. Since Len spoke about three words to every 90 of Greg's, their exchange consisted mostly of cursing and smiling. They reminded me of a couple married for 58 years.

Being creative himself, Greg could come up with an obscenity for any occasion. Upon my sweeping of their work area, Greg would announce in his husky voice, "Len, it's so clean up here you could just sh**". I would wonder how many people besides Greg associate cleanliness with doing number 2. On one occasion something caught my eye on Greg's work table, some kind of design that looked interesting but a little unusual. I leaned the push broom up against a box and asked Greg what that meant. Before I completed the last syllable of my question, he turned to me and said, "It means f*** nosy kids." I returned to my sweeping. Greg was a Cub fan, and if he heard that they won, he'd exclaim, "Hey, the pr*cks!" If he heard that they lost, he'd exclaim, "Hey, the pr*cks!"

Our warehouse collected all sorts of promotional gimmicks and displays designed to increase awareness for products and generate revenue for the booze industry. One time we had this monkey made of foam nestled in a frame. It ran on batteries, and turning this contraption on resulted in the monkey gyrating all four limbs, head, and tail. It would probably catch your eye walking down the aisle of a liquor store. At break one afternoon Greg takes a walk to this mobile. "This ought to be good," is what the rest of us thought as we watched a perverse mastermind in action. After a couple of simple adjustments, the monkey's hand is relocated to his crotch area as he now moves with obscene convulsions. Fifteen seconds of hearty laughter roared from the six of us.

To dismiss Greg and Len as just a couple of vulgar and eccentric guys would be a mistake. Len with his artistry and Greg with his mechanical aptitude created wonderful things. In their corner of the warehouse stands photos pieced together that celebrate their diverse and attractive work over many years. Splendid mobiles, paintings, sets, and woodwork adorn this collage. This tremendous testimony to brilliant and creative capabilities overwhelm the superficial eccentrics and obscenities. I learned from them, to which Greg would undoubtedly respond, "Shit, yeah!"

GAME 49: PHILADELPHIA PHILLIES VS. CHICAGO CUBS
SUNDAY, APRIL 18

"Yesterday, April 17, 1976, is a day that will live in Cub infamy."

That was the day that Mike Schmidt bombed Wrigley Field. Unsuspecting to most Chicagoans, Schmidt's attack snuck up on us, even while some ambassadors from Philadelphia were in Chicago when it happened.

During this game the Cubs owned an insurmountable lead for any major league team with a major league pitching staff ... which meant that the Cubs lead was in jeopardy. Four home runs later by Mike Schmidt and the Phils cap a most improbable comeback.

So as an Easter treat our whole family watches and hopes that the Cubs can come back to life. I travel home from Notre Dame during Easter break, knowing that several friends had witnessed yesterday's disaster and bound to give me all sorts of razzing. I hoped desperately that today would yield a different outcome.

It's already been documented that my dad would rather have a root canal than go to Wrigley Field, so to hear his enthusiastic support of the home team caught me a bit off-guard. To be honest, it was more a bashing of the Phils than support of the Cubs, but I'll take it. It came in the top of the 2nd inning as Schmidt, probably exhausted from running 360 feet on four separate occasions yesterday, struck out in his first plate appearance. He looked funny returning back to the dugout, body language that said something like, "I should not whiff against Cub pitching." My dad noticed this non-verbal message, and responded with a verbal one that went like this, "Hey, Schmidt, you're not gonna homer every time up." I thought the comment a bit odd, but what would baseball be without heckling.

True to form, the Phillies and Schmidt would have the last laugh again. In fact, after Ray Burris whiffs Dick Allen and Schmidt to start the 2nd, he yields three doubles and a walk, with the big blow a two-run two-bagger from the opposing pitcher, Larry Christensen. I guess Burris used up all his quality pitches on Schmidt, and at this point I was merely hoping for a non-embarrassing game.

Four homers again sailed out of the Confines this day, and three by Chicago: Jose Cardenal, Rick Monday, and Andy Thornton. Take a wild guess who homered for the Phillies. The good news is that Schmidt was also responsible for five outs—the aforementioned strikeout, two pop outs, and a double play grounder in his last at-bat. Cubs were not embarrassed too much, but still lost 8-5.

Forgive me if I sound like a broken record, but as Harry Caray did multiple times in his career, I'd like to do yet again: Let's look at these line-ups: For the Phillies: Dave Cash, Larry Bowa, Jay Johnstone, Greg Luzinski, Allen, Schmidt (why is he hitting 6th and Johnstone 3rd?) Garry Maddox, and Bob Boone hitting against Ray Burris. So much for a level playing field. This Philadelphia lineup had precisely one easy out, the pitcher, and he hit a two run double! The Cubs meanwhile, had several automatic out-makers: Steve Swisher, Dave Rosello, and the pitcher. Taken together, this begs a few questions:

- Couldn't the Cubs' higher-ups see this problem?
- Did they care?
- Couldn't they do something to be a little more competitive?
- And why do I keep going?

I suppose in fairness if I can't answer the last question how could I expect Cub management to answer the first three?

NO GAME: SAN DIEGO PADRES VS. CHICAGO CUBS
SATURDAY, MAY 15

Big blue tarp with the beloved Cub logo, lots of raindrops plopping on the tarp, and a rain out. You've seen the bumper stickers that say, "*A bad day of fishing is better than a good day at work?*" I think of that as I have in my possession two virgin scorecards with not a starting lineup, not an out recorded, not a pencil mark, and not even a mustard stain. I have nothing else to do except sit in the upper deck cheering hard for sunshine. "*Watching a rainout at Wrigley Field is better than most days at work.*"

GAME 50: TEXAS RANGERS VS. CHICAGO
WHITE SOX MONDAY, MAY 31

Chicago Bear fans thirty and older may remember "The Fog Bowl." On January 1, 1990, the Bears hosted the Philadelphia Eagles in a playoff game. How often does a football game, let alone a playoff game, take second billing to the elements? I can think of only a few: The Ice Bowl, of course (Dallas vs. Green Bay at Lambeau Field), the Vikings during the Chuck Foreman era mucking out a win in a torrential downpour in LA against the Rams, the snow conditions leading to Tom Brady's infamous "Tuck Rule" between the Raiders and the Patriots, and this one--the Fog Bowl. How bad were the conditions? So bad that cameras from the booth could not capture all the players (I wonder how many things players got away with. Imagine how much the refs couldn't see). Fortunately for Bear fans, the home team saw well enough and long enough to defeat the Beagles and proceed to the next round.

Tonight's contest serves as baseball's version of the fog bowl. I've seen numerous times when players lose the ball in the sun—right field in Wrigley comes to mind immediately, and I recall some left field difficulties in Oakland's ballpark when the A's played day games in the post-season. I've seen balls get lost in the lights; earlier in his career Bill Melton of the White Sox loses a foul popup in Baltimore and has a broken nose to show for it. And there have been times when outfielders in the old Metrodome in Minnesota lost the ball in the roof. But never have I seen nor even heard of a player losing the ball in the fog. Until now.

Sox bat in the first, bases loaded, two out, and they already trail, 2-0. Chet Lemon lofts a routine fly ball to left field. My friend Jorge and I get excited as the left fielder, Tom Grieve, panics. He looks as helpless as Charlie Brown, Good Grieve, and we know he has no chance of making the play. Juan Beniquez, the centerfielder, can't offer much help. Consequently the Chisox play ring around the bases as Lemon winds up with a gift triple.

Here's another time when a kid's sense of fair play would trump decisions made in the adult world. Kids in a pickup game would undoubtedly declare a "Do-over," and all the runners would have to return to their bases. When the fog lifted and players could see, play would resume. Now I suppose that Grieve could have hollered for a timeout or something, but I'm thinking that visibility could have drastically changed between the time the pitch was thrown and the time when the ball landed in the outfield grass. The umps do enforce a "fog delay", but not until counting the White Sox three tallies. I'd go bananas and probably be ejected if I were Frank Lucchesi, skipper of the Rangers. Maybe he was and I couldn't see it. In any case, the fog did lift, the runs counted, and the rout was on. The early lead by Texas ended up in a lopsided 9-4 victory for the home team.

Nelson Briles, a Cub nemesis for many seasons (Cardinals and Pirates) departs in the 3rd inning. Jorge Orta saw well enough to pull a homer in the 3rd, and then proceeds to single twice more and score three times. The gentleman following him in the batting orta, Jim Spencer, does some one upmanship by singling four times in five at bats. It was no contest, really, but a fan of Texas could argue that this game was significantly tainted. Had the Sox not been awarded those three propitious runs in the first inning, would they have been relaxed enough to tally six more times? My gut says the Sox still win. My head, on the other hand, doesn't have the foggiest.

GAME 51: NEW YORK YANKEES VS. CHICAGO WHITE SOX
SUNDAY, JUNE 20

My friend Petey and I went our separate ways during the school season. He was a "public" and I attended schools that were named St. Domitilla and Immaculate Conception. Petey didn't live very close, not even by bike. He played the real hockey on ice: I couldn't skate but loved the game of street hockey. He'd party and I didn't. And his knowledge of baseball trivia was unmatched, until he met me.

Because of baseball we hung out together during the summer months. In the Pony League tournaments (age 14-16) Petey played shortstop and I played third. He was a marvelous athlete who would slap the ball and run fast; in the field he had this oversized glove that would intercept balls headed for the outfield. You old-timers might remember his glove model—it was signed by Denny McLain and was at least twice the size of the typical infielder's mitt. I believe it was a Wilson. Later it came as a surprise to learn that gloves for the infielders should be relatively small so the exchange to the throwing hand happens as cleanly as possible. I thought of Petey's "elephant ear"—the name he gave his glove—and thought this mitt served him very well in the infield. One of life's lessons that I guess I had to unlearn.

These tournaments we played in were fun, and we won our share. But I always had the sense that the adults—coaches, parents, tournament directors, etc.—were way more into these games than we were. I recall travelling over a 3-4 day stretch to a tournament site in Naperville. The car ride lasted about forty minutes or so, but it seemed to me that we had to be close to Iowa by the time we arrived—much more open space and even some corn fields. In the days before smart phones when people actually talked with one another, we engaged in baseball trivia quiz, Part 2 (Part 1 was waiting for the El after a Cub loss to Pittsburgh, you might recall).

Me: Name two Cubs on the '69 team who used to play for the *Milwaukee* Braves.

Petey: Gene Oliver and, um, …

Me (Starting to gloat and trying to get into his head): Time's running out, give up?

Petey would deftly change the subject to whom we were playing to buy some time.

Petey (triumphantly): … and Al Spangler!

Me (in the voice of Kip Dynamite): Dang it.

Petey: Okay, name four Sox players who used to play for the Angels.

Me: Jay Johnstone, Rick Reichardt, Tom Bradley, and Steve Kealey.

Petey: How did you get Kealey?

Me: It wasn't that tough—actually there's one more, Tom Egan.

This would go on for the entire trip, every day. By the end of the second day of travel, the other bemused travelers in the car simply shook their head. Usually the topic of conversation on the return trip centered on key plays, who did what to turn the game around. This was fun too. Even in defeat the mood was we'll get 'em tomorrow. At that point in my playing days, I hate to admit it, but I was a selfish player. You know how the major leaguers' clichés run: *"My job is to keep the team in the game." "I don't care how I play; I just want the team to win." "I'll do whatever it takes to win."* Seems like players are forced to memorize such drivel before playing in the majors. And it's mostly BS. Here's how I know—watch how many players shorten their swings with two strikes. Not many. They still swing mightily because as the old expression goes, "Home run hitters drive Cadillacs" (or Porsches or Hummers or if they hail from the South--trucks). More evidence to show how the "team" concept is a farce: watch the majority of players try to bunt. It looks to me like they'd be more comfortable delivering kidney stones. And then there are pitchers—some take the "Five and fly" approach so they pitch just long enough to get the win. And others never want to leave a game, even if they lost their effectiveness several batters ago. This latter group seems more admirable and more competitive, but I have to think they're thinking more of themselves than the team. "Buddy, **you** just don't have it anymore." Can't you, after a few weeks if not shorter, just tell who the players are that really do put the team first? I got to believe that the team with the most players like this wins.

Like I said, I was selfish growing up, which probably explains why the teams I played on didn't win many championships. Self-centered guys like me ruin things. Then a transformation occurs when I really put winning ahead of personal glory. And you know what? We still lost. No, just kidding, favorable outcomes increased as my ego decreased. The teams I played on started winning more regularly—I'm glad I came to this realization, but sorry it took so long to figure it out. Winning is really more fun than doing well individually and losing.

These days of "Baseball Jeopardy on Car Rides" took place in the summers of 1971-72. Some marvelous music from that era. Topping the list of favorites was "Brandy" by the *Looking Glass*. Another one I liked featured an artist more from our parents' or even grandparents' era, Sammy Davis Junior. His big hit that summer … "The Candy Man." Admittedly I was not averse to bubble gum music, nor disco in the years ahead, and I paid for it with a lot of abuse from friends and family. Mentally, if not literally, I'd flip off such harassment and keep listening to stuff I liked.

Fast forward to 1976. Petey and I went our separate ways in so many ways, but re-united on an American Legion baseball team. A few subtle differences—we shifted from the left side to the right side of the infield. He now played second and I first. Plus we could drive ourselves to games and tournaments without playing "Baseball Jeopardy." But the one constant in our lives, the one passion that we still shared, the deepest part of our souls remained the same—politics (yeah, right).

This Sunday we took ourselves to the Sox-Yankee game. Actually Petey drove and got lost as I gave him lousy directions in the pre-Mapquest and GPS days. The O'Donnell family moved several miles away to unincorporated North Elmhurst (I never knew what unincorporated meant as a kid, but I figured it had to do something with social class. An infrequent snobby remark from somebody in corporate South Elmhurst taught me that). So Petey and I finally connect in a gas station and take off for Comiskey. The highlight of this experience was listening to music from Petey's tapes. He was pretty hip when it came to music, and I enjoyed listening for the first time songs from *Heart* and *Boz Scaggs*.

The music remained with me much longer than the ballgame. Yanks win, 6-3, and it wasn't anywhere near as close as the final score might indicate. No drama whatsoever after New York bats around in the fifth, scoring five runs off George Brett's brother, Ken. The hurler for the visitors, the colorful Dock Ellis, was known for several things:

- Wearing hair curlers in the bullpen (light years before locks or do-rags were fashionable)
- Allegedly throwing a no-hitter while on LSD
- Beaning the first 4 or 5 Cincinnati Red hitters to start a game, and then being removed by the manager
- Giving up that mammoth home run to Reggie Jackson in the '71 All-Star game at Tiger Stadium

With the Yankees comfortably ahead by 6, the Sox halved the margin with a 2-run homer by Jack Brohamer and an RBI double by Pat Kelly (normally a lead-off guy, Kelly hit clean-up this game. Clean-up for a guy who would slug 5 homers that year. A pop-gun offense in spacious Comiskey Park was the order of the day, I suppose, for Manager Paul Richards and White Sox management).

The day wasn't a total loss because of music: the initial time I heard songs like "Crazy on You" and "Georgia" to and from the ballpark.

GAME 52: NEW YORK METS VS. CHICAGO CUBS
SUNDAY, JUNE 27

Time for another New York team to administer another pasting of a Chicago team on a Sunday in June. This time the Reuschel brothers, Rick then Paul, got lit up like fireworks one week prior to the bi-centennial bash of our country. A lead-off homer by Mike Phillips did not bode well, especially since it was followed by an eight-run second. A double by Dave Kingman (more on him later) and a two-run homer by the Original Met who shares the same birthday with me, Ed Kranepool, puts this game away early. If I weren't a kid, I'd leave very early and try somehow to salvage the day. But I hang around to watch the Cubs swat a couple of meaningless homers, one by Bill Madlock and another by "Tarzan" Joe Wallis.

Wouldn't it be nice if the managers and players would tell the media after the game that we just gave up and wanted in the worst way to get out of there? "We rolled over and mailed it in," would be refreshing to hear. But again with the clichés, "I'm proud of the way these guys battled." "The one thing about this team is that it never quits." Blah-blah-blah. Wouldn't it be more charitable if baseball did what they do sometimes in chess, just lay down your piece (or bat) and declare the game over? That way fans can take the rest of the day off and go to the zoo or something. They'd probably meet some of the players and their families already there.

Final score: NY Giants 13, Chicago Bears 3.

GAME 53: ATLANTA BRAVES VS. NEW YORK METS
MONDAY, JULY 19

A vacation takes the O'Donnells to the upper deck in Shea Stadium. So high were these nose bleed seats that my brother, Denny, jokes of a ball hit a mile in the air. He acts as if he's in his seat watching the ball keep ascending, and ascending, and ascending—all the while looking downward from his seat. Then he speaks of the frequent interruptions of airplanes flying to and from nearby LaGuardia airport. He'd complain that these jets would obstruct his view of the game.

Truth be told, I did not make this trip. Choosing to play ball over a vacation, my folks let me stay put in Elmhurst. Looking at the scorecard that they brought home, I sometimes wished I joined them.

The Braves lineup was nothing special since this was the post-Aaron era and the pre-Dale Murphy days. But the Mets, who I recently saw demolish the Cubs, had an interesting assortment of players. Three of my favorites would be in the lineup that day: Joe Torre, Dave Kingman, and Mickey Lolich. All three you'd associate with other teams, but for a brief while they were together and employed by the New York National League Ballclub. It's difficult to have something nice to say for anything Met-like after 1969, but these three were okay.

Torre amazed me with his physical transformation. I recall getting his baseball card when he broke in as a catcher with the Milwaukee Braves. He was a hefty guy, and that's being charitable. He had this sleepy look behind his omnipresent five o'clock shadow. A very good pudgy hitter with the Braves grows into a very good, svelte hitter later with other teams (for the Cardinals in '71, he led the league in average (.363), hits (230), and RBI's (137). As a part-time player this year in the twilight of his playing days, he would hit over .300 for the fifth time.

Dave Kingman. A man perpetually ripped by the media. I'm sure they have their reasons, but I didn't care at all about the media nor with any problems they had with uncooperative athletes. I simply liked the way he could bash the ball 500 feet with some regularity. At the close of tonight's game, Kingman will have homered for the 31st time this season. The next closest players on the playing field this evening were Jimmy Wynn with 11, and teammate John Milner with 10.

And then there's the hero from the 1968 World Series, Mickey Lolich, a folk hero among couch potatoes. I remember reading a quote from Lolich explaining his popularity. It went something like this:

"A lot of guys could relate to me. A guy on the couch with an empty beer can in his hand watches the game on television and hollers out to his wife, 'Honey, come in and look at this guy pitching. He looks just like me. And please get me another beer.'"

Rotund, unassuming, durable, clutch, motorcycle rider and donut maker—that's Mickey Lolich. Today, a starting pitcher is praised who logs 200 innings. In 1971, Lolich threw 376 innings. That's the equivalent of *forty-one* complete games. For the record, Lolich tossed an incredible 29 complete games that year. And he did this by playing second banana to the more highly publicized Denny McLains, Al Kalines, Willie Hortons, etc. But in '68 all of his team-mates, and the great Bob Gibson, and the Redbirds were the bridesmaids to the guy who owned a beer gut . . . and three World Series wins.

Back to the game at hand--Lolich hurls a nifty two-hit shutout. This complete game victory (what new?) drops his ERA to under 2.90 and elevates his record to 5-10. Not a whole lot of run support, it seems. He'd finish the year with an 8-13 mark and an ERA of 3.23.

Kingman's homer leading off the fourth accounted for half of the Mets' scoring. I heard it went a long way—big surprise. The other Met who scored in the heat of the night was Roy Staiger—that's Roy Staiger and not Rod Steiger. Staiger crosses home on one of three Felix Milan's singles, and the home team claims a tidy 2-0 victory. I enjoyed this game vicariously through family members' stories, and of course, the scorecard.

GAMES 54 & 55: DETROIT TIGERS VS. CHICAGO WHITE SOX
WEDNESDAY, JULY 21

The Bird. In the summer of '76, that's really all you had to say or know in the world of baseball. The Bird. It was the word.

Mark Fidrych enchanted and owned baseball for a summer. His hair resembled Harpo Marx, and come to think of it, so did his antics. How could you not like a guy who patted the mound dirt with his hands, verbally instructed the baseball what to do before he pitched it, and shook hands with his fielders after they made plays while the opposition was still at-bat. Best of all, for me at least, was his unabashed exuberance and his disarming honesty. To paraphrase one of his more revealing quotes about status and salary, he wondered aloud, "Why should I be upset about making the minimum baseball salary while my friends back home are making a whole lot less pumping gas?" I detect three things:

1. Fidrych's guileless simplicity
2. That in the 70's there were jobs for people at service stations who pumped gas
3. A journalist looks to stir things up a bit.

God bless the media—they really need it. Still, the management had to be making it hand-over-fist as media folk report on the spike in attendance when it was The Bird's turn to pitch.

Now if Bird was a bust on the mound, none of this would have mattered. But he was far from a bust. In spite of a late entry into Detroit's rotation, Fidrych managed to not only make the All-Star team, but start the game for the American League. He would go on to lead the league in two impressive categories: ERA (2.34) and Complete Games (24). I see something telling in his win total of 19. It is an incomplete number in that it's one short of the coveted 20 mark, it's an odd number, and it's a prime number. What three things can better describe the Bird—incomplete, odd, and prime?

So my friend Jorge and I, doubling our chances to go Bird watching, get tickets for a twi-nite double header. Unfortunately, he pitched in neither.

But there are worse things to do than watching six hours of evening baseball. Playing in mid-July when days are near their longest, the lights would not take effect until the latter innings of Game 1. For Game 2, that refulgent glow, especially reflected off batting helmets, impressed me then and still does today. Nighttime baseball just seems to have a surreal quality with the magic amped up around 8 o'clock on a summer's evening, at least on the South Side of Chicago.

So the Tigers called upon to pitch were Vern Ruhle in Game 1 and Dave Lemanczyk in Game 2. Not only a far cry from the Bird, but a far cry from Denny McLain, Mickey Lolich, Earl Wilson, Joe Sparma, Joe Coleman, etc. Heck, I'd even take a Dave Wickersham, just because I like the name (reminds me of that elderly lady in Great Expectations). The Sox counter with a couple of good young arms in Chris Knapp and Bart Johnson.

In fairness, the pitchers on both sides acquitted themselves well. Especially effective were the hurlers for the home team. Here's a situation— the dangerous leadoff guy for Detroit, Ron LeFlore, walks and scores in the first inning of the first game. One of those nights, right? But only if you're a Tiger fan, because Knapp and Johnson combine to record 54 outs without another Bengal crossing the plate. Two dominating performances, reminiscent of those Sox teams in the 60's. Pitch, defend, scratch out a run or two, and win both games. Turning our attention to the Detroit situation, did you ever notice how a sense of melancholy envelops a team when it is in transition? Now, mind you, nothing melancholy took place when the Bird did his thing, but when he wasn't pitching, a closer look at the Tiger roster leaves me feeling a bit empty. As previously documented, this club was one of my favorites ever since I started following the game around '63 or so. They had personnel you could depend on for so many years—it was comforting to know who'd be in right field, who'd be catching, who'd be at first base, second base, left field, even platooning in center field. But now those familiar names and faces I've come to know through my baseball card collection had dwindled to a precious few. These Tigers still had some claw to them even though they were in the twi-light of their careers. For the record, their names and their performances for the evening were …

- Willie Horton, who was 1 for 8 in both games
- Bill Freehan, 1 for 3 in Game 2
- Mickey Stanley, did not play in either game

On the glass half-full side, Detroit brought in a couple of players who were new to the team but performed at a high level, the aforementioned Fidrych and LeFlore, with Rusty Staub. And a blast from the past whose name is synonymous with discord: Alex Johnson. Throw in an Alex Rodriguez, a Jason Thompson, and a Ralph Houk as manager and you have a team still searching for an identity. Perhaps the most telling sign of confusion was this: four catchers. Two, of course, three, maybe, but 4? One is Bill Freehan. Now if you happen to be a Tiger fan from this era, you earn an "A for the Day" if you can name 2 of the other 3 backstops. Okay, guess (I'll just double check my scorecard for the right answer, to give you some time to think). Okay, time's up. Who do you have?

The guys who tried to fill the spikes of that perennial All-Star, Bill Freehan, were—in no particular order—Milt May, Bruce Kimm, and John Wockenfuss (Holy cow--Wockenfuss spelled backwards is ...) Did anybody out there get Wockenfuss? If you really did, give me a call—I'd like to shake your hand. Do you now see why I called this a melancholy stage for the Tigers, in spite of Mark Fidyrich? If Freehan got the mumps, look who would have to catch the Bird.

Next to the pitching exploits, the most remarkable quality about this evening was efficiency: 2 wins in less than five hours. Just enough offense with 2 RBI's by Lamar Johnson in the first game, and a 2-run triple by Bucky Dent in the nightcap. Bottom line for the evening: Chicago 4-3, Detroit 1-0.

Permit me to share one minor mishap from this satisfying night. In the early innings of Game 1 my tummy was grumbly so I passed on my scorecard to Jorge to look for some delicious ballpark victuals. In fact, with some sleuth work I see that it was the second inning when this search occurred because the new scorekeeper, Jorge, would mark a walk in this fashion: "BB", just like my ol man. I, on the other hand, put a "W" in the box. I know, I know, fascinating stuff. Well, anyway, in '76 the White Sox had this tremendous treat at the ballpark: chicken dinner in a box. It consisted of 2-3 pieces of *fried* chicken—none of this healthy stuff—a roll, and slaw. This would be washed down by an ice cold Nehi pop served in an assortment of flavors. For a guy who didn't eat after work today in order to get to the ballpark on time, this combination of food and drink sounded yummy. Trouble is, the point of purchase is way upstairs, and our seats were pretty good—only a couple rows from the Tiger on-deck circle. This meant that my return trip with these delicacies could be a tad tricky.

To make a short story long, by the time I reached Jorge it is the top of the third inning. Unfortunately, having to navigate my way over a myriad of steps with little to balance myself, there was very little precious Nehi liquid left in the cup upon my return; most had found its way to my pants. You know how they say that people are often too self-conscious? You think that everyone is looking at you when in reality no one is? Well, that's not always true. I got some funny looks from people sitting around us (remember, this is the high rent district) and I just had to tell them that everything's okay, this is just Nehi pop on my pants. Jorge laughed for an inning and a third. No lie.

PAUL

"He's never had a bad day in his life."

For three months in the summer and one month in the winter, my daily contact with Paul confirmed my dad's assessment of this man. Paul supervised me at work, as did many others. Paul's blend of size, strength, humor and gentleness made for yet another memorable character at the warehouse. Picture a middle-aged man with salt and pepper hair, broad shoulders, a collared shirt, navy pants, and work shoes. Add a ready smile and a talkative nature and you have Paul—someone who's very easy to be with. Whereas instructions from other folks in charge sound authoritative, Paul's directives were more like suggestions. "Well, John, why don't we clean up some stuff downstairs," and off we'd go to the cellar of the warehouse.

Three distinct recollections I have of Paul go a long way in defining the man. The first just a simple remark he reserved for me. When I'd mess up, which was not an extremely rare occurrence, Paul would make it a point to say, with a smile in his voice, "Wrong again, John." Not taking myself or the job too seriously, I'd laugh along with him. Fortunately a mistake in the warehouse was nothing like a mistake in the operating room or a mistake by one of the flying Wallendas. These problems were easily fixable and seldom left a mark. An example occurred one day as Alan and I thought we were supposed to pick up a display at a downtown liquor establishment. We approached the owner and announced that we were here to pick up something. "Pick up, PICK UP!!??" The curmudgeon spoke with increasing volume and with blood vessels bulging. "You're not supposed to pick up—You Are SUPPOSE TO *DELIVER!!!*" Alan and I high tailed it out of there back to the sanctuary of the warehouse. When Paul got the news, we shared a good laugh and he said, "Wrong again, John."

The second incident was so routine that I almost missed it. We unload a truck one humid summer afternoon as Paul talks to the truck driver. It's just the three of us, working at a steady clip but not killing ourselves. The conversation shifts to music, a topic of interest at the warehouse because of the great variation in tastes. Just the three college kids alone have their own radio stations, with one preferring hard rock, the other light rock, and the third R & B.

Paul leans toward the two types of music they play in rural regions: Country and Western. How a guy who lives on the South Side of Chicago which is mega miles north of the Mason-Dixon Line could like Country-Western is beyond me, but he did. The truck drivers who frequent our place also like country. But now the conversation turns to country singers, and this is where I get a life-long lesson.

> Truck driver: I like blah, blah, and blah in country music.
> Paul: I like Charlie Pride. (I know this name. Charlie Pride was a baseball aficionado who did a guest appearance on Monday Night Baseball once. And he was black).
> Truck driver: Ain't he a nigger?
> Paul: So?

I've read countless articles on prejudice and racism of all kinds. I've heard speeches and sermons on the subject. I've seen people cruelly treated by other people and I hate it. But the most enlightening, compelling, convincing response on racism comes to me that day from Paul. Here is a real guy from the real world who soundly defeats bigotry that day with one two-letter word. The truck driver sheepishly changes the subject, but I never forgot.

The other fact about Paul that raised him to practically celebrity status had to do with his family. Paul has a son, let's call him Paul as well, who plays in the big leagues. My dad would occasionally run this by me at home, but it never really sunk in until I started working at the warehouse. "My gosh, I am talking with a guy whose kid plays for the Montreal Expos!"

So you can imagine how much time we spent, and how much time Paul spent, talking about his son's adventures at the major league level. I almost never tired hearing of these stories, stories of what it was like to play for Billy Martin and Gene Mauch, stories of rooming with Gary Carter and breaking in with Larry Parrish. And the story of what it was like for Paul Senior to watch his son clobber a homer as an Expo in Wrigley Field (probably doubly sweet, since Paul and his son pledged their allegiance to the White Sox).

Paul tells us how his son is a bit disgruntled as he returns to the dugout after touching all the bases. The reason he's put off is because as he looks into the stands to see his family, all he notices is his father sitting down and eating peanuts. "What was I supposed to do?" argues Paul Sr. "I stood and clapped for a moment or two, then went back to my peanuts." At least his pants weren't pop stained.

Paul's pride in all his children shone through on a daily basis. He mentions how he roots for Rich Gossage on the Sox because he looks so much like one of his sons. (I worked with this son briefly, and he did indeed look like the Goose). By coincidence, our family and his family crossed paths a couple times in the classroom. My sister taught his daughter a Spanish class at the junior high level, and then I had the privilege of teaching Paul's granddaughter at the high school level some fifteen years later. I recall his grandkid, who had the anomaly of one blue eye and one green eye, as a gregarious, intelligent, and delightful girl.

Paul's frequent tales of his children's exploits would sometimes get old. While I loved him and most of the stories, I promised myself that should I ever have kids, I wouldn't talk so glowingly about them. Better to let other people praise my kids than have myself do it so often. Fast forward several decades from my warehouse days, and what happens? After twenty-plus years of raising kids, and then talking about my kids, I could hear Paul say, "Wrong again, John."

GAME 56: ST. LOUIS CARDINALS VS. CHICAGO CUBS
SUNDAY, AUGUST 1

I look up the word "enigma" in the dictionary (there are still a few around) and wouldn't you know it--there is a picture of Ray Burris. Tall, long-legged, and erratic righty hurler on the Cubs from 1973-1978. Lifetime mark of 108-134 with an ERA of 4.17. To illustrate the enigma-like quality of Burris, I present you with his performance in the post-season with Montreal in '81. In the first round, Ray starts the third game against the Phillies, and loses 6-2. He doesn't make it through the sixth inning. The Expos win that round, however, and now face the Dodgers in the NLCS. In this round Burris starts Games 2 & 5, pitching 17 innings and giving up just one earned run. In the first round of the playoffs his ERA is 5.06; in the second round it's 0.50. I'd say, "Go figure," but I guess you can't do that with enigmas.

His work with the Cubs was just as perplexing. He owns a 55-56 mark over six seasons. I learned this about Burris: if you want to see him pitch, wait till July or August. Ray was not one of those guys who'd be good half the time you saw him—like if he pitched poorly on Tuesday he'd have a good game on Sunday. Nope, he'd either be atrocious or unhittable for lengthy chunks of time. I learned that he pitched so much better in the second half of the season when the Cubs engaged in meaningless games. Following this pattern for several seasons, he could drive a fan crazy with his inconsistency. I could only imagine how his coaches felt.

Since we're now in August, we should be in good shape with Burris on the hill. The arch-rival Cardinals, foes for today, possess a potent lineup with one aberration—batting second and playing shortstop is Don Kessinger. So former Cubbies reside in the first two holes: Lou Brock and Kessinger. I was just glad to see that Billy Williams wasn't hitting third.

A pitcher's duel deluxe ensued: John Denny of San Looie matching goose-eggs with Burris for seven complete innings. The Cubs break through in the 8th with a two out walk to Bill Madlock followed with a couple of singles from Jerry Morales and Pete LaCock.

In a game like this one run seems like five, so with three outs to go, life looks pretty good. But then a major boo-boo by Jose Cardenal in left has

Willie Crawford (I think by now he's not mad anymore) on 3rd with one out. Heartbreak city is temporarily thwarted when Burris retires Ted Simmons, pinch hitting for Joe Ferguson. He grounds out with Crawford unable to advance. Then heartbreak reigns supreme as the next hitter, Keith Hernandez, *also* reaches on an error, with the tying run scoring. How can a team play errorless ball for 8 1/3 innings and then commit two with two outs to go? Only the Cubs can snatch defeat from the jaws of victory with such play.

But wait, St. Louis does not accept this gift today. The score remains tied at 1 in the top of the 10th as Brock attempts to steal but fails, courtesy of the Baron, George Mitterwald. Since this caught stealing retires the side, the Cubs feed off that momentum into their half of the 10th and end the game with singles by Joe Wallis, Morales, and LaCock.

The line on Burris: 10 IP, 0 earned runs, 5 hits.

The line on Denny: 9 2/3 IP, 2 earned runs, 5 hits (by the way, Denny had a no-hitter through 7 2/3).

Time of the game: Not very long.

Attendance: Quite a few people, but not a sell-out.

GAMES 57 & 58: BOSTON RED SOX VS. CHICAGO WHITE SOX TUESDAY, AUGUST 17

My brother's birthday. Two baseball games. Under the lights. A family affair.

Now for the bad news: Lynn, Yaz, Rice, Fisk, and Evans hitting 3 through 7. Yikes. Throw in a Cecil Cooper, Rick Burleson and this makes one wonder how does such a lineup not contend? Two hypotheses: A) Pitching B) Road games. Sounds familiar to North Siders, no? It's just not conducive to baseball's best interests for the Red Sox to play all their games in a cozy ballpark that rewards big boppers and forgives suspect pitching.

That being said, how can the Chisox compete with a team that boasts *three* Hall-of-Famers in the middle of the lineup? Especially when you're middle sluggers are Bill Stein, Jim Spencer, Brian Downing, and Jerry Hairston? But at the end of the game, the box score informs us that the middle of the Boston order is a combined 3-16, while the Chicago hitters in those slots went 3-13.

Since this wasn't a game about the sluggers, let's turn our attention to the true heroes: Ken Kravec (7 IP, 1 ER, 10 K's), Clay Carroll (2 IP, 1 H, 0 ER) and Pat Kelly (3-4, 1 R, 1 RBI). The Right Sox win with a walk-off 2-1 victory in the bottom of the 9th.

Lasting memory … PK on first base and off with the pitch, as the hitter drives the ball into the deep pastures of the outfield but not beyond the outfielders. The defense tarries a bit too long, and Kelly scores from first on a *single*. This truly inspired me. Made me think that if he could go from first to home on a single, I should be able to go from first to third on a single. My dad got my attention and wanted me to take note of what good things can happen when a player truly hustles.

The second game? Forgetaboutit! The Sox hitters did abuse Boston pitching to the tune of 7 runs on 13 hits. But Boston, on the same number of hits, tallied 11 times. John "Blue Moon" Odom started for the White Sox, but got the hook in the 4th. Our family left in the 5th after we witness the Red Sox erupt for 5 to grab an insurmountable lead of 11-3. "Enough of this," my dad grumbles, "I got work tomorrow." With the White Sox losing 97 times in '76, one can't be too upset with a split against the defending AL champs.

GAME 59: BALTIMORE ORIOLES VS. CHICAGO WHITE SOX
SATURDAY, AUGUST 21

Magneto and Titanium Man"—one of two songs I have stuck in my head this day. Ever had a song you associate with an experience—like you know exactly where you were in life when this song was popular? What were the popular songs when you were a senior in high school? What was a popular song that made you think of that special someone? What song do you associate with a time of pure fun? And it works the other way—what was a pretty popular song but you couldn't get to the radio dial fast enough to change the station? (For all you youngsters out there, back in the day people did listen to music on the radio).

"Magneto and Titanium Man." Due to the heavy traffic along the Damn Ryan and Eisenstopper "expressways," I heard this Paul McCartney tune a few times. Pretty weird, yet typical of Macca music in that it's easy on the ears. But there was one other thing today that was not easy on the eyes: today marked they day the Sox played in short pants. Since this traumatic episode—probably not unlike seeing a parent partially clothed—I've tried to rid myself of the image of Lamar Johnson in shorts. I think a few more years of therapy should do the trick. I can now tell my grandkids that we watched grown men play baseball in short pants on a warm afternoon in 1976. Thank you, Bill Veeck. Amnesia does have its perks. "We love baseball, hot dogs, apple pie, and Lamar Johnson in short pants."

The O's at this point in the season seemed to be in an in-between phase. A good team, no doubt, but really no match for the Yankees. Their roster held some holdovers from the glory years of the World Series—players like Brooks Robinson, Paul Blair, Mike Cuellar, and Jim Palmer. But Father Time reared his head as Robinson and Blair sat the bench and Cuellar worked out of the bullpen. Some up and coming talent dotted the lineup—names like Ken Singleton (former Expo), Bobby Grich, and Doug DeCinces. But one name in the middle of the batting order jumps out at you—Reggie Jackson. For a brief interval between the dynasties of the A's and Yankees, Jackson spent a year playing ball with the Birds.

Not to bash Reggie's accomplishments, but I could never see him as a good fit with Baltimore. Reggie said so himself, as he's quoted as saying that he couldn't sign with Baltimore because there just weren't enough reporters around. Imagine the clubhouse that year—not only did you have the eternal feud between Palmer and Earl Weaver, the O's now had to deal with the ego of Reggie.

I do recall this one Reggie story where he hangs around the O's batting cage and strikes up a conversation with a much underrated slugger, Lee May, big brother of our Carlos May.

Reggie: Hey Mo (May's nickname).

May: Yo.

Reggie: I was just checking out our stats the other day and saw that we had so many numbers the same. So then I got to wondering, how come I make so much more money than you? Do you know why?

May: No.

Reggie: Because I put asses in the seats.

The O's bat around in the first inning, and when the leadoff man (Mark Belanger) singles to start the second, it's an early shower for Sox starter Bart Johnson, as a young Terry Forster relieves him. It was not your typical game in the spacious confines of Comiskey this day. No, the ball seemed to be carrying extremely well. Reggie & others may be reaching those a**es in the outfield seats. The relatively soft hitting Sox drove balls to the warning track in consecutive at-bats in the second inning off Rudy May. After these two loud outs, Jack Brohamer muscles one out to right, and I felt some vindication for the previous two near misses. "Hah, catch that one, Reggie!" I chirp as Jackson in right looks up and out.

This brief comeback is brave but futile as the Orioles bat around again in the third inning. It was one of those times when a 6-2 deficit could have been a whole lot worse, for with the bags loaded, Lee May pulverizes a ball to deep, deep center field. Chet Lemon, the colorful and skilled center fielder for Chicago, races back as fast as he can and nabs the ball with his back to the wall, some 440' away from home plate. It was one of those plays where a speedy man could have tagged up and scored from second, maybe even first. Instead of a 10-2 score, the Sox were only 4 behind with 21 outs with which to work.

In the middle innings, seated near the Oriole dugout, my kid brother, for some inexplicable reason, sticks his head into the visitors' lair and proclaims that "DeCinces sucks eggs." At first I was surprised to hear such an expression—I doubt I heard it before or since—but then a wave of pride came over me. Way to go, kid, give the other team a hard time, they're kicking our butts. Go ahead and get in their heads. But then with DeCinces' very next at-bat, he lines a rocket to the deep reaches of the lower deck in left. I think the ball disabled three empty wooden seats as it left the playing field in a hurry. I gave my brother a "nice going" kind of look as DeCinces trotted around the bases, but I was still proud of him (my brother, that is, not DeCinces).

Then in the 6th, my other kid brother loses his temper and his scorecard, simultaneously. Maybe it was pent up angst over traffic jams, a lopsided score or gross looking legs. But the real reason was, I believe, was Al Bumbry. The diminutive center fielder for Baltimore drives a pitch to deep right center. The Sox right fielder, Jerry Hairston, takes a horrendous route to the ball and looks like something from the Keystone Cops in trying to track it down. The ball, as it collides with the wall, takes a sharp left turn. So now it's up to Lemon to do some damage control. As he hustles the ball back into the infield, Bumbry, the fastest Bird on the team, circles the bases. Voila, an inside-the-park home run. Sorry, but not much Lemon aid this time. If we weren't so disgusted we'd be happy with the novelty of a home run within the premises. But my brother writes something not-so-nice about the play of Mr. Hairston, and abruptly discards his scorecard.

Highly unorthodox play, usually reserved for Wrigley Field, continues to unfold this afternoon. In the 6th, it's the Sox turn to bat around, sending 11 men—all wearing shorts—to the plate. Five cross home, and the scoreboard now reads, 8-7 Baltimore. From then on it becomes a tennis match/track meet. The O's score in the 7th and lead, 9-7. Sox score twice after the stretch to tie the game at 9. With a lead off triple by Bumbry, who came a *single* shy of hitting for the cycle, the Orioles reclaim the lead, 10-9. We're now down to the last out. Pat Kelly, who would later go on and do fine things for Mr. Weaver as an employee of Baltimore, batted for the Sox with the tying run on second. PK singles home the tying run and we head for overtime: Colts

10, Bears 10 (The Ravens did not play in Baltimore until the 90's; the Colts played in Baltimore until the mid 80's).

In the top of the 12th, more drama. After watching the game for about four hours, Brooks Robinson is called upon to pinch hit with two outs and the go-ahead run at second. A lefty from the Sox bullpen, Dave Hamilton, is asked to get out a Future Hall-of-Famer with the game on the line. Let's make a friendly wager—at this point in the game, who stands in a better position to win, Orioles or White Sox. Or to put it another way, if I were to give you 4:1 odds and let you have Hamilton and I'd take Robinson, would you take it? Great game, isn't it, because there's no slam dunks in the sport. A journeyman pitcher who was traded 5 times might retire one of the top clutch performers in my lifetime. With the game in the balance, Brooks grounds out to second.

So how do you like the Sox chances now? In the bottom of the 12th, Bill Stein does what Brooks couldn't do, and that is drive in the winning run in the person of Jim Essian from second base with two outs. We depart gleefully, humming the melody to … never mind.

(PS. The other song that I remember from this day was a hit by Hall and Oates, "She's Gone." I think one day Hawk Harrelson will do a remake of it and call it "He Gone").

(PPS. Alan, not a Top 40 fan, thought for the longest time that the name of this group was Hauling Oats. "You know," he explained, "like hauling ass, hauling wheat, hauling oats." Reasonable misunderstanding).

GAME 60: ATLANTA BRAVES VS. CHICAGO CUBS
SATURDAY, AUGUST 28

Another bad case of the back-to-school blues. I'm not looking forward to my second year in college any more than I looked forward to my second year in grade school. I have a cure, albeit temporary. It starts with baseball and ends with game. I think this was the first of many games that I'd watch solo. It did add a bit to the sadness, but going to a game was my way to extend denial. If memory serves, that following evening I'd be settled in what became my second home for four years, Morrissey Hall. But for now I just got to get one more game in, and try not to let the imminent school year come any sooner that it must.

Here's what we have this afternoon: two teams eliminated from contention months ago. Two mediocre pitchers facing two mediocre lineups. Two managers (Dave Bristol and Jim Marshall) soon to be released. A small crowd (15 K) on a pleasant sunny day. Should be fun.

And it was. The Cubs out homer the Braves, 2-1 (Rick Monday and Jerry Morales for Chicago, Ken Henderson for Atlanta). The Cubs win the game as well, 5-2. A nice, neatly packaged triumph with sufficient hitting and effective pitching by Steve Renko. He tosses 7 innings of two run ball, and then the Cubs' most valuable commodity, Bruce Sutter, gets the last six outs (remarkable how often saves by Sutter and those from his era would often extend beyond one inning. Today it's front page news if a save requires more than three outs). In spite of Atlanta's two runs, the Cubs face only three men over the minimum.

By the looks of these last two games, a slug-fest and a low scoring affair, I'm thinking that the players from the White Sox and Cubs switched places. Maybe it is time to get back to school.

POST-SEASON 1976

The World Series was anti-climactic this year. Reds sweep Yankees, ho-hum.

The real story was the ALCS, KC vs. NY. Midwest vs. Big Apple. Cornfields vs. Broadway. Heart of the country vs. Wall Street. Dorothy (Kansas is close enough) vs. Lil Orphan Annie. But the most captivating for me was George Brett vs. Yankee pitchers.

In the deciding Game 5, with the Royals trailing by 3 in the 8th with two runners on base, Brett faces Grant Jackson, a southpaw. I'm taking a break from the futile studying of accounting, and glued to the television. Brett drives a pitch way, way back into the upper regions of Yankee Stadium. I can't control myself. Before the ball lands, I sprint out of the dorm room, down the hallway, and nearly kill myself on a set of stairs. I miss all five and land face first on the carpet, but pain never felt so good. I can't say what I enjoyed more: watching a fine team from the Midwest do well behind the heroics of a young and talented Brett, or delaying an inevitable and probably arrogant Yankee celebration.

But this unadulterated joy was short-lived. Leading off the ninth in a tie game, Yankee Chris Chambliss homers off Royal reliever Mark Littell. Horrors. The Yankees in the Series after a 12 year hiatus. The Yankee-Cardinal Series of '64 is the first I remember, and now I must suffer through seeing the Pinstripes on baseball's biggest stage again. What adds to the pain is the media—going on and on about how long a drought it's been for the Yankees, and now they're back where they're supposed to be, Yada, Yada, Yada . . . Obviously these insensitive reporters don't realize that Cub fans may be in their audience. Complaining about not being in the World Series for 12 years to a Cub fan is like complaining of a paper cut to someone who's about to face the guillotine.

As Chambliss circles the bases, I wonder for the 10 millionth time if it's better to have love and lost than not having loved at all. No, not really, but I do think of something similarly painful—is it better to watch George Brett tie the game only to get your heart broken later, or would it have been better if Brett popped up and lost in less dramatic fashion? What do you think? A roller coaster of explosive joy followed by sudden death, or to go meekly into that dark night of defeat? Oh whatever. Go Reds.

1977

PRE-SEASON, 1977

Changes on both sides of town. Trades and transactions affecting the look and feel for each club. The Sox got themselves some power by adding a Richie Zisk, an Oscar Gamble, and an Eric Soderholm to complement the nucleus of a Chet Lemon, Jim Spencer, and Jorge Orta. Setting the table for these capable hitters were high average guys like Ralph Garr and Alan Bannister. On paper this looked like a team that would score, perhaps prolifically. The bad news is that with less than outstanding pitching and glaring holes on defense, their offense would have to score mega runs just to be close. True story—I had a college classmate from Atlanta, and he told me that Ralph Garr may be the only player in history to one day own a higher batting average than fielding percentage. He was not kidding. Nevertheless, I could see the fireworks getting quite a work out on the South Side, which makes for fun nights, long games, and lots of beer.

On the North Side we have two big trades: Bill Madlock to San Francisco for Bobby Murcer, and Rick Monday to Los Angeles for Bill Buckner and Ivan DeJesus. The former trade got people excited at first, getting the person who at one time was pegged as the heir apparent for Mickey Mantle. Still, you're trading a perennial batting champ contender for a guy who is on the downside of his career. The latter trade, however, looked promising. The Dodgers did not get cheated because Monday is a quality player (and quite the patriot if you remember the flag incident at Dodger Stadium) who would pay huge dividends by crushing a legendary home run in the '81 playoffs against the Expos. But I think the Cubs got more than they gave with the acquisition of Bill Buckner. A hitter nearly as consistent as Madlock (both would win batting titles in Chicago), Buckner was a guy who would play hard and play hurt. A gamer, no doubt, and the Cubs desperately needed some of them—just too much indifferent play over the years. DeJesus would perform steadily and unspectacularly at shortstop. The Cubs, like the Sox, would be an offense first kind of team. Not often the recipe for championships, but given the teams' track record so far in the 70's, why not take a Gamble?

JIDGE AND HAMMER

The hot dog vendor smiles. A dark haired, heavy set man raises his hand to get the vendor's attention.

"I'll take six," the customer says.

"Six? That'll be twenty-one bucks."

The gentleman grunts as he wriggles free his wallet from his back pocket. He yanks out a twenty and a ten. "Keep it, kid," he barks, "and don't forget about us."

"No sir, I won't. Thanks," then turning back to the grandstands, "hey hot dogs, get your red hots here! Who's hungry now? Red hots!"

The big, burly gentleman turns to the fellow sitting on his right and offers him three red hots.

His friend smiles and politely shakes his head, "I'm okay with one, Jidge. I had breakfast not too long ago."

"So?" said his companion, "I had six donuts, six eggs, five coffees, and three beers a couple hours ago. Here," he compromises by offering his partner two, "take a couple at least. A skinny guy like you has to keep his strength up."

"Thanks," his partner chuckles as he accepts the hot dogs. "You know, Jidge, baseball food never gets old. You can have your fine cuisine; I'll take hot dogs. I hope they're at ballparks forever."

"Nothing's forever, Hammer. Bonds proved that."

"Yeah, but today all that stuff's tainted. I mean look at all the charges against him and so many other guys he played with. Then compare those accomplishments with stuff I went through."

"Whatcha mean by that?"

"I had to deal with death threats. Lots of folks, many in the South where I played, didn't want me to break your record. They wanted us to win, of course, and maybe even pulled for me to do well, but not too well, if you know what I mean."

"Yeah, I think I do. And I know about that BS, too. Bastards on other teams really rode me hard cuz me and my teammates used to beat their brains out."

"How bad did it get?"

"Lemme put it this way …. You weren't the only one of us called n-word."

"You serious?"

"Yeah, and that set me off. I even told the bastards that they could call me anything they want except that word. And of course they called me that word."

"Were they color blind?"

"No, just a bunch of a**holes-- oh, sorry ma'am," Jidge looks up and sees a young mom with two kids shooting him a dirty look.

"Like I was saying, Hammer, a bunch of jerks. Yeah, I had to deal with bench jockeying and all that crap. The one who managed here a few years ago," pointing to the third base dugout, "might have been the biggest tool of all."

"Leo? How's that?"

"For a guy who couldn't hit, he had a mouth on him that never quit. Ya know what I called him? The All-American out." Hammer laughs. "That's right, the All-American out cuz he was. Especially on our team. But he sure could tick off the other team."

"Yeah, he was something," Hammer grimaces as a bad memory comes back. "He got on us pretty bad, too. 'Stick it in his ear' and all that. He did my friend, Ernie, wrong when he managed this team. Here Ernie is at the end of his career, and the manager shows him no respect. I guess he couldn't stand anyone getting more attention than himself."

"Yeah, but look at where Ernie, you and I are compared to him."

Jerry Morales, Cub outfielder, launches a home run to make the score 9-7, Phillies, in the fourth inning.

"And they accuse me of playing in a launching pad," Hammer exclaims as Morales slowly and awkwardly rounds the bases.

"Why's he hot-dogging his way around second and third? Hasn't he ever done this before?" Jidge asks.

"Guess not. Hot dogging and his team's still losing. Say, I wonder how many homers we'd hit if we played here?"

"Oh, probably 30-35."

"What?"

"Yeah, you'd hit 35 cuz you're 40 something and I'd hit 30 cuz I been dead for 30 years."

Hammer laughs. "But could you imagine playing here with the wind blowing out?"

"I think the folks living across the street would want us to get traded or take up plumbing."

Two batters later Bobby Murcer cracks a wind-blown homer into the bleachers in right. Now the game's tied at 9.

"Ya know, that kid's all right … a former Yankee, I might add. He had to put up with all that pressure of being the second coming of Mickey Mantle. Not fair. DiMaggio couldn't replace me, Mantle couldn't replace DiMaggio, and Murcer couldn't replace Mantle. It don't work that way."

"Yeah, I think you're right. Say, speaking of pressure—do you know which brothers in baseball combined for the most homers?"

"I'm guessing the guys I just mentioned … the DiMaggios."

"Nope."

"How about the Griffeys?"

"They're not brothers—they're a father and son team."

"Oh, yeah, I forgot. Okay, I give up."

"Me and Tommie."

"No shit. (Turning to the lady in front) AHH, Ma'am, shit's not even that bad a word. But I'll watch my mouth just for you and your boys. Here, have a hot dog. (Turning back to Hammer) Really, it was you?"

"Yep. One to remember if you want to sting your buddies next time at the bar and collect some easy cash. Tommie played long enough to knock out 13. Bobby and Barry Bonds hit more, but like the Griffeys, they're father-son, not brothers. Well, they were brothers, but they weren't. Know what I mean?"

Jidge laughs. "I get it. And the thing about you two—you were clean. How many guys hit homers when they're on the juice?"

"Too many to count."

Mike Schmidt connects for his second homer of the game. 12-10, Phillies.

"There's a guy who could play in my era," Jidge says. "Say, since he's hit so many here, I wonder if he'd ever call his shot?"

"Did you really do that?"

"Ask me no questions and I'll tell you no lies."

"C'mon, Jidge. (Turning to the aisle) Hey, beer man, over here. (Back to Jidge) Tell me the truth and I'll buy you a beer."

"Make it two and you got a deal."

"Okay, two beers for my friend, Old Style man. Now Jidge, is that made up or not?"

"I pointed at the monkeys in the dugout . . . see, I didn't say 'bastards', ma'am . . . held up a finger or two, and knocked one out."

"So you didn't call it?"

"Like I said before, sort of. I told the catcher" (Jidge lowers his voice) "I told him, I'll show those bastards of yours. And I did. But I tell you, Hammer, if the pitcher saw me point, the next pitch was in my ear. I'm no dummy. But if you look at the replays, I gave them the business all the way around the bases."

"Yeah, I did see that. This place hasn't changed much, has it?" He hands him twenty dollars for a $12.50 fare and said, "Vendor, keep the change."

"Nah, this place is the same, 'cept it never had the wind blowin' like it is today."

"I saw the wind do funny tricks here. Cost us a no-hitter once."

"Really, you guys lost out on a no-hitter cuz of a fluky homer?"

"No, they (pointing again to the third base dugout) got ME because of the wind. Holtzman, Kenny Holtzman, a lefty, got us. I hit one over there. See where the wall curves in on left field?"

Jidge nods as he starts working on his second brew and third hot dog.

"Well, Billy Williams—another Hall-of-Famer from Alabama—goes back and does this complete turnaround in the well. Wouldn't you know it--the wind pushes the ball back on the field and he catches it. Some say it was 10-15 over the fence before the wind knocked it back. I couldn't believe it."

"Tough break, kid. Reminds me of the time when we lost a World Series because some fat head was out trying to steal second with two outs in the last inning of the last game."

"Man, what sucker did that?"

"Me."

Both laugh through the next two outs.

"Well, kid, gotta go. I'm playing with the Angels now, not the ones from California, and we gotta game soon. I'm pitching—I like that. Look me up when it's your time. We got a helluva team. Sorry ma'am."

"I betcha got a good team, Jidge, I bet you do. You take care of yourself. Food good there?"

Jidge guffaws and points at his ample belly. "What do you think?" (Turning serious) "Oh, and by the way, nice job. If someone broke my record, I'm glad it was you—a class act."

"Thanks. Like I said ... I didn't want nobody to forget about you. I just wanted folks to remember me."

"You did just that ... see ya around, kid."

GAME 61: KANSAS CITY ROYALS VS. CHICAGO WHITE SOX
WEDNESDAY, MAY 18

I'd like to play a game of telepathy with you. A few warm-up questions first, then when the baseball question strikes, that's when the mind reading begins. Okay, ready?

- Who do you think of when you think of the Rolling Stones?
- What hockey team is associated with octopi?
- What is the suspense as Rob Petrie enters the living room at the beginning of the Dick Van Dyke Show?

All right, now that you're mentally warmed up, it's time to read your mind. The decade is the 1970's, of course. Think of the first person you think of when you picture the Kansas City Royals and their powder blue uniforms. Got it? Now remove the very last letter of the person's last name. Then change the vowel to an "A". You're now thinking of a word that can be eaten or can be spoiled? Am I right?

Silly, I know, but the point is this—I doubt if any player was the face of a team as much as George Brett was to the KC Royals. In the modern era, Tony Gwynn of the Padres might be a match, I'll give you that. But it's not even close after that. Amos Otis, Bret Saberhagen, Frank White, Hal McRae, and Paul Splitorff compose a wonderful supporting cast, but no one approaches the royal status of Brett. Not to belabor the point, but for evidence here's what you can do—check out the all-time statistical leaders for the Kansas City Royal ballclub. Then note how many times Brett's name appears.

With such a grandiose introduction, you'd think that Brett had the game of his life this day. Nope, didn't even play. Mixed feelings—sad like I was as a 7-year-old fan who didn't see Willie Mays play when Frisco rolled into town, but glad because the home team stood a better chance to win. In fact, the Sox handle the Royals with relative ease, 7-4. One of those games that wasn't as close as the score might indicate because the home team erupts for five runs in the second inning, and KC pushes across two in the 9th.

Chris Knapp, a young and unassuming righty, goes 8 strong and gives up 2 runs on 6 hits. Darrel Porter led the mild Royal attack with a homer, and Cookie Rojas who as Brett's substitute chipped in with a single and a double. For the White Sox, the big blast came courtesy of Oscar Gamble, one of Bill Veeck's one and done rent-a-players. Gamble and his magnificent 'fro jogged around the bases after nailing a three run homer in the second inning off Dennis Leonard. It was never close after that. Leonard, as an FYI, owned one of the most animated nicknames from that era: Yosemite Sam.

This Sox team of '77 could flat out rake. I dare say not an easy out in the lineup, and pretty deep when you can afford to have an All-Star in Chet Lemon bat seventh. Their nickname this season, the South Side Hit Men, was well earned. Trouble is, like the Lumber Company in Pittsburgh, the club could not bat forever. And when they took the field, how strong up the middle could they be with a DP combination of Jorge Orta and Alan Bannister. The team would be much better served if they could afford to use Orta and Bannister as a DH combination. I'm guessing here, but whoever finished second in errors to this tandem must have been a distant second. Jim Spencer kept busy at first base this summer, coming up with throws well wide or short of the mark. I recall one time late in the summer when a reporter got under Spencer's skin by asking why he couldn't save a teammate from a throwing error. Jim's curt response: "I ain't a bleeping Houdini!"

The Sox outfield defense wasn't much better. In fact, the corners were awful. Richie Zisk in right field and Ralph Garr in left. Again, prime candidates for the DH role. As Spencer worked his less-than-Houdini magic in the infield, the same fell upon Lemon in center field. Anything from foul line to foul line that he could catch, I'm sure that Garr in left, Zisk in right, the infielders, the pitcher, the manager, the broadcasters, the front office, and White Sox fans everywhere would give their complete consent.

So with such a sub-par defense the pitching must have been brilliant, right? I mean, you had to get outs some way, right?

Truth be told, the pitching did not excel ... and that's being charitable. The aforementioned Knapp, the late Francisco Barrios, Steve Stone, and a couple of Kens--Brett and Kravec—comprised the starting rotation. (Brett was traded to the Angels in mid-June). The bullpen? That was a no-go, too.

If this conjures up football scores, sloppy play, and lots of fireworks, you got the picture. The Good News is that the South Side Hit Men kept the club competitive and in many games. The Bad News is that their pitching and defense often prevented them from winning those games.

GAME 62: CHICAGO CUBS VS. ST. LOUIS CARDINALS
SATURDAY, JULY 2

Some of the differences when you travel to a ballpark outside Chicago and support the visiting team:

- Standing up three outs early for the 7th inning stretch
- Hoping the game does not go extra innings. Like losing the overtime coin toss in an NFL game, extra innings has a decided disadvantage for the visiting team. Consider that if the visitors do not score in extra innings, the home team is guaranteed six outs before they can lose the game. The visitors are guaranteed zero. To me that is a significant psychological edge.
- Seating in the upper tiers isn't as good: it's usually much higher and this perspective can be confusing on balls hit in the air. Is that a line drive to the outfielder or a fly ball?
- Trying to find that fine line of rooting for the visitors without offending the folks around you. I hate it when loud and obnoxious fans cheering for the other team sit by me, so I try to remember that when I'm on the road.
- Checking out all the electronic gizmos on the scoreboard.
- Comparing the amounts of advertising at other stadiums to the places back home.
- Appreciating the whiteness of the home team's uniform. The Cardinals had these powder-puff blue things on the road—pretty lame. But at home they decked out in these bleach-white spotless threads that radiated and maybe even intimidated. They looked good.
- Observing different ways that ballpark employees do things. For instance, I pitied the poor hot dog hawker. For every sale he had to … 1. Extract the bun. 2. Extract a hot dog. 3. Insert hot dog into the bun. 4. Ask the customer if he wished for condiments 5. Wrap product in wrapper. 6. Pass on hot dog. 7. Collect money. 8. Issue change. 9. Receive generous tip (I hope). This all seemed like a lot

of work. Back home the vendors flipped me my red hots already wrapped, grabbed my cash, and went on the prowl for the next sucke, er, customer.

- Checking out the music. Organ? Recorded top 40's? Elevator?
- Checking out the crowd. Families? Elderly? Blue collar? Couples? Affluent? Kids? Drunks?
- Checking out what the crowd wears. It must be a rule that people attending a ballgame in St. Louis must wear red. Are there no non-conformists? Imagine the satire Mark Twain would toss at his kin-folk.
- Noticing how the crowd reacts: How often do they cheer? How loudly? Do they boo? (In Minnesota, the answer is no). Do they acknowledge exceptional play by the other team? Do they pay attention to other games being played? Do they do The Wave?
- Checking out the ballpark employees. Do they seem content? Friendly? Courteous? Harried? Impatient? Suck-ups? Do the vendors do subtle things to accumulate tips? (As in any profession, there are a few tricks of the trades to supplement income).
- Food and drink. This one never has been high on my list—I'm going to a ballgame, not a restaurant. Yet I still am interested in things like the brand that is offered and the size of product. (Portland's Triple-A ballclub served beer in 1980 that was the size of a horse trough...you needed both hands to hold it). What interests me the most are items germane to the area. For instance, the Miami Marlins offer dolphin sandwiches. After watching many Flipper episodes on Saturday evenings, I'd have to pass on porpoise.
- The mascots. Since Chicago didn't have any in my formative years, mascots at other places caught my eye. Fredbird in St. Louis, the Pittsburgh Parrot, the Phillie Fanatic, and of course the San Diego Chicken. I enjoyed them. Working as a vendor one day, the Phillie Fanatic visited our ballpark, gave me a big hug, and with his free hand reached into my peanut bag and flipped a half-dozen or so bags into the crowd. Most of us were highly amused.

All these considerations make for a busy experience when taking in a game at a new venue. At Wrigley Field or Comiskey Park, I might catch one novel thing every few months. But on the road, there are at least a dozen new things to absorb.

Scorecards. I'd be terribly remiss if I didn't mention scorecards--one of the lasting impressions of my visit to St. Louis. Here in Cardinal territory in the 70's you open your scorecard and you're in for a surprise, or at least I am. They have printed out all nine slots of the lineup for both teams, complete with the batting average for the first eight spaces followed by the pitcher and his won-loss record. It's efficient and nice to look at, but I got two complaints: first, I'd rather write the names in myself, thank you. The second is accuracy. On *both* days that we went, the Cub lineup that took the field had several alterations from the Cub lineup posted in the scorecard. Now making these changes is no big deal because I write small, but I wonder how common an occurrence this was if the folks in charge were 0 for 2 in accuracy for these weekend games. On the plus side was having the averages listed. Lofty averages from both teams dominated the lineups and the season was nearly half-spent. The Cubs trotted out two regulars hitting above .300 (Manny Trillo and Jerry Morales), while the Cards could boast four—Gary Templeton, Ted Simmons, Keith Hernandez, and Jerry Mumphrey.

To break it down further, here's what you'd see should you invest in a St. Louis Cardinal scorecard on this date: for the home team—Brock .295, Templeton .318, Scott .309 (part-time player), Simmons. 343, Hernandez .311, Reitz .294, Anderson .186 (Mumphrey who played more was hitting .335, explaining why he played more), Tyson .231 and Falcone 3-6. For your Chicago Cubs—DeJesus (Ivan, not David) .276, Clines .324 (he only played against lefties, Greg Gross played against righties), Buckner .254 (he'd finish the season 30 points higher), Murcer .278, Morales .310, Trillo .336 (I had to do a double take on that one), Ontiveros .284, Swisher (Nick's dad) .182, and Bonham 8-6.

Looking at these numbers you would think that the pitchers have their work cut out for them. You'd be half right. A brutal game from the get-go. The broadcasters at the end of the first Cardinal at-bat would say ... "four runs, on four hits, and four errors." The ball, when it was not being hit hard, was being kicked, muffed, and thrown all over the lot by the visitors. Cardinals were flying everywhere, taking the extra base at will as the Cubs fumbled another play. The next two plus hours was simply a matter of playing out the string. By the time the Cubs scored thrice late in the game, the Deadbirds had built a 10-love advantage. Fortunately, we had tickets for tomorrow's game.

GAME 63: CHICAGO CUBS VS. ST. LOUIS CARDINALS
SUNDAY, JULY 3

Can anything compare to mid-summer heat in St. Louis? Oppressively hot. So hot that when you first go outside in the morning the heat suffocates you for a moment, literally taking your breath away. But small price to pay, especially when taking a road trip and staying at the home of a college friend. My friend, we called him Bird, loved watching sports and playing basketball. Add in beer and studying, and you got the four pillars of the college experience. So if you take out the studying part, you got an idea as to how this weekend went. Bird and his folks put me up for the weekend, fed me, took me to and from the train station, and got me tix to see the Cub-Cardinal games. Sometimes you don't have to die to experience heavenly hospitality.

After that dog of a game Saturday, Sunday's game turned out to be a gem (guess who won?). Eric Rasmussen of the Cardinals, sporting a 6-9 record, baffles the Cubs through 7 innings: no runs on a measly five singles. Luckily, Cub ace Rick Reuschel matched him: 6 innings, no runs, two singles. Unluckily, the intense heat got to Reuschel in the bottom of the seventh. After two outs, Simmons and Hernandez single. The Cub manager, Herman Franks (love that name) pulls him and brings in … the closer!!?? Yep, with seven outs to go in regulation time, the ace of the bullpen, if not the ace of the league, Bruce Sutter enters the game. After walking Reitz to load the bases, Sutter fans Mumphrey. Much joy, happiness, and relief.

Now the Cubs have some momentum and it's their turn to KO the Cardinal starter. With two on and two out, the Mad Hungarian (I'll give you a few lines to come up with his real name) takes the ball to face the Cubs' best clutch hitter (again, see if you can name him). Anyway, the stage is set: an inferno of an afternoon, two ancient rivals playing good ball, late innings of a scoreless game, and their best reliever facing our best hitter with the game on the line. So here's what happens next: Deep in the count, Al Hrabosky delivers a pitch to Bill Buckner. Buckner squares it up and the ball jumps off his bat headed deep down the right field line. Two immediate and important questions: Home run distance or just short? Fair or foul? Our upper deck perches along the third base line provide us with a spectacular view as we follow the flight of the ball. I gaze in disbelief as the ball lands a couple feet fair and a couple feet over the fence. Three run homer. Much more joy and happiness.

Every story has falling action, so here it is: the Cubs tack on a run in the ninth, Sutter retires the last seven Redbirds in order, and the Cubs win 4-0.

This makes my train ride home so much more fun. After saying our good-byes, I hop on Amtrak, grateful for the weekend and appreciating the amber waves of grain that grace the landscape from St. Louis to Chicago.

My mind wanders from baseball for an extended period as I contemplate a much more important topic: world hunger. In my simple mind, I don't understand how there can be world hunger issues when for a 4 ½ hour trip, I see nothing, and I mean nothing, but corn. So many crops, so many hungry people. I had no clue then, and I'm still at a loss and frustrated by it today. Why?

GAME 64: MONTREAL EXPOS VS. CHICAGO CUBS
WEDNESDAY, JULY 6

"A home run?" spoken sadly.

A despondent nod of the head.

A few moments pass. *"A grand slam?"* The words a little louder and sharper.

A grimmer nod.

Then the horror is fully realized. *"BY THE PITCHER!!??"*

Imagine the most pathetic nod ever.

What these two brothers of mine communicate in a paucity of words captures the top of the second inning. As the older brother makes his way from the concession stand to his seat, he notices a bevy of Expos congregating and celebrating around home plate. Incrementally does the tragedy dawn upon him. Expo pitcher, Don Stanhouse, better known for his days as an Oriole under Earl Weaver, would have 135 official major league at bats. This would be his only hit that ever left the yard. And it came with the bases loaded against the Cubs, of course.

Meanwhile about seven miles to the south and west of Wrigley Field, their older brother (me) angrily tosses a box unto a truck at the warehouse as he hears these events broadcast over the radio. I was ticked and Paul, who had a son playing for Montreal, enjoyed himself. He saw my frustrations and snickered. Why not, his kid's team had just slammed the Cubs and grabbed a 5-1 advantage.

But he who snickers last snickers best. The Cubs' pitchers, Bill Bonham, Pete Broberg, Willie Hernandez, and Bruce Sutter, allow just one more tally—a solo shot by Ellis Valentine in the 7th—giving their team a chance to come back.

Speaking of Valentine, I remember the hoopla and praise lavished upon the trio of young Expo outfielders: Valentine, Warren Cromartie, and Andre Dawson. Turns out we were witnessing the proceedings of two fine careers that didn't last long in Valentine & Cromartie, and one Hall-of-Famer who would one day roam right in Wrigley. This is just a guess, but maybe the reason Expo careers got cut short had to due with the wicked playing surface in

Montreal. A friend told me that he learned from former Expo third basemen Larry Parrish that not one Expo from that era who played significant innings did not have some kind of lower body issue due to their turf. The players played on simple fuzzy grass on top of concrete—not great for the knees, eh Hawk?

Trailing by four, the Cubs start chipping away. Some pundits coined this Cub lineup as the "Rush Street Offense"—a lot of singles but not much scoring. Today, though, some power emerges from unlikely sources. A two-run homer by Larry Biittner highlights a three run third. And then something almost as unlikely as a grand slam by the pitcher occurs. Greg Gross, who never homered in 1500 at-bats, connects for his first home run *ever* in the 6th. Gross would muscle out four more homers this season, and connect for two more in his entire career, leaving him with a grand total of 7 homers in 3,745 official trips to the plate. So while highly unusual, Gross' hit was pretty clutch when you consider that with two outs and two men on, Gross turns a 5-4 deficit into a 7-5 lead. Cubs would eventually survive the ignominious grand slam by Stanhouse and win, 8-6.

One of the thousands of things I like about baseball is that points can be earned in bunches. It's been well documented how the big inning matters in the final outcome of the game, and I've noticed that in baseball, one play, one pitch, and one swing can add as many as four points. No one can score a hat trick in hockey with just one shot, and even a good shooter in basketball can only add three points to his team's total. But the complexion of a baseball game can shift dramatically with one good swing, especially with teammates on base.

GAMES 65 & 66: HOUSTON ASTROS VS. CHICAGO CUBS (DOUBLEHEADER)
SUNDAY, JULY 25

Now wouldn't you think that scoring ten runs in the course of two games would qualify for at least a split? But the bottom line reads … Astros 10-6, Cubs 6-4. In the opener, we watched the bad Ray Burris pitch, giving up 6 hits and 4 runs in 3 innings. As mentioned earlier, this is what you got with Burris—a shellacking or complete domination—nothing in between.

A few other noteworthy items from this sweep:

1. My friends and I sat in the bleachers. It wasn't my idea. Sometimes you just have to go along to get along.
2. The bleacherites cleverly placed the letter 'P' in front of Enos Cabell's forename when they screamed his name as he came to bat. I could tell that it really upsets him since he homers in both games.
3. The abuse poured on Cesar Cedeno was relentless. Up for manslaughter charges from an off-season incident, the chant from the right field bleachers went something like this: "A tisket, a tasket, Cesar put her in the casket." Sensitive folks, those bleacher bums.
4. A long homer to right from the Cubs' Bobby Murcer nearly lands in our lap. It gives the Cubs a short-lived lead, but with the exception of Paul Reuschel (Rick's brother) none of the pitchers on the home team did anything special. Most gave up multiple runs.
5. The heat and the drunkards take its toll after six hours of baseball. The 'Stros are a team I generally see the Cubs handle, but not today.

GAME 67: LOS ANGELES DODGERS VS. CHICAGO CUBS
FRIDAY, AUGUST 20

He's a guy who can figure out square roots in his head faster than you can using a calculator. In fourth grade, he flew through times tables at the speed of light. I could match him, but I don't think I bested him in these competitions that drew such VIP's as the school principal. And he's also one of the biggest Cub fans I know, perhaps the second biggest at that. His name is Stephan.

Today we sit in the grandstands in the last row of the upper deck directly behind home plate. I sat recently with him in his favorite location—the bleachers—so now he returns the favor.

We're treated to a well-played, highly contested game. Here's what transpires: scoreless after 3 (Doug Rau vs. Bill Bonham), 1-0 LA after 4 (Dusty Baker scores), 1-1 after 5 (George Mitterwald homers), 2-1 LA after 6 (Steve Yeager now has both LA RBI's), 3-1 LA in the middle of the 7th (Bill Russell with an RBI single). Cubs are battling, but find themselves trailing an awfully good Dodger team. With two on and one out, Mike Garman (former Cub) gets the call from the bullpen to face Jose Cardenal. Junior whiffs, leaving it up to Billy Buck (the pet name that Tommy Lasorda, current Dodger manager, bestows on him). Buckner drives the ball just far enough to make the basket in left-center. The Cubs now lead 4-3, and ecstasy reigns as Billy Buck hobbles around the bases. Talk about clutch. But with an uncharacteristic misplay by the reliable Manny Trillo at second, the Dodgers tie the game in the 8th at 4. The Cubs manufacture a run in the bottom of the 8th with a walk, a bunt, and another clutch hit by Mitterwald.

That takes us to our Play of the Day. With Reggie Smith on first and one out, the veteran Dave Giusti attempts to close the game for the Cubs. (I'm guessing Bruce Sutter's banged up or needs a day off). With Ron Cey batting, the outfielders shift to their right as the Penguin is a powerful pull hitter. So wouldn't you know it, Cey slugs the ball a long way to the deepest part of the ballpark, which is about fifteen feet <u>right</u> of dead center. Jerry Morales, an adequate but not great outfielder, with average speed at best, gives chase. From our vantage point upstairs, we can see the ball slicing away from Morales. It's almost like the faster he runs, the more the ball moves away from him. In what seemed like hours, the ball, the wall, and the outfielder are on a collision course. Undoubtedly a moment worth the price of admission. So Morales fully extends his left arm and, AND, **AND ...** he catches the baseball!!! Smith scampers back to first base. Stephan leans over to me and lets me know that that baseball had extra bases written all over it. But it doesn't get any easier. Standing in the way of a victory is probably the Dodgers' Mr. Clutch, Steve Garvey (just think back to Game 4 of the 1984 NLCS, or on second thought, don't). But Garvey flies out to Murcer in right, and the Cubs knock off a perennial playoff team by one run.

How good was this Dodger team? Well, you probably noticed that a barometer for me is the lineup exam. I like keeping score because it gives me a chance to study on hard copy how the enemy is lined up to attack us (that's not too dramatic, is it?). I usually have a litany of questions that go like this: How many hitters should we pitch around? How many easy outs are there? And perhaps most importantly, who bats in the 6-7-8 holes? Why, you ask? Because I figure that every major league club should have decent hitters 1 through 5, but how difficult is it to retire the bottom of the order?

On this afternoon, the 6-7-8 hitters for LA were Rick Monday, Dusty Baker, and Steve Yeager. Not too shabby. And a recap of the scorecard shows that the Cubs were not going to let Baker beat them, as the Cubs walked him thrice, twice intentionally. But the #8 hitter, Yeager, ruined that strategy not once but twice. Only in the 8th does walking Dusty pay off, and Yeager whiffs with the go-ahead run in scoring positon. Then in the late innings, Manager Lasorda has the luxury of two quality pinch hitters: Manny Mota and Vic Davalillo. With such a strong starting lineup, guys like Mota and Davalillo understand their roles and their value to the team. So with fantastic regulars and a tremendous bench, how was the pitching? Running starters out there like Don Sutton, Tommy John, Burt Hooton, Rick Rhoden and Doug Rau ... wow, a few runs should be enough for a win. If the Dodgers had an Achilles heel, it was probably their bullpen. The knuckle balling Charlie Hough and the tough Elias Sosa (ERA under 2) did most of the work.

Final thought of the day: it took a good game by the Cubs to beat this good team, and they pulled it off.

GAME 68: BALTIMORE ORIOLES VS. CHICAGO WHITE SOX
SATURDAY, SEPTEMBER 3

"One of these nights,
One of these cold and lonely nights,
Gonna find out …"
"…Coming right behind you
Swear I'm gonna find you
Get you baby one of these nights …"

I'm lying down in the back of my roommate's van listening to the Eagles. I never did like this group, maybe because I didn't like this one roommate who did. But this song got me thinking of my girl friend, come to think of it, breathing got me thinking about my girl friend. She studied abroad during this school year while I remained in Indiana. I visited her less than a month ago in her Florida home—in the days before Marlins and Rays. So I had to settle for visiting Disney World and had a farewell at the airport loaded with drama. A year separated from someone with whom you've grown attached seems more like a decade. She assured me that everything would be fine, just like George Custer was assured that those were friendly Native Americans. In other words, both Custer and I had reservations. "One of those cold and lonely nights" fit the mood.

Then there was this other roommate whose song and philosophy was, "Love the one you're with." He related to the opposite gender in this fashion, bless him, but I couldn't subscribe. "A girl is a girl is a girl until you meet that special someone," is how he explained his approach and also explains why I'm opposed to my daughters dating until they're 35. Some guys begin to mature by then. So while prowling and loving the one he's with, I'm brooding in the back of the van to the whiney lyrics of the Eagles.

Okay, so what's with all this Dr. Ruth talk in a baseball book? Fair question. Well, you see counsellor, my roommates (all seven of them) and I decide to hop in the van and travel to Comiskey. Not a long trip at all, even if I had to listen to the Beagles. And one of these roommates was a huge Oriole fan who took baseball as seriously as I. No kidding. When the O's lost the '79 Series after being up 3 games to 1, he sequestered himself in his room for days. This roommate, named Dinger, had a bad case of Oriole fever. The Birds were once again in the thick of the divisional race (I know pennant race sounds much better, but it is less accurate) and Dinger planned to cheer his team on to victory on enemy turf.

You know how coaches love to parade the words, "That's not our kind of baseball; that's not ___ baseball." (Fill in the blank with the team's nickname). Well, 96% of the time I think of that as a bogus and macho expression that really doesn't mean much. But I really do think there is something to a select few teams claiming this title—like "Oriole Baseball" having a team built around defense and pitching. Ditto for "Dodger Baseball" throughout the 60's, and maybe even calling Cincinnati "The Big Red Machine" has some merit. The Go-go Sox of the 50's had a style comparable to the Orioles and Dodgers, but if anyone was to say "that's not Chicago baseball," I'd have to shake my head and object by saying that they (Cubs & Sox) weren't good enough to have a kind of baseball.

So Dinger supports this Earl Weaver team that has good pitching, good defense, and timely hitting … in that order. Now it's fairly well known that Weaver disdained the bunt and small ball, opting instead for his favorite play, the three run homer. But truth be told, if baseball was just about the long ball, the Cubs and Red Sox would have met each other in the World Series numerous times. Instead, with an obvious lack of pitching depth, slugging teams without pitching usually went golfing in October. Whereas the O's and LA run out four quality starters, many teams struggle after their top two guys. The names on these quality organizations may change, but the success at the end of the year stays in place. That's why the Orioles of the late 70's with a Scott McGregor and a Mike Flanagan can compete nearly as well with the Orioles of the 60's with their Mike Cuellar and Dave McNally. The one common element that bridged both ball clubs defined pitching greatness—Jim Palmer. You might have heard the question that goes like this: if you had to pick one pitcher to win a game, and your life depended on it, who would you take? Well, who *would* you take? (I'll take a commercial break and give you some time to think) . . .

"Say, if you're in the market for reading an excellent baseball book about Chicago baseball from 1964-1969, we have just the thing. Pick up a copy of the classic, <u>Like Night and Day</u>, written by John O'Donnell. It's an easy read, it's nostalgic, it's fun, and it's not that expensive. So go ahead and order yours today on *Amazon*. Operators on duty now. That's <u>Like Night and Day</u>, A Look at Chicago Baseball, 1964-1969. You'll be glad you did."

COMMERCIAL OVER

I'd like to know who you would choose to pitch for the game of your life. I really would. For me, the aforementioned Jim Palmer would be my second choice right behind Bob Gibson.

Pitchers, even the dominant ones who pose in underwear, need help. That's when fielders earn their keep. Stories circulate how Gibson adamantly insisted on an abysmal hitter, Dal Maxvill, to play shortstop when he pitched. Gibson didn't give a hoot (one of Gibson's nicknames) about Maxvill's offense, but he needed him in the middle of the field to catch the ball should opposing hitters make contact.

The O's had their own Maxvill in the person of Mark Belanger, AKA 'The Blade.' Belanger, skinny as a blade, would struggle to hit his weight. No matter because boppers like Frank Robinson and Boog Powell in the 60's and now guys like Eddie Murray and Lee May could handle the heavy lifting on offense. So for a couple of decades, with defenders like Belanger and Paul Blair and Bobby Grich and Al Bumbry roaming the middle of the field, hits by the opposition had to be legitimate.

For this contest, the Sox had to deal with Belanger but not Palmer. Ross Grimsley, a talented lefty, got the start against Francisco Barrios, the Sox hefty righty. Perusing Chicago's lineup, they strike me as the antithesis of "Oriole Baseball." Mediocre pitching, not a lick of defense, but plenty of guys who could hit (now take a wild guess as to which team is in contention in September). The White Sox figure to have a pretty fair offense when a young Brian Downing hits *ninth*. The table setters on top, Ralph Garr and Alan

Bannister, each reach base twice tonight. Both they and each of the next four hitters—Chet Lemon, Richie Zisk, Lamar Johnson, and Eric Soderholm— would drive in a run. Two three run innings by the Sox in the 3rd and 7th decide the game. Sox victorious by a score of 6-3, but out of consideration toward Dinger, very little celebrating took place on the return trip to our dorm. (I found it quite amusing that when his team showed signs of life on offense and would mount a rally, he'd scream at the top of his lungs, "LET'S GO YOU HAIRY BIRDS." Must be a Baltimore thing, along with "Thank God I'm a Country Boy" and crabcakes).

As you know, Dinger's rally fell short, and I didn't give him too hard a time. But the Sox win took some of the sting out of one of those cold and lonely nights as we drove back to South Bend.

GAME 69: PITTSBURGH PIRATES VS. CHICAGO CUBS
SATURDAY, SEPTEMBER 24

The setting: a crisp autumn Saturday on arguably the most hallowed football campus in America. The first few weeks of the season mean the Fighting Irish are probably playing one of their Big Ten opponents. The games against the service academies, USC, Stanford, and Boston College come later. Today happens to be a road game.

So what do a couple of friends and I do? You can tell by the sub-heading above; we drive to Wrigley to watch an absolutely meaningless game between the Cubs and Pirates. Why? Because we had access to a car (not something us carless students take for granted), tickets (thanks pops), and a sickness for baseball (Dinger, the Oriole fan whom you met before, and "D", a huge Pirate fan). With one ear on the ND-Purdue game, we set sail for Wrigley Field.

Against certain teams over the past decade, my winning percentage at Wrigley Field as a fan would turn your stomach. It would need to improve tremendously just to be labeled "atrocious." It got to the point that if the Cubs were playing the Phillies, Reds, or Pirates … a close game was a moral victory. Strangely enough, I never felt that way when watching the Sox play in person in the late 70's; I always felt that they had a good chance of winning, no matter who they played. But as soon as I'd see the red of the Reds, the maroon of the Phillies, or that horrid combination of whatever it was on the Pirates uniform, my stomach churned.

That being said, this one started with great promise as the first four Cubs reach base and they claim an early 2-0 lead. The only out recorded by the competent Jerry Reuss was not really recorded by him—Billy Buck was thrown out trying to go from first to third on a single. Reuss departs after the fourth batter (injury?) and is replaced by Terry Forster, now reunited with his old bullpen pal, Rich Gossage, and manager, Chuck Tanner. Forster restores order for the Pirate club, yielding only one run (a Bobby Murcer homer) heading into the sixth. For the Cub mounds men, the second and third time through the Buc lineup proved to be much more challenging than the first. Dave Roberts, who started, and Pete Broberg and Dave Giusti, who relieved, gave up 2 runs in the 4th and 4 runs 2 innings later. The hitting machine in the middle of the lineup called Al Oiver ripped a two run homer in the 4th and singled and scored in his following plate appearance. This ended about as well as can be expected, 6-3 Buccos.

As my favorite baseball team was losing in Chicago, my favorite college football team was losing in West Lafayette. "D" the Pirate fan, would occasionally give us gridiron updates with a simple ejaculation, "Oh, LORD!", as ND fell further and further behind. The exploits of the Boilermaker QB Mark Herrmann put Purdue well ahead. But as we got back into the car for the return trip to South Bend, the momentum of the football game changed dramatically. Coach Dan Devine replaced the struggling ND quarterback with a player named Joe Montana, perhaps you heard of him. Montana proceeds to slice and dice Purdue's defense, leading ND to late scores. Ultimately we (being an undergrad I use the pronoun 'we' even though I did very little blocking or tackling) snatched victory from sure defeat. So I guess the day ended with a split. This football team, by the way, would be crowned national champs a few months later after an arduous journey loaded with adversity.

The final thought of the Cubs season features a hero, Mr. Cub. Today the Cubs honored and celebrated Ernie Banks' election into the Hall-of-Fame. Today's scorecard highlights Ernie's image, smiling of course, and a replica of his autograph. In the upper right hand corner it showed the date of his inauguration at Cooperstown—August 8, 1977.

I bring this to light because I've read on several occasions the rough treatment Ernie received from one of his managers, Leo Durocher. Now no one knows for sure, but it has been suggested that Durocher did not care for Banks and wanted him replaced (with some great players like John Herrnstein). Anyway, Banks took this ill treatment as he took everything, with tremendous grace bordering on the transcendent. Nice guys finish last? Not on 8-8-77.

POST-SEASON, 1977

"KC, what do you want to put on the series?"

The speaker was short with dark hair and he talked fast. His demeanor was cocky and brash. He was also a Yankee fan. My nickname wasn't KC, but that's how he addressed me since I pulled for the Royals in the playoffs.

"So what do you want to put on it? 5? 10?" He repeated himself as we stood in line at the south dining hall. I stalled for time.

The Chicago fan in me is a curious blend of perpetual optimism laden with terror of the opposition. After yet another disappointing game, I say, "That's it, I'm not going to Wrigley Field again this year!" The next day a friend will call with a spare ticket. With no hesitation I say, "Sure, I'll go." And then when we arrive there we remember that the Cubs have to play another team. I ask, sometimes aloud, "What am I doing here? They're not gonna win." This has been going on now for six different decades.

So this classmate of mine assumed I was a KC fan. I didn't correct him. Of course I'd like to see a team from the Midwest (excluding the Cardinals) defeat teams from the East Coast, but it's more of a case of hating the Yankees rather than loving the Royals. I thought that hating the Yankees was about as American as apple pie. In college I found that some people actually rooted for the Pinstripes, with a former roommate being one of them (but he wasn't obnoxious; he was a classy guy and a classy fan. Still is.)

I mustered up bravado and placed some money on KC, figuring the Royals were due after Chris Chambliss terminated Royal Nation the previous year. The Royals were looking good after taking 2 of the first 3 games with the last two games in Missouri. After the Yanks took Game 4, Game 5 took on epic proportions. I should know by now that there's this weird correlation that exists in the world of fandom that goes like this: the more you want a team to win, the more likely it is that they will lose.

Don't laugh—it has happened way too often in my lifetime to be dismissed as coincidence. If I can stay nonchalant, the team I want to win usually does. It's when I get passionate and emotionally involved that bad things start to happen.

Naturally I'm up to my eyeballs with intensity for Game 5. The highlight for me came when George Brett slammed a ball in the outer regions of the Yankee defense and legged out a triple. So filled with emotion was Brett that upon his pop-up slide at third he took offense at a hard tag administered by Craig Nettles and slugged him. I mimicked his actions in the TV room where my mates and I were watching the game. So full of angst was I that I fancied myself taking a swipe at a Yankee, too. My friends were amused.

But I wasn't. For a second straight excruciating year, the Royals lost to the Yankees in the last inning. A KC 3-1 lead late in the game just added to the agony. 3 runs in the 9th gave the Yanks yet another pennant. I vaguely recall Paul Blair, a player that I _used_ to like, rap out a big hit, and after that everything went blank. I told one roommate who owed me money to pay another roommate who I now owed to make things square. I stormed out of the room, not just upset by this outcome, but knowing that the upcoming World Series would pit the Yankees against the Dodgers. Yuck. To root for one of these teams in the World Series is hardly fun, but I have to cheer for somebody. So go Dodgers.

I assume that since you're a baseball fan, all you need to know about this Series can be captured in two words: Reggie Jackson. He did lots of other things in his career, but no one can convince me that if Jackson hit 3 homers in a deciding World Series game for any team outside New York and Boston it would have received half the attention. (Do I sound bitter?). Don't get me wrong, Jackson's work in Game 7 is an incredible feat. But lots of other incredible things happen in baseball that don't get the recognition they deserve. Look up, for instance, the 1980 NLCS between the Astros and Phillies. Things in that series defy description, yet it hardly ever gets a mention.

About a week later my arrogant Yankee acquaintance and I cross paths. I paid up, and he initiated the conversation with some praise of KC's effort. If there had been a hint of condescension in his tone, I might have re-enacted the George Brett/Craig Nettles scene. But sensing his sincerity as he offered his words of consolation, I simply nodded my head and moved on.

1978

BILL, STAN, RICK AND JOE

Every day Joe wore a painter's hat. He stood 5'7", maybe. He told the worst jokes. He shared stories from World War II. When he smiled, which was often, gaping holes appeared where teeth should have been. The few teeth he had left were tainted a tobacco yellow. A baggy gray shirt and loose fitting pants comprised his wardrobe. We called his shoes "clodhoppers," today they'd be more charitably referred to as working shoes. This is what Joe wore whether it was 95 degrees and humid, or ten degrees below zero and windy. To the world he was an ordinary Joe. But as Clarence was to George Bailey, Joe was to me. Jesus saved me, but Joe gets an assist. He turned my life around.

"C'mon, Stan, isn't there some place we can put him? Isn't there something he could do?"

I was eavesdropping on a private conversation between Stan, a supervisor who I'll describe later, and Bill, owner of this small business.

Now if I have failed to do so already with descriptions and narratives, let me do so with direct language: *every* person I encounter in my first full-time job at this warehouse is a character. In all the time I worked there, I did not come across one boring individual, not one arrogant SOB, not one superficial person. Instead I found myself surrounded by people who had a ready laugh and readier curse. There was not a soul there who could be accused of not living. Together they formed a place that was as real as the world gets with no apologies, and I learned more lessons from that place than I did in college.

Bill, the owner, pleaded with Stan. This stunned me for this was never the voice Bill used when speaking to me. So this is why he's hiding out here, I thought, because he doesn't want to blow his image and show any sign of decency or compassion. It was fun sleuthing—looking like I was pushing a broom but hanging on every word that Bill said.

Bill was the kind of guy who had a sixth sense of employee slackness. Let's say I'd just spend ten minutes unloading a truck, with still many boxes to go. So I lean up against a wall and take a quick break. Without fail, precisely at that moment Bill would emerge from his office, walking with a purpose, and then stop in his tracks when he sees me.

"Attaboy, John," he'd yell. "Keep leaning up against that wall to make sure it doesn't fall down." The truck driver and my co-workers guffaw at my expense.

After his dig, I'd return to the boxes with a curse in my mind, if not on my lips. He'd rip me on a bi-weekly basis, almost as if it were on his "To Do" list. I used to think he had an alarm clock in his office that would occasionally go off to remind him . . . "Oh, I almost forgot, it's time to give John some shit." Upon my fourth summer of employment I mustered up enough courage to approach Bill and ask him for a raise. "A raise??!! Sure, we can talk about a raise. You're worth about a nickel an hour, so we can start our negotiations from there." In fairness, he did smile when he said this, and I did get a raise.

But now I catch my curmudgeon pleading with Stan to find something for this old World War II vet to do. In the school of hard knocks he must have adapted the management philosophy of "rip 'em in public, be sympathetic in private." From the moment that I caught Bill being decent, he could bust me 24/7, and at times it seemed he did, but I'd gladly accept. I'm just a college kid looking to help out with some tuition expense—this job didn't mean all that much to me. But for Joe, it could be his means of survival. I saw Bill for who he was—somewhat of a tool on the outside but a good man within. This is who he was all the time, I just happened to figure it out today. A jewel of a discovery.

So now Joe's a co-worker. He's inept as I am. In fact, Bill reminded me of this. One day, as Bill looks up the conveyor belt, he sees Joe and hollers something to him. Startled a bit, Joe knocks something off the belt. Bill, in disgust, looks at Joe and then at me and exclaims, "He is as useless as you are!" and storms back into his office.

This is how it went for the rest of the summer. The most mundane work with the most colorful characters. I think I'd rather have it that way than the other way around. Bill once observed that the toughest thing about the job was staying awake. True that, true that. But just before dozing off, someone would curse, laugh, or say something to make me laugh to rouse me from somnambulism.

One of the best laughs occurred right after lunch one day. Rick, an African-American fellow, worked briefly alongside me during my first summer. He was also a vet who had served during Vietnam. One day he returns from lunch after having one too many cocktails. We're both trying to look busy upstairs straightening up a few things, but hardly being productive. I get a sense that we're trying to stay hard to find until Rick sobers up a bit. Anyway, in the recesses of the warehouse, Rick comes across this huge sombrero (don't ask). He carefully places it on his head, making sure that the little green balls dangling off the sombrero's brim are in the right position. Now if you have never seen a black man who has had too much to drink put on an enormous sombrero and start singing and dancing like a Mexican, you really should. I laughed so hard that I didn't recognize the sound of my own laughter. I almost wanted Rick to stop with the fiesta and the Spanglish and the accent because my sides were really starting to hurt. Easily in the top five of the funniest things I've ever seen.

While Joe didn't have this "split your gut" humor, he did have, as previously mentioned, corny jokes that made you laugh with him or at him. Joe didn't care. Actually, he was the first to admit that his jokes were lame. But we laughed just the same. In his more serious moments, Joe entertained us with war stories. Some fabrication I'm sure, but the gist was reality: real war stories fought by real soldiers against the real Third Reich. Take away the exaggerations and you still have admirable stuff. Like the time Joe shared with us his version of the McAuliffe adventure (right away I think of the Tiger second baseman with a funny batting stance, but this McAuliffe was a different guy). Here's what happened, according to Joe …

"Our troops were surrounded by krauts; it was looking bad. One of the German officers sent McAuliffe a message telling him to surrender. Now the safe story goes that McAuliffe wrote a one word reponse—'Nuts'—and returned the message. I was there to see what McAuliffe wrote, and it wasn't 'nuts', but it still got the point across. We ain't surrendering."

Long story short—the Americans did not surrender, and against great odds, hold their ground and win the battle. I've always been partial to Joe's version more so than the history text books.

Fast forward to Christmas break. I work for about three weeks in late December/early January during my college years. I'm told that Joe's attendance has been spotty. One wintry day I show up before the shift even begins and see Joe sitting at our break table. He's wearing this foolish grin. Now at the ND campus you won't see characters like Joe, but I've seen that same grin at bars and at parties. Drunk as a skunk. Not good, but I keep my questions and concerns to myself.

Back to summer. No sign of Joe for weeks. I finally get the courage to ask Stan of Joe's whereabouts. Before I get to his reply, I need to introduce you to Stan. Here's the best way to put it—Stan's a second dad to me. I had a white dad at home and a black dad at work. He tipped the scales at 240--260 pounds. Big man. He stood about 6'2" with the Afro, about 5'9" without it. He and Paul were both dedicated family men. Paul had a run of sons and his last child was a girl. Stan had several daughters, and his last kid was a boy. One day at lunch I had an epiphany and asked them if they kept having kids until they had the complete set of both genders.

"Of course," they *both* replied, as if what I was asking was a stupid question. Their looks and not their words wondered if all college kids lacked smarts, or was I just special. Here I thought I was Sherlock Holmes and they made me feel like Inspector Clouseau. Paul continued, "They only come in two kinds, John." Not only did their kids matter the most to these two men, but having at least one of each mattered as well. They'd work overtime until they were 90, but they seemed determined to have both sons and daughters. I didn't forget that.

Stan had this unruly beard that had a mind of its own. He had a sleepy eye, a quick smile, and genuine interest in me. At this time in my life I was not the most responsible person on the planet. Nothing criminal, but I just did spacey things, especially at work when I'd get bored. In all this time covering four years, Stan lost his temper with me but once. I forget the occasion, might have been tossing a box on the wrong pile, but his anger consisted of a slight irritability in his voice tone. That was it. Some people speak harshly whenever they open their mouth; Stan did it once in four years.

One day as quitting time neared, Stan cornered me and asked me to help him tie a tie. I was honored. And he had this tendency to tap people on the arm when he had something of importance to say. When he finished, more often than not he'd explode in raucous laughter. That was cool, too. He spoke highly of my dad, whom he knew, and my dad reciprocated. I'll never forget one day when we were driving home my dad referred to Stan as "a beautiful man." Such sentiment from my old man went way beyond rare, but in Stan's case, it fit. I liked Stan from the very first day of work. It was after lunch and we were piling boxes on the conveyor belt. He looked at me and asked, "John, do you like baseball?" By the way he phrased the question, I could tell he was hoping for a 'yes' answer. Before I answered, I knew that working here over the next four years would be okay.

A few paragraphs ago I introduced the mystery of the missing Joe, and I asked Stan what happened to him. Stan informs me that Joe came to work drunk one too many times and they had to fire him. "Too bad," I said, and resumed working thinking that this would be the end of Joe and his corny jokes.

Wrong again, John. In mid-summer Joe shows up looking worse than ever. He gets a less-than-warm greeting from the warehouse workers, so I thought I'd approach Joe and try to lift his spirits, which seemed to be sagging. Did you ever get a feeling that getting involved in a situation is probably going to hurt, really hurt? I took a deep breath and asked Joe how he was getting along.

This is what Joe said: "Not good. I've done some things I'm ashamed of. After I got let go from here for drinking, I was in a bad way. I started drinking more and eating less. One day this bread truck stopped right in front of my apartment. The truck driver opened the back door and made a delivery to the little corner grocery store across the street. As he went inside, I snuck to the back of the truck and stole a loaf of bread. I couldn't help myself—my stomach was in knots from hunger. But I felt terrible for stealing."

"So what are you going to do now, Joe?"

"I came to get some bags. My brother runs an apple farm in Michigan. I'm here to ask for some bags so I can pick apples and work for him."

Just then Stan interrupted by telling Joe he couldn't take that many bags—he'd have to return some to the warehouse. Joe obeyed.

With our conversation winding down, I was feeling pretty helpless. "Here Joe," I said, reaching through the gate (at this point Joe stood outside the gate of the truck entrance and I stood within). "Take this." I handed him a buck. I was mad at myself for not having more cash on me.

"Thanks, John. I won't forget you."

"Take care, Joe."

We shook hands through the gate. Eye contact was difficult; all four were pretty moist by now. He left and I raced to the bathroom and wept for a good five minutes. I came out a different person.

Poverty had just smacked me in the face. Until now, "the poor" was a vague and generic term that consisted of many people globally and nationally. But I never shook hands with poverty like I just did. I felt a little ashamed, but mostly determined. A new perspective and a new purpose, if you will, that it's time to be other-centered way more than I have been. I had plenty, far more than the majority of the world, so why am I on the track to seek more and more? It struck me as overkill to grab more for myself, when the Joes of the world, WWII vets no less, are reduced to stealing bread. Time to change, time to see what I can do to improve the lot of others. And I have Joe to thank for that.

GAME 70: BOSTON RED SOX VS. CHICAGO WHITE SOX
SATURDAY, APRIL 8

Road trip. A couple of classmates from my marketing class and I make the 100 minute trek to Comiskey to witness the battle of the Soxes. This could be tense—an insufferable Red Sox fan (if there are any other kind, please point me in their direction) travels with us.

Early baseball games make my must-do list. So do games late in the year. So do games in the middle of the season. But in the first week or two of April, the husky voice of the vendors hawking peanuts, hot dogs, and even hot chocolate are sounds for sore ears. The concessions, save for beer, entice more now than in mid-August. Calories are needed to keep warm as play proceeds with temps in the 40's. The cooler conditions seem to amplify the crack of the bat. Line drives look and sound like line drives more in chilly weather with sparse attendance. The ball plopping in the gloves sounds louder, as does the encouraging and constant clapping of the coaches' hands. I may be imagining all of this because a six month absence does make the heart grow fonder. But maybe with fewer fans in the stands, the sounds are clearer and don't get absorbed into as many human cells. Games early in the year just sound better.

Then we see roster changes in the flesh. Something to look forward: seeing the ballplayers acquired in the off-season wearing different uniforms. Sometimes it looks okay, but frequently it looks funny and out-of-place; kind of like seeing your 2nd grade teacher at the grocery store. For instance, I could never get used to seeing Carlton Fisk in a White Sox uniform. He always will be, in my mind, a Red Sox player passionately waving his arms to direct a fly ball to stay fair. No matter how long or how well Pudge played for Chicago, it lacked legitimacy.

Seeing the Red Sox meant seeing a team with quality players. Love 'em or hate 'em, who wouldn't look forward to watching a Fisk (still with Boston), a Rice, a Lynn, and of course, Yaz.

And the White Sox continued to trot out "South Side Hit Men." As mentioned earlier, they had a team of capable hitters who at some point would have to defend. Familiar names like Garr, Bannister, and Orta at the top set the table for run producers like Johnson, Lemon, and Soderholm. Unfortunately,

Bill Veeck had to part ways with some of the more expensive hitters like Richie Zisk and Jim Spencer, but scoring would not be the problem with this team.

On this second day of the season, it looked like the Bosox would even their record at 1-1. On opening day the White Sox plated two runs in the ninth to win a thrilling 6-5 game, much to the delight of over 50,000 fans. Game 2—not so good: 5-0 Red Sox in the middle frames. Actually, holding a team to five runs that has Dwight Evans batting *eighth* isn't so bad. The Chisox bullpen did shut down Boston after they took this lead. Yet, I find it a bit deceptive when broadcasters give heaps of praise to a bullpen for shutting down a team that's already way ahead. They obviously deserve some credit in not letting the game get too far out of reach. However, I do think that in all sports it's only natural for the team that is dominating to let up. This isn't said aloud, but perhaps out of sportsmanship, perhaps out of conserving energy, perhaps out of complacency—the team that's cruising does seem to let up (especially in the NBA when you see an insurmountable gap turn into a close game in the later stages). You'll often see hitters squander at bats and not bear down as much when their team is comfortably in front. So you know what's coming—as on Opening Day, the White Sox stage a late inning rally.

I recall an exhilarating play for the home team when Garr lined a pitch into the right field corner. Normally, this is good for a double, but how I enjoyed watching the "Roadrunner" turn on the jets and slide safely into third. Then, with the score 5-3, Chet Lemon faces Bill Campbell with two runners on base. A double to center field ties the score, as the small (11,000) but vocal crowd goes bananas. The volume increases as the next batter, Eric Soderholm, singles off Bob Stanley to score Lemon. So it's 6-5, Right Sox, as we head into the 9th.

Two on, two out, as Lerrin LaGrow (sometimes called "La Groan" by certain parties) faces Jim Rice. If I'm a betting man, I'm putting money on Rice, who would go on to have more home runs, more total bases (a phenomenal 406) and more RBI's this season than anyone else in baseball. Rice or LaGrow—who would you take in this spot? I'd gladly lose money and win the game, which is precisely what would have happened as Rice flies out to left field. I return to South Bend one happy camper, and no, I did not rub it in to my Red Sox companion.

One last look at this game after a long cold lonely winter. Before the decisive rally, an inning or two earlier the White Sox start their comeback. And in the midst of this rally, I noticed something. I found myself in a complete "in-the-moment" moment. The only thing that mattered was the next White Sox hitter, as I was hoping, pleading, imagining, and willing him to keep the line moving. Pure hope and anticipation of something good. Honest, the world outside the ballpark could have been destroyed and I probably wouldn't have cared until the inning was over. Obsessive? Fanatical? Healthy? I dunno, but I do know that the escape that baseball can provide is timeless, and I think its zenith happens when the team for whom you're rooting stages a come-from-behind, late-inning rally.

GAME 71: PITTSBURGH PIRATES VS. CHICAGO CUBS
SATURDAY, APRIL 15

I know, I know. I'm a slow learner and a glutton for punishment. Once again, do I really think that Dennis Lamp, starting pitcher for the Cubs, will shut down the likes of a Willie Stargell, Dave Parker, and Rennie Stennett? Lamp did have success later in his career with the "Winning Ugly" White Sox team of '83, but at this point in his career, this was a mismatch. My brother and I used to jest that one of the highlights in the '78 season could be the time when Dennis Lamp threw a no-hit *inning*.

Actually on this chilly day in April, Lamp hurled two consecutive no-hit innings—the second and the third. Sandwiched around them, however, was a 2 run homer by Bill Robinson in the first and nine, that's right, nueve, runs in the 4th. Isn't there a baseball adage somewhere that says the team that scores nine runs in an inning usually wins? I hate it when your team gives up nine runs in an inning, and with the Cubs it happens more than you'd think. Look at the Pirate, Red, and Phillie lineups and then at the Cub pitching staff . . . and then duck.

To their credit, the Cubs did not roll over. As earlier documented, the Pirates can't run the bases forever, and the Cubs did manage to get three outs, eventually. And the Bucs on the field are like real Pirates on land—not nearly as dangerous. The Cubs went scoreless only in the 2nd, 4th, and 6th innings and had runners on base all afternoon. But they came a field goal short this frigid day, 13-10, Steelers over Bear-cubs.

GAME 72: CALIFORNIA ANGELS VS. CHICAGO WHITE SOX
TUESDAY, MAY 30

The Express. How's that for a nickname for one who throws pure heat? Easily one of the best nicknames from this era, The Express.

But I was never one to jump on the Ryan Express Lane. Strikeouts galore and unhittable more than anyone else, but wins? I know he didn't play on the greatest of teams, but if this guy was so good, then how come his record hovered only slightly above .500? And for all the years played and innings pitched, only two twenty-win seasons? Overwhelming stuff, but doesn't winning games trump strikeouts and even no-hitters? Seems that something's askew.

This particular game may yield insight into the Ryan record. The Sox with a fairly innocuous lineup got to Ryan for nine runs. Granted that five came in the last at-bat, but still how does a baseball legend give up nine earned runs to a team that would finish nineteen games below .500? In some ways years later a Kerry Wood was a poor man's Nolan Ryan. Both are super exciting, both could dominate like no one else, both were fan favorites, but I wouldn't want either pitching a game if my life depended on it. This approaches heresy to Ryan fans everywhere—if they're still reading—but it just didn't seem that Ryan mastered the craft of pitching the way that some of the greats did. He impressed me as a guy who didn't concern himself with the finer points of pitching. He just didn't have to.

This, I believe, explained how losses piled up. His ERA, well over 3.00 for most of his career, had nothing to do with poor run support or extremely shoddy defense. The Achilles Heel for Ryan had to be walks. But maybe that's a blessing for the sport. Had he the command of a Gibson or Seaver to go along with his stuff, other teams likely would have no chance, ever.

A brief look at this game reveals that Ryan walked six unintentionally to go with nine hits. That's fifteen baserunners in eight innings to go along with six K's. And not all these hits were cheap—a triple to center to the first man he faced, Ralph Garr. Then in the 8th, two homers. One struck by a legitimate hitter, Jorge Orta. But the other struck by Bill Nahorodny? First game we had

Lerrin LaGrow besting Jim Rice, and now we see Bill Nahorodny homering off Nolan Ryan. Wow.

The Sox win, 9-5, but the game was not that close. The Angels tag a tiring Steve Stone for four runs in the ninth. Up to that point, the Halos managed just one score on five hits.

I know I might be lynched in Texas for these remarks about Nolan Ryan. I really did enjoy watching him pitch, and his record speaks for itself—good and bad. I just prefer someone who wins games consistently and helps to get his team into the post-season.

PS Something of greater social significance took place on the South Side this summer. Namely, the second black manager was hired by Bill Veeck and the Chicago White Sox to replace Bob Lemon. His name? Larry Doby. And now for some irony: Doby was also the second black man to break the color barrier as a baseball player. More irony … both times the first person just ahead of Doby was someone called Robinson. Jackie as ballplayer and Frank as manager. Even more irony … Veeck was the owner for both occasions: when Doby broke in during the 1947 season in Cleveland and now in Chicago.

How did Doby fare as a manager? Not good (37-50). Like most skippers in Chicago in the 70's, he didn't have the horses to compete with the elite teams. But his contribution went well beyond wins & losses. Veeck and Doby paved the way for successful managers of color down the road … people like Cito Gaston, Ron Washington, and Dusty Baker.

GAME 73: PHILADELPHIA PHILLIES VS. CHICAGO CUBS
SUNDAY, JULY 2

Let's see … middle of summer, which means the wind often blows out; the Friendly Confines won't hold a ball that travels 369 feet to the power alleys; sluggers like Luzinski, Schmidt, and Murcer; and the starting pitchers are Randy Lerch and Dennis Lamp. You may be thinking, wait a minute, could this be that famous 23-22 game?

Good try, but you're a year off. This turns out to be the less-than-famous 2-1 game. In what other sport could you find the same two teams playing on the same field in consecutive years engage in one run games in which 48 runs were scored altogether? How could you have such a great disparity with 3 runs scored one year, then the following year the teams combine to score 45? By comparison, would the NFL scores yield such a range? Would the Bears and Eagles play a game that ended 7-6 one year, and then the very next year run up the score to something like 74-73? I can't see that happening. And while a 23-22 score is a serious aberration, on any given day in baseball you'll find scores that present a diverse blend of pitching duels and slugfests.

One thing that held the score down on this day was the absence of one Michael Jack Schmidt. His performance in Wrigley Field over his career simply blows away reason and Cub pitching. I did the "Hustle" when I heard that #18 and not #20 was playing third base for the Phils. This replacement, Richie Hebner, was a capable batsman in his own right. Three things stand out about Hebner: 1) He labored as a grave digger. 2) He also played my second favorite sport, hockey. 3) He had this habit of pulling the back of his jersey up toward the top of his neck when he entered the batter's box. I never saw another hitter do this—and such quirky things entertain and make a lasting impression.

But this was not a day for hitters. In such a tight, low-scoring game plays get magnified. Halfway through the game Philadelphia had 2 runs, one on a Ted Sizemore RBI single that scored Hebner, and a lead-off homer in the 5th by the clutch-hitting catcher, Bob Boone. On the Cubs' ledger, not only did they have no runs, but they had no hits. But the third time through the lineup the Cubs' offense did show signs of life.

I've learned this about the key moments in baseball—they don't always happen in the last inning. You may not win the game with a good 4th inning, but you could sure lose the game with a bad one. These middle innings are like middle children in that they're often overlooked and taken for granted. But if mismanaged and neglected, these middle innings can come back and haunt you, just like middle children. With slow-footed Larry Biittner on first with two outs, the eighth place hitter, Larry Cox, doubles to right. Here's some second guessing now and some first guessing as the play unfolded: why not try to score Biittner? There are two outs so he's running on contact, and Trillo with a strong arm is NOT the relay man for the Phils but on this day it's Sizemore. Most of all, the pitcher batting next, Dennis Lamp, has about as much a chance of getting a hit in this situation as you, dear reader. I think this is where the manager and 3rd base coach need to be on the same page. If you're not taking out Lamp for a pinch-hitter, then I think you've got to send Biittner. But alas, Biitner holds at third, and with the tying runs in scoring position, Lamp whiffs.

On to the next inning. With two out, the middle of the lineup—Bobby Murcer hitting third and Manny Trillo (Trillo hitting cleanup? That's another story) and Mike Vail string singles together. This produces a run, and once again the tying run is in scoring position. Biittner, again in the middle of things, lines out to the pitcher. Game of inches—a few either way and the game is tied. So while a bit discouraging, it looks like the Cubs are starting to get to Lerch (I wonder if he answers the phone in the bullpen like this, "You Rang?")

But this optimism crashes and burns in the person of Ron Reed. The tall righty who played hoops at Notre Dame slams the door on the Cub offense over the last three innings. A nine out save with 9 up and 9 down and 5 K's. Thank you for coming, please drive home safely.

The point? In baseball, score while you can. Here are a few principles that might come in handy next time you find yourself managing a baseball game ...

- Win today, it might rain tomorrow
- Get the lead now, it might rain in the 6th inning
- Momentum is only as good as tomorrow's starting pitcher (or the next relief pitcher)
- When you see a chance, take it . . .
- Score before they bring in that blankety-blank stud reliever from the bullpen

GAMES 74 & 75: LOS ANGELES DODGERS VS. CHICAGO CUBS (DH) SUNDAY, JULY 16

Game 1

One of the teams is down to their "last bullet." It's a one-run game, it's been a well-played game, definitely a well-pitched game, and now one pitch stands between your team and a victory. The pitcher, who has a plaque in Cooperstown, rears back and cuts loose. The ball dives downward drastically as it intersects home plate. The batter wisely checks his swing at an unhittable pitch. To the delight of the crowd, and to the amazement of my kid brother and yours truly, the umpire raises his right arm. Ballgame. The hitter protests, but to no avail. He, nor any of his mates, proved no match for this ace out of the bullpen. So if this game ended prematurely by a pitch or two, it really didn't make a difference … no way were they going to hit this guy.

Bruce Sutter. Probably the most dominant relief pitcher I've ever seen in person. You've probably heard how one pitch can rejuvenate a career. The split finger (that's forkball to the old-timers) came to Sutter via the tutorage of a coach named Fred Martin. The ubiquitous pitch today was cutting edge in the 70's. When on, which Sutter usually was during his time with the Cubs, his split finger frustrated the best of hitters. On occasion he'd hang one, as I remember watching Ken Griffey Senior drive one such pitch into the bleachers. When the closer hangs one, 150 minutes or so of the team's hard fought advantage evaporates immediately.

But not today. Sutter enters the ballgame in the eighth inning with the tying run on second and nobody out. The first three batters he faces are Bill Russell, Michael Jordan, and Wilt Chamberlain. No, just kidding—they were in fact Bill Russell, then Steve Garvey and Ron Cey. Should he survive the 8th, due up in the ninth were Dusty Baker, Rick Monday, and Bill North. The point is that Sutter would have to face at least six quality hitters and retire them without the tying run scoring to earn his save. We saw Ron Reed go nine up and nine down against the Cubs not too long ago, now Sutter is asked to get the six toughest outs of the game.

But these six could be anything from Murderer's Row to your local Little League team, they weren't going to score today. As a team, the Cubs ERA stood at 3.93. Sutter's was 1.71. The entire Cub pitching staff gave up 754 hits in 763 innings. Sutter gave up 37 hits in 58 innings. If you're manager Herman Franks, the plan is to shorten the game and have a lead after 7. Then turn it over to #42, the Sutter the better. Two ground outs, one fly out, two swinging strikeouts and the aforementioned caught looking close the game. Cubs win 3-2.

Kudos to Sutter's battery mate, Dave Rader. One of my brother's favorite players, Rader drives in all Cub runs in this game with a two-run double and a sacrifice fly. Ivan DeJesus, former Dodger, smacks three singles and scores twice thanks to Rader's clutch hitting. Quite a bonus to get such productivity out of your seventh and eighth-place hitters.

Game 2

As pitching giveth, pitching taketh away. Ray Burris, the enigma, did not make it out of inning number one. Hits, walks, and a lack of patience re-sulted in a very early appearance of Lynn McGlothlen. He held the Dodgers in check, and kept the Cubs in the game chasing three runs with plenty of baseball left in this one.

But the Cubs had formidable obstacles to overcome. Foremost on the list is an impotent offense. With Dave Kingman on the DL, the leading home run hitter for the Cubs, in Game *87,* was Bobby Murcer with 5. Not a '2' in front of the 5, not even a '1' in front of the 5, just 5 by its lonesome. As in cinco. Manny Trillo, who in an earlier game batted clean-up for the Cubs, had a grand total of 2. Rush Street Offense indeed.

But in fairness that's only half the story. At least 50% of the nightcap was about LA's starting pitcher, Burt Hooton. Hooton struggled when he pitched for the Cubs, finishing his time with them with a record of 10 more losses than wins. Then practically overnight he enjoyed a remarkable resurgence with the Dodgers. In '75 he started the year 0-2 with the Cubs, got traded on May 2 to LA for pitchers Geoff Zahn and Eddie Solomon, and then took off. He went 18-7 for the rest of '75, another 18 wins in '76, and reached 19 in '78. He finished his career winning 15 more games than he lost. By looking at those numbers, some critics might argue that the Cubs gave up on Hooton and his knuckle curve too soon, and that the proverbial trade for Solomon was just not wise. But the counter point holds that pitching for a much better ballclub can do wonders for a pitcher's win-loss record.

In this game Hooton had the Cubs' number. He beat them with his bat—driving in a run with a single—and his arm. He'd allow a tally here, a rally there, but overall not much to speak of. In addition to the Cubs' inept offense and non-existing power, a brisk breeze blew in from center field, unusual given the time of year.

In the middle innings, the play that most impressed me, my brother, and many in attendance came when the Dodgers were batting. Dusty Baker swung mightily and squared one up. With the wind blowing in, I feared not and expected the ball to be caught by the left fielder. To my surprise and chagrin, the ball kept travelling. Over the left fielder's head, over the left field ivy, over the heads of the bleacherites, and onto Waveland Avenue. I had to wonder what would have happened with no wind, or heaven help us, if the wind had been blowing out. In light of a popular song back them, my brother turned to me and suggested that in honor of Dusty's mighty wallop, that Waveland Ave. should now change its name to Baker Street.

That pretty much was your ballgame, 5-3 Dodgers. So the teams broke even on this Sunday afternoon: Chicago 3-3, Los Angeles 2-5. Plenty of good things this day; the best just spending time with my brother.

POST-SEASON 1978

The fall of '78 brought younger Catholics something new to their world—the election of a pope. John Paul I's abrupt death necessitated a second election in several weeks after not having one for a decade and a half. Among many other things, John Paul II's election represented two significant novelties: A) a pope who wasn't Italian, and B) a pope who travelled extensively. Prior to his papacy, Catholics made the pilgrimage to the Vatican. Now in role reversal, the pope became the pilgrim, visiting people all over the globe. My folks had the opportunity to attend Mass with John Paul II as the celebrant in Chicago's Grant Park. I wonder how many people knew at that time that they'd be worshiping with a canonized saint.

On the baseball front, THE signature playoff game that's been discussed and analyzed ad nauseam took place between the Red Sox and Yankees (once again the cynic in me asks if we would know a fraction of this contest had it occurred between two other teams). Admittedly, high drama in several scintillating moments … Lou Pinella's poise in right field after losing a ball in the sun (did I just use Pinella and poise in the same sentence?), Bucky Dent requiring a different bat just prior to launching THE home run, and of course Yaz facing Gossage with the pennant hanging in the balance. Begrudgingly, a classic (but must we be reminded of it as often as we are?)

After this playoff game the post season was déjà vu all over again. The New York Yankees knock off the Royals in the playoffs and the Dodgers down the Phillies. Ho-hum. On to the World Series. Okay, there was this one electric confrontation between Bob Welch pitching and Reggie Jackson batting. After a marathon at-bat, with tension rising with each delivery, Jackson swings and finally misses. Welch wins the battle and LA goes up 2 zip. But the fortunes for the Pinstripes change in New York. This time it's not Reggie's bat but his hip that makes contact with the baseball, deflecting a critical double play opportunity. Manager Tommy Lasorda protests, but the play stands. The Yankess take all three in the Big Apple, and finish the Dodgers in six games.

Changing subjects and raising spirits, we'll talk Notre Dame football. A few games into the season, a solid Purdue team visits South Bend. Their tailback is a player by the name of Russell Pope. Amidst the Vatican election, the opportunistic school newspaper, *The Observer*, shares this bulletin: "Purdue running back named Pope." (I guess you had to be there). Anway, the previous season the Irish football team claimed the national championship with the rout of the previously unbeaten #1 Texas Longhorns in the Cotton Bowl, 38-10. Prior to the BCS playoff structure, Notre Dame leapfrogged a few teams after the bowl games. ND's ascent resulted in mild but not major controversy. The team under the direction of Coach Dan Devine and the resourceful play of Joe Montana got on a roll toward the end of the season and dominated their opponents. I was glad that their early season struggles, which included a stunning loss at Ole Miss, didn't prevent them from a shot at the championship.

1979

(Note to reader: skip the next seven pages if you want to read more baseball. You won't hurt my feelings).

Believe it or not, baseball did not take top priority as the '79 season commenced. These two things usurped the game: 1. graduating college 2. confronting the question--NOW WHAT?

Neither of these issues was a slam-dunk. Good grades, heck, sometimes passing grades did not come easy for me in college. I thought I'd be clever and wrap out my academic career by "investing" in an investment class. I planned on taking this Investment class Pass/Fail. After the first exam, it looks like I'll be taking it Fail/Fail. As profs often do before returning tests to students, they indicate the range of scores. You've probably heard versions of it before. It goes something like this: "Well, some of you did well and some not so well. The scores on your test ranged from a '98' to a '48'."

Now when some of my cut-throat classmates got this bit of information, they're likely thinking, "Gee, did anyone beside me get the '98'? I sure hope not." By contrast, this is what I'm thinking, "Please, Lord, please, please, please don't let me be the '48'."

So now the exams get returned. I ask you to pause and think back to a difficult class you've taken, anything from Phonics to Physics. Now recollect the classroom atmosphere when a difficult test was being returned. Many things in education have changed—but this isn't one of them. I've been on both sides as a student and as a teacher. Nothing a teacher can do to reduce the anxiety. Go ahead and pull out your most hilarious material, tell the world's funniest joke, distribute PEZ to the students, and the response you get is … NOTHING. A bunch of strained faces, some may be trying to act cool but they're not, a bunch of strained faces glaring at the teacher wanting him/her to shut up and give me back my test NOW … please.

Upon receiving my test, I calmly scream, "Oh #*@*#^%*##," or something like that. Everyone—the kid that's always asleep in the back of the room, the janitor in the hallway, students playing Frisbee outside, the campus security, the cafeteria ladies, that is, everyone---takes a momentary break from a self-absorbed existence and peers at me.

"Well, we know who got the '48', wonder who got the '98'?"

In complete panic mode, I rush to the teacher, the academic dean, the priest, the RA, the Grotto, the palm reader, the therapist, former roommates (all 13 of them), Dear Abby, Lourdes, and Senior Bar for consolation and advice. Then on to Plan B: Take three mini-courses to replace the investment class. Passing all three (again, all Pass-Fail) insures graduation on time. If it took 132 credit hours to get that diploma, then by golly I was going to graduate with nothing less, and definitely nothing more, than that magic number of 132. (I believe this was also the Cubs' magic number at Labor Day that year). Cutting it so close like this means that I was either … A) quite efficient in my studies, or B) never really liked school and wanted to take no more than the bare minimum to graduate. Before answering that multiple choice question, here's a clue to the right answer: it's not 'A'.

I'm obliged to take three mini-courses over the last eight weeks of my college career. So whereas my senior pals have checked out from anywhere between three months to three years ago, I'm now looking at the equivalent of cramming 21 credit hours into my schedule (the standard lies between 12-15). Here I am, a business major, taking three Arts & Parties classes like "Book as World--British Literature from the Romantic Era," "French Resistance during World War 2," and "Antiquity and Philosophy." Now if you're a practical person, and what business major isn't, how are you going to use these classes in the world of commerce? I can already picture an interview with a Fortune 500 company offering me a position because I was able to correctly identify several types of satire in *Tristan Shandy*.

But one has to do what one has to do and the classes weren't that bad. The history one really stood out. I took it with a friend named Kyle who resided in the same dorm. He took great notes, but notes that had nothing to do with the subject. He'd get bored easily, and then take out his notebook and keep a running tally as to how many times the instructor (a young, pretty and conscientious recent grad) would say "Uh-Hum" whenever a student spoke. On some days these tallies went on and on. Noteworthy because many tallies meant that students were talking a lot, and this meant that we would not be accountable for as much material on the next quiz. So Kyle kept records, and we rooted for these records to be broken.

Across campuses everywhere, students carry their mates through courses. In this history class it soon became apparent that I was responsible for both Kyle and me passing this class. Class began at 2:20 PM on M-W-F. He'd come in at 2:19, pull up a chair next to me, and ask what was on the last reading assignment. Normally we wouldn't care, second semester seniors and all, but we had a quiz in five minutes. Having read the stuff, I proceeded—with examples, quotes, metaphors and all other things that teachers love to see—to highlight the 435 page reading assignment in four minutes. Kyle's recall was like Dustin Hoffman's in *Rainman*. So when Kyle got the quiz back, without reading a page of material (I doubt he even bought the book) and relying on what I told him, he scored higher than his personal tutor. No lie. But at least I scored higher than a 48 (I think).

It's now late April, standing between me and my degree is one last round of finals. For decades after my final final, I have been haunted by this recurring nightmare. It goes like this ….

I'm scheduled to take this class in college. I just learned about this class moments ago.
It's been meeting now for a couple of months, and I've been absent all that time.
So I finally show up and discover that it's the day of the Final Exam.
The instructor's Eddie Poe and there's this pendulum blade
Right above my desk, and it descends after
Each incorrect answer, swinging
Lower, and LOWER, and
LOWER … until
I wake up.

With my sheets soaked, I rouse myself in bemusement. My dreams about final exams persist to absurd degrees. I've even asked the teacher in these nightmares to please double-check your records because I'm in my fifties and have four kids, two in college. Friends my age retired years ago. Are you sure I have to take this test?

So the class before the history final arrives and it's the typical "pump the teacher for as many answers" session. Any nugget of info to boost our score by a percentage point is the intention of the class. Some would sacrifice their left arm and all their red-headed children for one or two fewer blemishes left by the scan-tron machine. So at the end of all this "learning", I raise my hand and ask if seniors are exempt from taking the final exam. Some muffled and some not-so-muffled laughter creeps out from where we sit. In a mini-course like this one, the final exam **is** your grade, basically. I thought I'd throw it out there to evoke a laugh or two. But then something very strange happens. The class collectively gasps as the young teacher clears her throat and responds,

"Is this senior exemption common at this university?'

"Oh yes," the seniors lie, trying to sound earnest but failing.

"Uh-Hum, uh-hum," our teacher replies. Kyle makes a couple more tallies in his notebook.

"Yes," I offer, "if seniors are getting a passing grade going into the final, then they have the option of not taking it." (Hey, there's NO WAY she's going to buy this, is there? About 10% of me feels bad for pushing it this far. Could she get fired over this?)

"Uh-hum," she says, "well, let me check my grade book and see who qualifies."

Did you ever get the feeling that you're holding the mega-lotto ticket and the first four numbers match?

"Okay, wait," this young teacher continues. My stomach sinks. No Lotto for you. "How many of you are seniors?"

Everybody's hand goes up. Some raise both. There are two high school kids in the back of the room just visiting the campus for the weekend. Their hands go up.

"Uh-hum, oh I see. Well, let me see if you can *exercise your senior option.*"

Alleluia, Alleluia, ALLELUIA, ALL-LAY-HAY-YOU-LA (I'm singing, not saying, these words at my desk).

She begins to go through the list in her gradebook. "Yes, uh-hum, Andersome you may exercise your senior option. Bilkis, yes. Caustic, yes. Hickee, yes. Horn, yes, Kraduk, sure …" There's not one "NO" so far! My innards are doing somersaults as she approaches the O's. "Maddun, yes; McEnernie, yes. O'C, ok". Here it comes. "O'Donnell …" a pause, why a pause? "Uh-Hum, you may exercise your senior option. Peters … yes, Quinn …"

It's all a blur. I won the Lotto, for me and for the whole class. I don't know whether to go to Disney World, the chapel, or the Senior Bar. Perhaps all three. All because I spouted off for a joke. That line you hear all the time is true… the one that says that the only bad question is the one not asked.

I think it was Andy Warhol who said that we all are given five minutes of fame. That line is not true. That evening, at this one social engagement, I had a few hours of fame. "Hey, here's that guy that got us out of taking the final. Let me get you something."

"Aw shucks, guys, it was nothing, but I am a little thirsty …"

Years later, I have an insight. Picture this--candles adorn a small dining room table. Soft jazz music floats in the air. Wine, cheese, and crackers whet the appetite. A young and relaxed history grad student leans toward her fiancée and says …

"Can you believe it? They think they pulled one over on me. Senior exemptions for a mini-course, yeah, right. You didn't hear about it? Some clown in the French Resistance class asked if seniors were exempt from taking the final. I played dumb and asked them what the school policy was. When they told me what it was, I acted like I was looking at their grades." She holds up her gradebook to her friend. It's empty. They laugh. "I told them all that they could 'exercise their senior option,' whatever that is. They believed me. Now I don't have to come up with inane questions about de Gaulle and the Vichy movement. And better yet, I don't have to read their drivel. You ought to look at their quizzes—I swear half don't even read the book. Honey, could you pour me some more Boone's Farm?"

Glasses filled and clinked together.

"And that's not even the best part," she giggles.

"What would that be?"

"The guy who asked if he could be exempt, I *do* happen to know *his* grade going into the final. Do you know what it is?"

"I've got no idea."

"48. Uh-Hum."

FIVE DAYS LATER ...

Okay, so I'll graduate. Then what? Our beloved institution, the Senior Bar, had our backs with this custom. For every rejection letter a senior earned from a potential employer, the management at this establishment would reward said student with a free beer. So naturally, we went on as many interviews as possible, asking the interviewer toward the end of the interview as to when we can expect to hear from them. A classic win-win situation: A job offer or a free beer. Many arguments over which is more valuable.

I had my fair share of rejections. But there's a roommate of mine whom you met last September, his name was 'D'. His consistent lack of a work ethic, his nonchalance about his studies, and his interest in socializing now pay huge dividends. He was a man with a vision. D was more prepared for "Rejection Night" at Senior Bar than he was for any class. He had this three ring binder bursting with follow-up letters from companies that start with ... "Thank you for taking the time to ....", and conclude with something like, "there's no way in hell we'd ever hire you; enjoy your parents' basement." After receiving this much anticipated correspondence via snail mail, he'd whip out his trusty hole puncher and add it to his collection. That way he didn't have to take each letter out but just have the bartender initial it and pour a cold one. 'D' had his five minutes of fame and then some that night. He bought rounds many times over—a truly enjoyable evening thanks to my roommate capitalizing on four years of indifference.

But I needed to address my second priority—what do I do now? Like 'D', I went on many job interviews and the next job offer would be my first. They would ask how I did in investments class. Oddly enough though, I was in a better place than many of my classmates, and it wasn't because of the Senior Bar largesse. For some time I had been going through a change of heart with the world of commerce—it was rapidly and definitively losing its appeal. It might have been that my indifference caused these rejections, or that these rejections caused my indifference. But foremost to my metanoia was last summer's encounter with Joe.

So I did something that no business major in his right mind would do—I looked into volunteer work. Now this just had to thrill my folks no end. Imagine spending mega-bucks for grade school, and high school, and college tuition, only to learn that upon graduation your kid was going to work for free. Isn't that a nice return on your investment?

This whole experience reminded me of something somebody once said on a day of reflection. This one fat and funny guy (think John Candy) was asked to describe the perfect girl for him. Without hesitation, his deadpan response was, "One who would go out with me."

I find myself hoping to get accepted into this program and work in the Great Northwest (Portland, OR) for a stipend of $50 per month. The benevolent folks in charge of this program (called Holy Cross Associates) asked me why I wanted to do this. I thought about the question and about the fat funny guy with girl issues, and said, "Because no one else will hire me." They laughed, assumed I was joking, and I laughed with them (I didn't mean for it to be funny, but I don't like to pass on a laugh). Later they offered me a position, and I signed up before they could renege. I'm psyched—knowing that I get to see big trees, big mountains, big water, and the Trail Blazers. I'm confident that I'll finagle my way to a Mariners' game or three, and happy that I think I'll be doing good work—fundraising for the Association for Retarded Citizens, coaching, and serving as a teacher's aid in a special ed. classroom. As cheesy as it sounds, I really did want to make the world a better place, but if I can take in beautiful nature while doing it, why not? Plus, I wouldn't be the

Lone Ranger: eight other recent grads from ND/St. Mary's decided to do this for a year, and we'd reside in two simple homes right next to the University of Portland.

So now that I'm more at peace because the next year of my life is decided, I can turn my attention back to baseball.

JOHNNY CALLISON

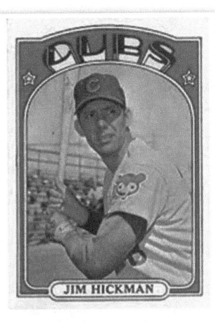

JIM HICKMAN

FERGIE
JENKINS
CHICAGO CUBS

PITCHER

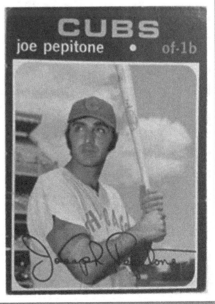

CUBS
joe pepitone   •   of-1b

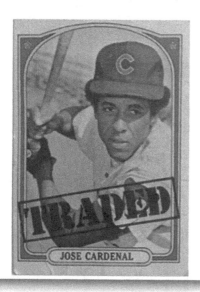

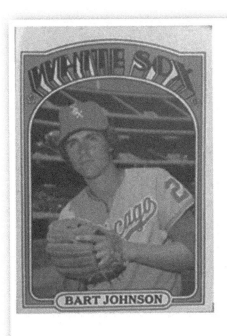

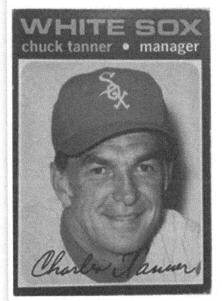

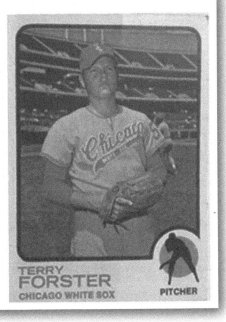

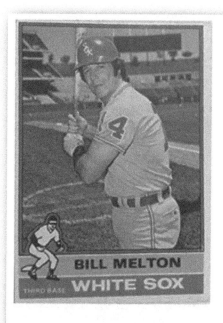

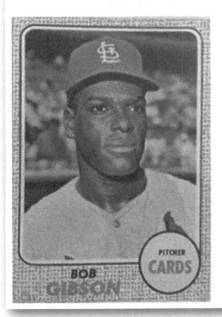

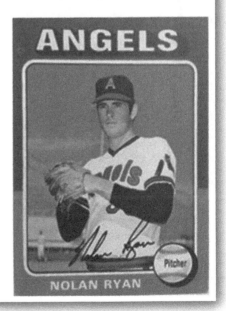

BILLY WILLIAMS

GEORGE BRETT

DAVE
KINGMAN
SAN FRANCISCO GIANTS
1st BASE

MIKE
TORREZ
MONTREAL EXPOS
PITCHER

GAME 76: NEW YORK YANKEES VS. CHICAGO WHITE SOX FRIDAY, APRIL 13

This had trouble written all over it. First, it was Good Friday. Probably a day I should have refrained from sports since this was the day I received stitches in my knee after sliding into third base (first time I ever got stitched up) and the day I broke my ankle playing basketball (first broken bone below the waist). Good Friday taught me that it's better to lay low and ponder the significance of this day.

But no, my friend Gary and I had to go see the White Sox play. More like the White Sox getting killed by the Yankees. And if Good Friday was not enough of an omen, check out the date. At least it's not a night game so that Freddy or Jason or Michael wouldn't jump us in the parking lot when it was pitch dark. And I'd be remiss if we didn't discuss the folks playing in the game itself. For the Yankees, their second-to-last batter possessed more power than anyone in the White Sox lineup. Embarrassing, really, when you have a Cliff Johnson following sluggers like Munson, Jackson, Chamblisss, and Nettles. Then we have the pitching matchup: Rich Wortham (Sox) vs. Luis Tiant (Yankees). At this point in their careers, Tiant and Wortham combined for 207 wins in the big leagues, with Tiant claimng 204 of them. The defending champs with 100 wins from the previous year vs. a team that had lost 90 games. The question wasn't so much if the Sox were going to get destroyed, but how badly?

So we watch the game from the upper deck box along the first base side and get hypnotized by Tiant's delivery. And Gary and I witness three homers struck that day. You have to figure Reggie is good for 1, 2 or all 3. Maybe Nettles smacked one—he had some marvelous April's in his career. Or Chambliss, the hero from two years ago, or Johnson, the guy who scuffled with Goose and did some damage to him in the clubhouse.

Sorry, no. None of those boppers went yard. Then it must have been a Munson or Rivers. No and no, and nobody off the bench either. So who was it? The three bombs delivered by Chet Lemon, Jorge Orta, and Alan Bannister. Decent hitters all, but none will ever be confused with Babe Ruth, Willie Mays or Harmon Killebrew. The Sox knocked out 15 other hits to go along with the three bangers. They even bested the Bronx Bombers in errors, committing "only" three to the Yankees' four. A most gratifying surprise on this Good Friday. For the reord, White Sox 12, Yankees 2.

GAME 77: PITTSBURGH PIRATES VS. CHICAGO CUBS
FRIDAY, MAY 25

"This would be a pretty nice place if it weren't for school." … words from a dorm mate.

Senior week gave us ample time with absolutely nothing to do save graduation ceremonies. It's your last fling before entering the real world (for most people), grad school (for some people), or volunteer work (me). I'm guessing that one of the intents for this week from an administrative perspective is to allow the soon-to-be grad an opportunity to reflect on the lessons learned over one's whirlwind college experience. And of course a chance to relax and spend time with confreres who you may not see for a while, after constant interaction with them over the past three years and nine months. Noble designs, but we had other plans, like seeing how much fun can be crammed into a week.

Of course that meant trips to the ballpark. My dad got us six tickets for Thursday and Friday's game, and we were even able to find cheap housing—my folks' house.

It may not have been living the dream, but it was pretty close. The day before "pushing and shoving" our vehicles through the tremendously congested highways of Chicago on the way to a ballgame, Gary and I went fishing in a remote pond in northern Indiana. I caught a nap, some sunburn, the Cub game on the radio, but no fish. Isolated with Gary, whose folks owned this property, I appreciate the contrast between the sublime serenity of fishing with the big city noise we'll encounter tomorrow.

The following morning marked the start of our pilgrimage to Wrigley Field. I called one of the absent pilgrims and had to cajole him in to coming. From the sound of his voice, it sounded like he had a rough evening. He had drinker's elbow, so I couldn't do a whole lot of arm twisting, but we were finally able to convince him to join us.

Good thing, too, or else he would have missed out on history. No hyperbole needed for this affair—how many 23-22 games have you seen? What made it all the sweeter for my reluctant friend is that he's an unabashed Sox fan, Cardinal fan, and Cub hater. It would have killed him to miss out on this memorable Cub defeat. And following a pleasant night of watching Walter

Davis and the Phoenix Suns in the NBA playoffs at a local bar and grill, we slept a few hours and made the return trip to Wrigley the following day as they opened a series with the Buccos.

Throughout the years of taking in games at *Cubs' Park* (a term used by some of the more veteran fans), it struck me that some players just seemed too big for the ballpark. Now I never had this feeling at Comiskey, even though muscle men existed (Jim Rice, Frank Howard, Willie Horton, Boog Powell, Harmon Killebrew, and Eddie Murray) and the dimensions were similar. But at Wrigley Field, it seemed like it was almost dangerous to have some sluggers in the batter's box staring down the 368' power alleys with the wind blowing out. Players like Greg Luzinski, Willie Stargell, Willie McCovey, Adam Dunn, George Foster, Mike Schmidt, and of course, Dave Kingman reminded me of college kids playing on a grade school field. They outgrew it and should be playing somewhere else.

Schmidt maimed the Cubs yesterday, and today it would be Stargell's turn. But the game's real blow belonged to Kingman of the Cubs. He launched a tape measure blast in the early innings off John Candelaria. The ball seemed to be in orbit for many moments before it started its descent toward Kenmore Avenue. This gave mighty Kong four long flies in the last 24 hours. I began calculating what 4 home runs in a day's time would lead to—maybe an occasional Cub victory? But not yesterday nor today: Pirates 9 Cubs 5.

GAME 78: CLEVELAND INDIANS VS. CHICAGO WHITE SOX
TUESDAY, MAY 29

In my fifteen years of going to baseball games, this will be my first as a college graduate. (Hey, I know that's not saying much, but this game was such a dog I had to come up with something).

The second most noteworthy tidbit in this reporter's eyes is the heart of the Tribe's batting order: Bobby Bonds, Andre Thornton and Cliff Johnson (recently traded from the Yankees) all at one time played for the Cubbies. Bonds got to play on both sides of town albeit very shortly. But the starting pitcher for Cleveland trumps all other items of note. His name—David Clyde. You may think of him as a Texas Ranger, breaking into the baseball scene with tremendous fanfare. How a kid just days removed from his high school graduation starts a game for the major league club in Arlington got a lot of attention. He took the league by storm, and I'm sure the Ranger front office capitalized on thi$. But then he fizzled, got injured, and wound up being traded to the Indians. He didn't last long there, either. A heartbreak, really, and probably a reason that some clubs have been overly cautious in the development of young and talented arms (see Stephen Strasburg, 2012). For his career Clyde would win only 18 games, with this being one of them. Indians 7 White Sox 2 in a totally forgettable game.

GAME 79: SAN FRANCISCO GIANTS VS. CHICAGO CUBS
SATURDAY, JUNE 2

An entertaining slugfest. Wind blowing out on a summer afternoon provides for potent offense, but not at the expense of shoddy defense. Impressive lineups on both sides: Larry Herndon, Jack Clark, Bill Madlock, and Willie McCovey for Frisco; Bill Buckner, Jerry Martin, Bobby Murcer, and Dave Kingman for the Cubs. Clark and McCovey go back-to-back, while Kingman homers once and Martin twice for the home team. Giants prevail, 8-6.

The highlight of this scorecard, however, is not the lead marks showing runs scored and long balls. Nope, instead it's a signature from a Cub broadcaster who to me was a splendid blend of baseball knowledge and class.

Lou Boudreau. Where to begin? Player-manager, innovator, basketball star, baseball sage, broadcaster, Hall-of-Famer. Quite a resume'. Classic case of local boy, sort of, (Harvey, IL) makes good. Yet what impressed me the most was the fact that he was Denny McLain's father-in-law. Silly, I know, but I was captured by the fact that this guy who I frequently listened to on the radio is related to one of the best and most colorful and most controversial pitchers of my time. Watching McLain pitch and listening to Boudreau talk baseball were two pleasures in my life, and to think that they were related intrigued me.

As my baseball IQ grew, so did my appreciation for Boudreau. His colleague for many years, Jack Brickhouse, boasted of Boudreau, "I defy any listener who listens to Lou Boudreau broadcast a game and NOT learn something." True, and I have proof. In my later years of playing baseball I was relegated to the outfield. I recall a routine play that gave me fits: a high lazy pop fly between me and the infield. I'd make the play, but was bugged by the fact that as I hustled in to make the catch, the ball always seemed to be bouncing in the air. It turned an easy out into a challenging play. Then one day another distressed outfielder brought this exact same problem to Mr. Boudreau's attention. Lou suggested that to eliminate this bouncing dilemma that the outfielder should run on the balls of his feet. I tried doing this and discovered that my life in the outfield just got a whole lot better. Just like that. Makes me wonder how many other times and in what other ways Boudreau helped players improve their game.

Veteran poise. Rookies have unbridled enthusiasm (or at least they should), sophomores have their jinxes, and veterans have poise. Boudreau had this quality in spades. There was this time in the late innings of a close game, his partner (I don't believe it was Vince Lloyd) got very excited about a fairly routine play that the Cubs handled easily. Boudreau calmly advised his sidekick to relax and that everything's okay. Minor incident? Yes and no. On one hand it is merely a singular comment from a meaningless game. (Let's face it—if the Cubs were playing a game in the 70's, it was probably meaningless). But on a broader scale, I pictured Boudreau as manager and how he probably had to calm the fears of players in his charge, putting them at ease just like he did with his broadcasting partner. He knew that poise is vital to maintain equilibrium when things aren't going well, to survive the storms so to speak, and to perform well when the opportunity arises. All this on the field from the boy manager, the shift inventor, and the Hall-of-Famer. And off the field, with McLain as a son-in-law with daughter Sharon his bride, Lou probably had many opportunities to have his poise tested.

GAME 80: PHILADELPHIA PHILLIES VS. CHICAGO CUBS
TUESDAY, JUNE 26

Catholics are big on penance, and they believe that suffering can be redemptive. So why not watch the Phillies hammer the Cubs one more time this decade?

Truth be said, it's easy to see how this Philadelphia team contended every year and won it all in '80. Imagine you're a pitching coach and your starter is set to face this lineup: Bake McBride, Larry Bowa, Pete Rose (Pete Rose—why 3rd?), Mike Schmidt, Greg Luzinski, Greg Maddox, Manny Trillo, and Bob Boone. Now what the heck could you as pitching coach possibly tell him? You either have an above average offensive player, an All-Star, or a Hall-of-Famer at every position. Overkill, that's what it is. If you guaranteed me that Schmidt would get at least four at-bats at Wrigley Field with the wind blowing out, I'd take my chances with him and eight of us from IC High School provided we'd have Lefty Carlton pitching. Yet suffering at the hands of this lineup for many years, the one guy (excluding Schmidt) that I did not want to see batting with the game on the line was Bob Boone. I thought he was a big-time clutch hitter and his sons weren't too bad, either.

Offensively the Cubs had a monster of their own in the middle of their lineup, Dave Kingman. Healthy all year, Kong would belt one less homer this year than the entire Houston Astro *team*. You could look it up. And giving Kingman some protection was Jerry Martin hitting fifth. With Buckner batting third, Kingman would often bat with men on base. The Cubs had a major league offense this year, something that couldn't always be said in the 70's.

Take this game, for example. With two outs in the fifth, Kingman singles, Martin homers, and a couple batters later Barry Foote doubles home Steve Ontiveros. So at the end of 5 the Cubs lead 3-0. I'm ready to leave and count it as a half-win.

But alas, Mike Schmidt has two more at bats. Of course he homers, this time to cap off a four run sixth. Bob Boone adds an insurance tater in the 9th. Final score: Phillies 5, Cubs 3. It's like Lent in June.

GAMES 81 & 82: HOUSTON ASTROS VS. CHICAGO CUBS
SATURDAY, JULY 7

The Cubs are to the Phillies as the Astros are to the Cubs, at least when I go to the game. Historically, the Cubs played terribly in the Astrodome, and that's being kind. Yet it seems that they more than made up for it when they played Houston at Wrigley Field. And playing twice today without having to face Joe Niekro, who was a genuine knuckle ball star at this point in his career, or J.R. Richard, who was a pitching freak with over 600 K's in two seasons, I like the Cubs' chances.

Game 1

Is it better to be too young or too old? (I'll pause and allow time for reflection).

Coach Mike Ditka of da Bears frequently began a philosophical point with these two words, "In life ..." I shall now copy that style: In life, a person in his career has years of peak performance. He is at the apex of productivity, glad that obstacles and adversity faced in getting to this point did not cause him to quit or look for other employment. Prior to this prime period, he's too young and is often groping to find his way. After the optimal time, when this same person seems to be owning the world, things start to decline. Studies show gradual decline creeps in at 30, more rapid decline at 35. So now let me repeat the question: "Is it better to be too young and haven't quite reached the top of your ability yet, or is it better to be too old and to be on the down side of the Ferris wheel?"

I'm guessing that in the world of major league baseball, executives if forced to choose one would probably opt for "too young." They'll likely endure the immaturity, the mistakes, the over aggressiveness, etc. because the future promises to be better than the present. After all, there is the celebrated "Rookie of the Year" award, but none for "Geezer of the Year".

On the other hand, experience goes a long way, even if it's too much experience. Unflappability is a marvelous word and a splendid quality to possess (and yes, it is a word, I looked it up). A person past his prime but still functioning has so much to fall back on. It's almost as if a sixth or a seventh sense takes over and they let their body go into auto-pilot, not wanting to interfere with what it knows. They can step aside and see things that are going to happen well before they actually do. Brett Favre, in his waning days, informed the mob of reporters that … "I do know what to do. It's a matter of my body being able to do it."

Kenny Holtzman in the Durocher years epitomized the kid with unlimited potential. He pitched in the majors while still a teen. He was a perfect 9-0 at 21, and he tossed two no-hitters by age 25. If I had a dollar for every time I heard him compared to Sandy Koufax, I'd have two bleacher tickets to the next Cub game with enough money left over for a hot dog and a bag of peanuts. And while Holtzman fell short of reaching Koufax status (like everyone else), he did enjoy a fine career. For what it's worth: Holtzman did wind up with nine more career victories than Koufax: 174 to 165. You might win some money on those stats, if you ask it cleverly enough.

As a kid growing up watching black and white television, I distinctly remember Holtzman pitching the second game of Sunday double-headers. Maybe this was Durocher's way of breaking him in easy, as the regulars often sat out the nightcap. Advantage pitcher. I can still see #30 rotate his body as no other pitcher—a style so unique and so hard to imitate. My friends could do Fergie, I imitated Hands, but no one even attempted Holtzman. Come to think of it, the great lefties from the Sox—guys like Gary Peters, Tommy John, and before them, Billy Pierce—had these fluid and original deliveries as well. Joel Horlen, the righty, we could handle, but the southpaws were beyond us. And this Cub southpaw, with his "12 to 6" curve ball, piled up a lot of strikeouts in the second games of doubleheaders. Makes me wonder how well that 9-0 season in '67 might have turned out if it wasn't cut short by military duty.

Fast forward to 1979. Holtzman doesn't play for Durocher any more, but for Herman Franks. No, he doesn't have the infield of Santo-Kessinger-Beckert-Banks behind him. (Those four names in that sequence just roll off the tongue). No, he doesn't have Hands and Jenkins along side him in the rotation. No, his stuff is no longer unhittable. No, he definitely isn't a kid; and no, he's no longer compared to Koufax.

But yes, he has played on teams that won World Series championships—three in fact. And yes, he had a significant role in that success--with Catfish

Hunter, Vida Blue and Blue Moon Odom—they comprised an outstanding rotation. And yes, he played in the other league for quality clubs like Oakland, Baltimore and New York. So yes, while Holtzman was past his prime, he could rely on his wealth of experience and put these upstart Astros in their place.

And he did, at least today. Aside from being the first and not the second game of the doubleheader, it seemed like old times. This elder Holtzman held Houston in check by scattering three measly singles (remember, as a team Houston had 49 homers). Offensively the Cubs pestered Houston to death, with 6 runs on 13 singles and one double. Scot Thompson led the way with a 5 for 5 performance. But the day belonged to the experience on the mound; vintage Holtzman as he let his defense do the work. He struck out only two Astroids (which are two more strikeouts than he claimed in his no-hitter in '69). One Astro reached second base, one Astro reached third base, but no Astros reached home base. He concluded the game by retiring the last ten batters. Not bad for a guy past his prime--this game a true masterpiece.

Game 2

My theory that pitching has the edge in the nightcap holds true today. Well, at least for one team. Dennis Lamp of the Cubs allows two hits through six innings. For Houston's offense, that's a grand total of 5 hits and no runs over 15 innings of baseball. This impotence comes against a guy who's past his prime and another guy who won't reach his prime for a while (Lamp went 11-0 as a reliever with Toronto in '85). By the time Houston finally scored, the Cubs were comfortably ahead after batting around in the second inning and jumping out to an 8-0 lead. Lamp shined brightly, but he was not the only star of the game. Mike Vail, the right handed hitting right fielder who played against lefties, slugged a two run homer. He and Thompson combined for a perfect 8 for 8 performance from the right field position over both games. The Astros scratched out a few runs late, but that was it.

Final scores: Chicago 6-8, Houston 0-3.

GAME 83: DETROIT TIGERS VS. CHICAGO WHITE SOX THURSDAY, JULY 12

"I knew we were in trouble when I saw people climbing down the foul pole."

This quote, my brother's eyewitness account of Disco Demolition night, pretty much says it all. The yellow foul pole in Old Comiskey stood a couple stories high. Like a scene from a zombie movie, folks stoned out of their mind were trying to navigate their way to the field below by shinnying down something that was probably never climbed before or since. My brother, a red-blooded anti-disco and classic rock enthusiast, could appreciate tonight's attraction in several ways. For a small fee (I think it was 99 cents because the rock station sponsoring this had 99 in its call number) anyone could attend the Sox-Tiger doubleheader, provided that they bring a disco '45' that was to be sacrificed between games *in center field*. That's right—first a ballgame, then a literal demolition of records on the field of play, and then another ballgame. To use the words my dad often said to me, and the words I have sometimes spoken to my kids, "What were you thinking?"

For 99 cents and a song, literally, every druggie within a 100 mile radius gets to unload his angst toward music he loathed. Heck, Mr. Veeck, why not have nickel beer and nickel bag night to go along with it? Looking back, I think the White Sox organization got off easy with only having the second game cancelled. It's a minor miracle that the entire ballpark wasn't razed.

Sources say that the audience this evening was not your typical baseball crowd. Fans got the sense that the ballgame served as the warmup act to the explosion of records. (I guess records were made to be broken). It was kind of like sitting through a set of Barry Manilow songs when the main act everyone wanted to see was Black Sabbath. I don't know if the Guinness Book of Records people who keep track of everything keep track of records being blowed up, but the way this event went down, I doubt that there'll ever be a second try at it.

Game one, won by the Tigers, excited the crowd as much as that "Mandy" song. But soon after the final out, the fun began. The DJ who led this assault to topple disco queens and kings everywhere was dressed in army fatigues. Shouldn't that tell you something right there? It's one thing to have the Village

People to do it, but it's quite another to have the MC decked out this way. It just fanned the flames of folks whose sobriety left them hours ago.

Here's another scenario: think of a Friday afternoon in a high school from the 1970's and you're the teacher. The bell rings, so now it's officially the weekend. As students leap from their desks and sprint to the door, knocking each other over as if at a Who concert, you remember that there's this home-work assignment you want them to do. You call out to your students to return to their seats. They don't. So you raise your voice a little above the din and try again. Still nothing. Finally you scream, "Your assignment for Monday is to read chapter 7 and answer the review questions."

Now how many papers do you think you'll be receiving come Monday?

Think of Bill Veeck as that teacher. He requested, pleaded, cajoled, and begged the fans to return to their seats. At one point he got on the PA and asked the fans to please get off the foul poles, according to my brother. Think of the absurdity. "Please get down off the foul poles," sounds to me like a teacher saying "Please stop passing that bong around in the back of the room." How did it ever get to this point? Now if 20-30 typical students turn a deaf ear to a teacher's plea when the bell rings, how is a motley mob of burnouts going to respond *once* the field has been taken over? Something like, "Oh, sorry Mr. Veeck. Yeah, I'll just climb *up* the foul pole back to my seat. My bad."

Poor Veeck. This attraction was the brainchild of his son, Mike, but of course as owner he feels the heat, literally, as center field is now on fire. So he tries another course of action. He starts singing "Take Me Out to the Ballgame" in an attempt to tame the troops. Probably as effective as singing "Kumbaya" at Alcatraz. But with the outfield now ablaze one could see smoke ascending from the grass as the participants smoked all kinds of grass. Nero fiddled while Rome burned, and Veeck sang while Comiskey burned.

To be playing the Tigers, of all teams. Could you think of a manager more indignant at these turn of events than Detroit's skipper, Sparky Anderson? Sparky has this penchant for going over the top with opinions on foolish things, like comparing his good players to legends. He once said Kirk Gibson is the next Mickey Mantle and his catcher Matt Nokes is heir apparent to

Johnny Bench. How do you think he'd handle this Veeck wreck in center field?

Not well. He wasn't caught up in the anti-disco spirit. He declared the field was unplayable for the second game. I seriously doubt if he was asked before giving his opinion. Nevertheless, the umpiring staff agreed. Word of this travesty travelled quickly. Sox forfeit the game. On this night I'm visiting my cousin, and we're chatting away over the background banter of Jack Brickhouse broadcasting the Cub game on TV. Suddenly, his voice changes. The kind of thing that caught your attention immediately, like a bulletin flash coming across the screen. His voice took on a solemnity you just didn't hear unless something really bad happened. "Uh-oh," I fear, "who's been shot?"

With more disgust than I thought Brickhouse had in him, he reports: "The second game of the White Sox-Tiger doubleheader has been cancelled." He goes on to give the reason why, pauses, and then adds, **"You call this baseball!!"** Jack was ticked, very seldom have I ever hear him speak in such a manner.

The closest may have been a bench-clearing brawl when he says in utter abhorrence, "Oh, this is a beaut! A real beaut!!" as players on both sides try to maim the opposition with haymakers and uppercuts.

But the voice he used tonight was worse. I'm sure parents from coast to coast reacted similarly. But being a kid, I couldn't share their condemnations. I didn't burst out laughing because people might have been hurt and we didn't have the details. Once we learned that there were no casualties save for the forfeit of a baseball game, I thought there was more than a little overreacting by the adult world. In all honesty, I found the matter amusing, like something out of a Monty Python skit.

Or better yet, a family dinner. I recall one Christmas in the 70's I asked for and received Cheech and Chong's Wedding Album. I smiled upon tearing off the wrap and thanked Santa profusely. Nothing celebrates the birth of my Savior more than an album produced by a couple of stoners. So I thought it would be a wonderful idea to listen to these comics during our Christmas dinner that featured roast beef and all the trimmings. I place the album on the hi-fi and turned up the volume so we could hear in the next room. Halfway through the meal, I started spitting out my roasted potatoes and ounces of milk came rushing through my nose as I listened to Cheech and Chong do their thing. I couldn't control my laughter at their outrageous material. To call their stuff "PG-13" would be a serious understatement. My dad, far from a righteous prude, insisted that we turn on something else and threatened that we return Santa's gift to the record store. Before dessert came around I flew into action by putting a halt to Cheech & Chong's inappropriateness and re-placing it with songs by Andy Williams. That bought me some time to save this album from my disapproving folks—they were right, of course, but I was a kid who valued few things more than laughter.

That's how I saw, and still see, people's disgust with the Disco Demolition episode. To the best of my ability I sympathize with the outrage that some folks display, but there's stuff that's much worse. Was the event totally impru-dent and ill-conceived? You bet. But at the end of the day, it's one less baseball game and that's about it—no one died and I doubt if anyone was scarred for life. They even played the following day.

GAME 84: DETROIT TIGERS VS. CHICAGO WHITE SOX
SATURDAY, JULY 14

Quick now—tell me who the United States hockey team defeated in 1980 to claim the gold medal. Hurry, don't even think of looking this up. Okay, if you proudly said the Soviet Union, take your proud self and go stand in the corner. That's the primary opponent in the movie Miracle, and that is the team that everyone remembers the U.S. defeating. That's the game where the goalie (Jim Craig) is draped in the American flag and all the players are engaged in wild celebrations. But defeating the Soviets was the semi-final game. Strange how this gold medal is like the P.S. at the bottom of a letter, but it is. Playing and defeating Sweden is what got the gold for Team USA.

That paragraph is a bit of a prelude to the game I went to a couple of nights after the infamous Disco Demolition. Everyone remembers the chaos from that evening, but I relish the game played two days later. You see, my brother not only got to see Disco Record Inferno, but as an added bonus, he scored free tickets to another game. And that would be on Saturday as my friend Kyle and I make our way to the healing ballpark.

The plan was to take in a game and then meet some friends at an Irish bar downtown. Coincidentally, the theme for this particular contest was Irish-American night. Now these promotions, I thought, were shrewd and fairly entertaining. Bill Veeck, fully aware of his blue collar ethnic fan base, would occasionally designate certain games for certain nationalities. He offered an "Italian-American Night," "Polish-American Night," and "Latin-American Night," among others that would be sure to highlight and celebrate different cultures. Clothes, music, dance, food, and a few politically incorrect jokes all showed up.

Some things worth noting: First, the ballpark didn't seem badly damaged at all. It was going to take more than thousands of druggies blowing up records to take down this baseball "Palace." Besides, old Comiskey used to host concerts in the outfield, so their pastures were hardly pure and pristine. I remember groups like "Foreigner" and "Aerosmith" performing on some hot days (my co-worker Alan used to go to them and fill me in. Once I heard there was a fairly serious fire in the upper deck regions of the ballpark.

Another time, Jimmy Piersall, Harry Caray's sidekick, once promoted an up-coming concert by informing the audience that the 'Foreigners' are coming to Comiskey Park to do a concert. I picture Jimmy turning to Caray between innings and asking him off-air, "Harry, why are we letting these foreigners on our field?"). If the old palace could take concert abuse in stride, surely some unruliness and record demoliton on the field was not going to cause irreparable damage.

Then next thing I recollect from this Saturday night game had to do with the noise. How could a lean crowd create such a racket? The stands were more than half empty as the dog days dragged on, but in terms of sheer volume I doubt if I ever heard Comiskey louder, and that includes a playoff game in '83. Every tally by the home team was supported with a thunderous explosion by the faithful fans. Today scoreboards across the country have to implore fans to make some noise. Bah.

Finally, Claudell Washington. The talented, well-travelled, and under-achieving Claudell Washington. After his playing days with the Sox concluded, some loyalists in the right field lower deck unfurled a banner on occasion that simply read: "Washington Slept Here." But this was Claudell's night as he homered not once, not twice, but thrice. This makes two times in one summer that I witnessed a hometown hero blast three long balls in one game. (The other incident I will describe to you in detail shortly). What made this even more impressive is the fact that he blasted them at the Grand Canyon of ballparks, Comiskey, where long fly balls go to die on the warning track. Speaking of which, Washington almost had the night of nights as one of the deep drives he hit was caught by the right fielder with his feet about six feet from the wall. Not too many cheapies here, and with each home run, Irish enthusiasm reaches a higher level in the stands. Washington and the Sox blasted their way to an easy 12-4 triumph, which happened to be the only White Sox victory in this infamous four game set.

THE GAME: PHILADELPHIA PHILLIES VS. CHICAGO CUBS
THURSDAY, MAY 24

"No, honest, this is a major league ballpark."

Seems like I spent a lot of time defending the legitimacy of Wrigley Field. Whether it'd be Sox fans who hated the Cubs, or out-of-towners who didn't quite appreciate the "deep" power alley of 368', I frequently fought off charges of this beloved "rinky-dink" landmark. A 15-14 defeat of the Big Red Machine just had to happen at home. These Tee-ball scores would make me defensive, as anti-Cub people said that these "unprofessional" and "Little League" results were merely a reflection of the home team's caliber of play.

But later in life a few things seemed to cool these attacks. The first had to do with wind direction. It just seemed as I got older that the wind blew *in* with more regularity. To support this hunch, a report surfaced showing that over a significant period of time (multiple seasons, I believe) the wind blew in three times as often as it blew out.

Then more homer happy ballparks emerged—precisely, one in each league. Coors Field in Colorado has probably done more harm than good to the Rockie hitter legacies over the years. For if the player in question excels as a hitter, he's not taken as seriously because of the way the ball carries in Colorado. And then there's U.S. Cellular Field, home of the Chisox. I can't remember seeing so many baseballs leave the premises over an expanded period of time. In recent years I seldom hear Sox fans bashing Wrigley Field as a bandbox, because they now know that their ballpark is worse. An oddity is when a well-hit ball on the South Side doesn't end up in the seats—the norm is that any well struck ball is gone. ERA's across both leagues have settled down, but there was a time when baseball scores resembled half-time scores from the NFL, if not the NBA. And while Wrigley has had way more than its share of slugfests, I no longer have to defend it the way I did in the past. But on this day in 1979, all arguments defending Wrigley Field's legitimacy were futile. I attended this game with several classmates who were hours away from college graduate status, and for at least one of them, this was their first encounter with the Friendly Confines.

Future grad #1: "The goal is to drink one beer per inning."

Future grad #2: "Why?" (The question was raised not in protest, or even surprise, but for the sake of friendly conversation).

Future grad #3: "Because it's the only way that this game will have meaning."

I'm thinking how proud their philosophy profs would be with such meta-physical reasoning. Who says you'd never use this stuff in the real world?

7-6 after one inning. On a warm day in late spring with the wind blowing out at 17 MPH, the hitters, bleacher fans, and beer vendors rejoice. My scorecard's already a mess, and with zero chance of rain, there are at least 45 more outs to go. I never liked it when a team batted around, because … A) it was usually against the Cubs or White Sox, and B) it made me make a difficult scorekeeping decision: do I place the second at-bat in the following inning or do I squish it together in one box for the same inning? Such big-time executive decisions would prepare me well for the world of business management, I thought. But neither scorekeeping option appealed to me as the Phillies resumed making a mockery of Cub pitching. Phillie hitters struggled more in batting practice than during the game. However as the Cubs answered with six of their own, it didn't take a degree in mathematics to realize that both clubs' ERA's were going to take a big hit.

21-9. That's an embarrassing score in the fat guys' softball league. But 21-9 was indeed the score of the Phils' lead in the middle innings. Three touchdowns allowed with only three field goals gained. Hardly competitive, but if you had to be losing by twelve runs, wouldn't it be better to trail 21-9 instead of 12-0?

But stuff started happening. A couple home runs here and there makes the score less atrocious. Nothing like three three-run innings and a six spot thrown in for good measure to tighten things up. As in any circus, there always seems to be an act or two that stands out. In this game, the runner-up memory goes to one Barry Foote, or as one of my roommates and I called him, Hairy Foote. We even tossed around the idea one night of making a banner and bringing it to the game which would simply read: WE HAVE A HAIRY FOOTE FETISH. Well, Hairy or not, Foote gave us a thrill as he cracked a double down the left field line and chased a runner across the plate. Now in a game like this a run scoring double stands out as much as a summer mosquito in Wisconsin. But what made this special was Hairy's approach into second base. The record books show that Hairy weighed 205 pounds. Yeah, right, just like I can bench 800 pounds. Heck, Hairy's left leg weighed over 200 pounds. Anyway, all that squatting and all that running of 140 feet tuckered out Hairy, so for the last 35 feet or so before second base he stopped running and walked the rest of the way. You know how it is when something really isn't that funny but you laugh hysterically anyway? Well, that's how this scene was. My roommate (the one with the Hairy Fetish) looked at me and just started cracking up. I did too; giddiness just seemed to fit the moment, the game, and the entire experience.

A few more Foote notes need to be shared. I recall reading in the off-season that key personnel in the front office waxed enthusiastically how the organization has sought far and wide for a large person to handle the catching responsibilities. Specifically, a behemoth behind the plate was wanted so that on those collisions at home plate, the Cub catcher would not be on the losing end. It was one of those statements where I first nodded upon reading it but then came to my senses and said, and I quote, "WHAT??!!" You're either completely snowing us, your fan base, or you're serious and perhaps putting together a search committee to find a catcher with size. Wouldn't it be wiser to find a catcher with talent? Think about it, how many violent collisions per year occur when the runner charging home tries to dislodge the ball by dismembering the catcher? Six? Ten? Twelve? So we're investing time and money on a guy who's not going to be knocked silly for a handful of plays? What about the dozens of times a runner from the opposing team steals or the hundreds of times a catcher bats with men on base? Shouldn't those considerations come first? I tell you, with that kind of master planning in the Cub front office, it's a wonder that the Cubs lose only 90-100 games every year.

On the upside, my roommate now gets his hairy foote fetish satisfied, and we get a hearty laugh watching this burly bear of a Cub walk to second base.

Top billing of the day belonged to #10 on the Cubs. After Santo and before Leon Durham, #10 belonged to Dave Kingman. Now he's gotten ample space already in this text, but just to get you caught up, Dave, the media's darling, slugged two homers in the early frames that cleared the fence by plenty. As he faces Ron Reed in the later innings, he really lets loose. To follow the flight of the ball would have reminded me of following rockets soaring from Cape Canaveral, except that I've never been to Cape Canaveral. It wasn't so much excitement as it was astonishment. Mouths open. Eyes stare. Beers almost drop. Incredible blast—in fifty years of attending games I've only seen one come close to it—Sammy Sosa blasting a ball on a Sunday afternoon against Hideo Nomo. But Sammy's did not reach the third house beyond Waveland; Kingman's did. Reports say the ball travelled 530 feet. I believe that as much as Barry Foote weighing 205 pounds. I've walked that distance from the bleachers outside Wrigley to that house Kingman reached, and burned many calories doing so. I think it might have had the length of two home runs. It was a blast for the ages in this game for the ages.

But it was Buckner, not Kingman, who was almost the difference maker. Hobbling to the batter's box comes Billy Buck, the guy with the gimpy leg, the guy who loves to play the game. He bats with the bags loaded facing Tug McGraw. As mentioned earlier, this is a time when the scoring in baseball can be delightful for its originality. Neither Bobby Hull nor Wayne Gretzky could ever claim four tallies with one shot, but right here and now, Billy Buck did just that (perhaps that's why I've yet to see the Blackhawks come back from a 21-9 deficit). One swing, and wah-lah, four Cubbies trot around the bases (or more accurately, three trot and one limps).

And then it was Foote's liner down the left field line that knots the score at 22. We're delirious. It's not every day you're down by 12 and come back to tie the score. To give up 22 runs and be tied is unusual, even at Wrigley Field. You might think if a team outscores it opponents 13-1 in the latter stages of the game, pure momentum would push the total to 14, sending the home crowd home happy.

But alas, the Cubs hit the wall, do not go ahead, and now I'm nervous. Ever notice when you're down by 12 that the pressure is off, but when you come back to tie, the pressure is back on? I got the old feeling of "Oh, no" when the Cubs failed to grab the lead, and I don't think I was alone. One thing worried me—#20 for the Phillies was still in the Philly lineup (memo to Phillie manager: shouldn't you rest your regulars when you're ahead by so much?)

Put this in analogy form: Mike Schmidt is to Wrigley Field & Cub pitching as _?_ is to _?_. What would be the best fit? The Globetrotters are to the Generals? Super Bowls are to Buffalo? Politicians are to integrity?

Two outs, nobody on base, tie game, and arguably the best reliever in the game—Bruce Sutter—facing Schmidt. What happens? Schmidt whiffs and Kong slugs his 4th homer in walk-off fashion as the ball sails over the center field scoreboard? This would be my ending. But corny endings can only happen in movies, I guess, so Schmidt homers. The Cubs are then retired *in order for the second straight inning.* There was this joke in the early 60's that goes like this: Len tells Greg that the pitcher on the Mets just threw a no-hitter (fictional). So Greg looks at Len and asks, "Did the Mets win?" (to be a nerd and ruin the joke, I'd like to say that I nearly attended a game where a pitcher for a New York team threw a no-hitter and lost the game. His name is Andy Hawkins, and it happened on July 1, 1990 in Old Comiskey). So now the joke goes like this—Stan tells Paul that the Cubs scored 22 runs today (nonfictional). Paul asks, "Did the Cubs win?" Please explain how a team can score **seven** times the mean score in a sport and still manage to lose?

Epilogue

So what do we make of baseball in the 70's? How do we label it? What are its contributions? Where does it stand compared to the decades surrounding it? How well will it be remembered?

How about this for the 70's label: Baseball in flux. The one universal constant is change, yet change defines some eras better than others. Baseball was never just a game, but the 70's almost scoff at the notion of baseball as game. I think with a careful look one can make a case that the economics of baseball was forever changed in this decade. Obviously Curt Flood's litigation and the emergence of free agency changed the landscape permanently. But money played a part in so many other ways; it changed the way players played. For instance, it no longer was an embarrassment to strike out. The days of a ballplayer slugging home runs as often as whiffing were never common (Joe DiMaggio being one exception) but once upon a time there was a stigma attached to the 'K'. I recall coaching a fine ballplayer in high school who set for himself the goal to never strike out for the entire season. I started to laugh but caught myself when I saw that he meant it. He didn't reach this goal, but came close. I wonder how many young players entertain such thoughts today. For decades now many batters will not adjust with two strikes; they'll swing from the heels if the count is 0-2, 3-0, or anything in between. Conversely, watch the congratulations a player receives for a successful sacrifice bunt. War heroes aren't honored as much. The reason is economical on two fronts: what is rare is precious and successful bunts are rare. Secondly, home run hitters' cars are the envy of everyone (chicks and agents dig the long ball). Earl Weaver and chicks may not dig small ball, but it has its place. Remember when Ernie Banks used to fake a bunt to draw in the third basemen? Let me know the last time you saw a 500 home run slugger square to bunt.

I can't argue that the 70's was Baseball's Golden Era. Not even close. I think that distinction goes to its older brothers from the 50's and 60's. I'm partial to the 60's because that's when I fell in love with the game (see Like Night and Day). The 60's were special—someone mentioned that more Hall-of-Famers played at this time than at any other. And there was the balance. Once the Yankee Empire melted like the Wicked Witch in the first half of the decade, no one team could claim a repeat championship. Pirates in 1960, then Yankees, Yankees, Dodgers, Cardinals, Dodgers, Orioles, Cardinals, Tigers, and Mets. As a bonus, an epic pennant race rivets us in 1967 as four American League teams battled to the last weekend, and three of them to the final day. You had your bad teams that never contended, but a few did, at least once in ten years. Like the Cubs and Mets.

In the 70's, with expansion to 24 teams, champions were anything but dark horses. First the A's, then the Reds, and for the second part of the decade you had the Yankees, Dodgers, Royals, and Phillies battling. With such little drama and suspense, it was almost as if you could cancel the regular season and have these four clubs play each other. Not nearly as much fun.

And compared to the 60's, the 70's came up significantly short on pitching. Heck, the rules had to be changed because of pitching's total dominance. Were there good pitchers in the 70's? Of course, but in '68 can you tell me how many .300 hitters dwelled in the American League? One, and with an average of .301, that barely qualifies. But that's what Yaz did, to win his second consecutive batting crown (until Miguel Cabrera, Yaz in '67 was the last Triple Crown winner). How can you fault the hitters when they faced folks like Gibson, Koufax, Marichal, Seaver, and Jenkins in one league, with Palmer, Hunter, Chance, McLain, and Peters in the other?

Nevertheless the 1950's did not have something that 60's did—expansion. And while the 60's had remarkable balance and performers, especially pitchers, it could claim a list of lemons for teams. Throughout the 60's the Mets, Astros, Angels and Kansas City (first Athletics and then Royals) seldom won.

Throw in traditional second division clubs like the Senators, Indians, Phillies and Cubs, and you had plenty of patsies. But the previous decade had its issues, too. Virtually no American League balance in the 50's, as the Yankees appear in every World Series excluding '54 and '59. How can that be good?

When it came to choosing which decade boasted better players, I think it's a coin flip. Look at who flourished in the 50's: Williams, Musial, Mantle and Mays. Banks and Aaron. Snider and Kaline. And South Side small ballers like Fox, Aparicio, and Pierce. All marvelous at what they did. And don't forget the traditional ballparks that add so much to urban identity like the Polo Grounds and Ebbetts Field. Tough to argue against all that evidence.

So I'm about 50/50 on the 50's as Baseball's Golden Era. Be it the 60's or the 50's, both were much better than the decade of this book. Close your eyes. When I say baseball in the 70's, what do you see? Here's what I get: funky uniforms with even funkier hair and lots of grass—the artificial kind and the kind you smoke. And some decent baseball. Without much competition for the five or six perennial contenders, the regular season could be hard to sustain fan interest, save for the occasional blip of the "South Side Hit Men" or a 23-22 game. And it just wasn't in Chicago, in the 70's up to three quarters of the teams were reduced to spoiler roles in August.

Why wasn't Chicago competitive? The Cubs were in the early years of the decade. Holdovers from the dynamic days of the sixties, with Durocher at the helm, gave fans a reason to hope. But the household names never quite got it done, and the Cubs went through a painful process of rebuilding. Since fans on the North Side flocked to the games you'd think they'd have the capital to get and retain quality players to replace the ones from the 60's. Alas, that didn't happen. How driven can the club be toward winning when players like Steve Swisher, George Mitterwald, Pete LaCock and even a Vic Harris started a substantial number of games? Yet fans kept paying to see such mediocrity.

The Sox had Bill Veeck. That right there would sell tickets. Sometimes baseball seemed to be an afterthought with cow milking contests and short pants, but wouldn't a guy with his guile find a way to sneak into the postseason at least once? Sorry, '77 was their best shot, but even then they were pretenders whenever they did anything except bat.

Perhaps, too, Bill Veeck had a little Connie Mack in him. Mack candidly reported once that he'd prefer to have a ballclub in contention for the first half of the year to whet fan interest. Then, fade toward the end of the season and finish in third or fourth place. Why? So he wouldn't have to pay his players as much if they had won. Mack's transparency is refreshing, and I wonder how common it is among baseball barons.

In spite of the aforementioned Cub players mired in mediocrity, some quality players did surface, just not enough of them. I can identify four right away—Bill Madlock who played and then was replaced by Bobby Murcer. And can't forget Rick Monday, who exchanged places with a gimpy but very capable player in Bill Buckner. Pity that these four quality players couldn't grace the lineup simultaneously. But the Cubs finally had a huge drawing card when they signed the much maligned Dave Kingman. Say what you will about him, and the sportswriters never tire of saying bad things about him, Kingman commanded attention. If he batted, the trip to the fridge or the concession stand would have to wait. When he stepped into the batter's box he was in scoring position. Kong was ahead of his time in constantly swinging for the fences; it didn't matter if he had zero strikes, one strike, or two strikes, he, the pitcher, and everyone paying attention knew that he was one swing away from a mammoth home run. Of course, he'd often find himself one swing and a miss away from a humble retreat to the dugout. Not shortening your swing is common today, but in the 70's you could really see most hitters concede power with two strikes in order to make contact. Not Kong. He was one of those boppers that when he batted, he wasn't just trying to make contact.

But Kong couldn't carry Cubs. I doubt if Babe Ruth *and* Hank Aaron could. Pitching and defense, right? Those two minutiae always seem to get away from us. How could the Cubs expect to compete when Rick Reuschel wasn't starting or Bruce Sutter wasn't relieving? But for a decade, it seemed, the Cubs ran tired arms, inexperienced arms, inconsistent arms and rag arms out to the mound. Would they have won with another stud pitcher? Probably not, but it might have tightened things up.

As for the White Sox? In truth, it was hard to take them seriously. Even with the fun in '77, the Sox just did not have enough. With the Ralph Garrs,

Alan Bannisters, and Jorge Ortas scrapping out every tidbit of production from their offensive skill set, they scarcely broke even with their offensive defense. In the early 70's, Carlos May, Dick Allen, and Bill Melton could hit. If only Wilbur Wood could pitch every day (it seemed for a while he was pitching every other day), the Sox might really have something. But this window shut quickly, as Allen, proclaimed by many to be the best ballplayer they played with or against, just didn't have staying power. This baseball gypsy ended up playing on six different clubs from 1969 to '77. (FYI: Some baseball experts claim that Allen's inaugural season of 1964 was the finest performance ever turned in by a rookie in the history of the sport).

I'm reminded by long-suffering White Sox fans that theirs is frequently a litany of "if only's." If only Carlos May did not lose part of his thumb and with it, his power, in a military accident. If only they had more patience with a talented but erratic reliever in Goose Gossage. If only Wilbur Wood's career didn't end pre-maturely with a line drive off the bat of Ron LeFlore that shattered his kneecap. (Notice how long knuckleballers like Hoyt Wilhelm stuck around). If only Jim Kaat was closer to his prime when he pitched for the Sox. If only the corps of Britt Burns, Rich Dotson, and Lamar Hoyt could have started their careers earlier so they could perform in '77 the way they did in '83. If only, if only ... but the 70's end and the 80's begin with a young Tony LaRussa managing a team with plenty of potential. Not only the aforementioned pitchers, but in the fold an unassuming, incredibly clutch young outfielder in Harold Baines. After many seasons of losing ugly the future promises its fans, at least for a season, a team that wins ugly.

As the Sox broke through in '83, the Cubs finally made it to the postseason in '84. After contending and pretending for a few years, the Cubs wandered in the second division wilderness wallowing below .500 for most of the decade ('77 saw Herman Franks' team finish with an 81-81 mark, causing my dad to exclaim how low the bar is when Chicago fans get excited over their team being as "good as they stink"). But here's something I believe is true: fan euphoria over the Sox and Cubs success in the 80's had much to do with persevering the trials of the 70's.

Economically the 1970's ushered in a new era for all teams, not just the Cubs and Sox. It has never been just a game since free agency. From Astroturf to the DH, from World Series being played at night, baseball decisions are far removed from the days of PK Wrigley, who insisted on reserving thousands of tickets every day for the walk-up crowd. Attractions such as Ladies Day or Senior Citizens Day today? Not a chance. Now, doubleheaders are never scheduled, and if played due to a rain out, they must be split so as not to lose a gate.

So let me leave you with a bit of nostalgic shopping: In 1979, a family of four could sit in the best seats at old Comiskey and not spend a dime more than twenty bucks. And if that family had 2 ladies 14 or older, the whole family could sit in the grandstand section at Wrigley Field for five dollars! Add four hot dogs, two Cokes, two beers, a bag of peanuts, a couple of Frosty Malts, an autographed baseball, and of course a scorecard and a pencil. Your total, ma'am/sir, comes to $11.95. Please pull up.

But wait, there's more. Throw in a couple of bucks for parking the car, with maybe a tip or two to those hard-working vendors, and this family could enjoy the whole baseball experience for something less than $20.00.

.... Years later ....

It's July of 2015. I drive to a baseball game. I spend $25.00 to park the car. Hmmm.

I didn't think about this until now, but on a personal note my life experience in the 70's dovetailed with Major League Baseball, almost to perfection. In my journey, I left behind the simple pre-teens, stumbled through adolescence, and finally had some sense of what I should be doing as the decade draws to a close. Isn't that the same tale of MLB? Bumbling its way through free agency, astro turf, sterile stadiums and funny uniforms? And settling down a bit in the 80's? So while I retain the same name, I'm not the same person. While baseball still uses a five ounce ball, it's not the same sport. Neither of us were ever going to be as young or as innocent. We grew up.

1970   (* denotes league leader)

WHITE SOX

- Final Record: 56-106 (6th place in Western Division)
- Managers: Don Gutteridge (49-97), Bill Adair (4-6), Chuck Tanner (3-13)
- Team Leaders:
  1. Average: Luis Aparacio (.313), Carlos May (.285), Ken Berry (.276)
  2. Home Runs: Bill Melton (33), Ed Herrmann (19), Carlos May (12)
  3. RBI's: Bill Melton (96), Carlos May (68), Ed Herrmann (52)
  4. Pitching Wins: Tommy John (12), Gerry Janeski (10), Wilbur Wood (9)
  5. Pitching ERA: Wilbur Wood (2.80), Tommy John (3.28), Jerry Crider (4.45)
  6. Saves: Wilbur Wood (21)

Season Attendance: 495,355

CUBS

- Final Record: 84-78 (2nd place in Eastern Division)
- Manager: Leo Durocher
- Team Leaders:
  1. Average: Billy Williams (.322), Jim Hickman (.315), Glenn Beckert (.288)
  2. Home Runs: Billy Williams (42), Jim Hickman (32), Ron Santo (26)
  3. RBI's: Billy Williams (129), Jim Hickman (115), Ron Santo (114)
  4. Pitching Wins: Fergie Jenkins (22), Bill Hands (18), Ken Holtzman (17)
  5. Pitching ERA: Milt Pappas (2.68), Ken Holtzman (3.38), Fergie Jenkins (3.39)
  6. Saves: Phil Regan (12)

Season Attendance: 1,642,705

1971

WHITE SOX

- Final Record: 79-83 (3rd place Western Division)
- Manager: Chuck Tanner
  1. Average: Carlos May (.294), Walt Williams (.294), Mike Andrews (.282)
  2. Home Runs: Bill Melton (33)*, Rick Reichardt (19), Jay Johnstone (16)
  3. RBI's: Bill Melton (86), Carlos May (70), Rick Reichardt (62)
  4. Pitching Wins: Wilbur Wood (22), Tom Bradley (15), Tommy John (13)
  5. ERA: Wilbur Wood (1.91), Bart Johnson (2.93), Tom Bradley (2.96)
  6. Saves: Bart Johnson (14)

Season Attendance: 833,891

CUBS

- Final Record: 83-79 (3rd place in Eastern Division)
- Manager: Leo Durocher
- Team Leaders:
  1. Average: Glenn Beckert (.342), Joe Pepitone (.307), Billy Williams (.301)
  2. Home Runs: Billy Williams (28), Ron Santo (21), Jim Hickman (19)
  3. RBI's: Billy Williams (93), Ron Santo (88), Joe Pepitone (61)
  4. Pitching Wins: Fergie Jenkins (24), Milt Pappas (17), Bill Hands (12)
  5. Pitching ERA: Fergie Jenkins (2.77), Bill Hands (3.42), Juan Pizarro (3.48)
  6. Saves: Phil Regan (6)

Season Attendance: 1,653,007

1972

WHITE SOX

- Final Record: 87-67 (2nd place Western Division)
- Manager: Chuck Tanner
    1. Average: Carlos May, Dick Allen (.308), Pat Kelly (.261)
    2. Home Runs: Dick Allen (37)*, Carlos May (12), Ed Herrmann (12)
    3. RBI's: Dick Allen (113)*, Carlos May (68), Mike Andrews (50)
    4. Pitching Wins: Wilbur Wood (24)*, Stan Bahnsen (21), Tom Bradley (15)
    5. ERA: Terry Forster (2.25), Wilbur Wood (2.51), Tom Bradley (2.98)
    6. Saves: Terry Forster (29)

Season Attendance: 1,117,318

CUBS

- Final Record: 83-79 (3rd place Eastern Division)
- Manager: Leo Durocher
    1. Average: Billy Williams (.333)*, Ron Santo (.302), Jose Cardenal (.291)
    2. Home Runs: Billy Williams (37), Ron Santo, Jim Hickman, Jose Cardenal (17)
    3. RBI's: Billy Williams (122), Ron Santo (74), Jose Cardenal (70)
    4. Pitching Wins: Fergie Jenkins (20), Milt Pappas (17), Bill Hands, Burt Hooton (11)
    5. ERA: Milt Pappas (2.77), Burt Hooton (2.80), Rick Reuschel (2.93)
    6. Saves: Jack Aker (17)

Season Attendance: 1,299,163

1973

WHITE SOX

- Final Record: 77-85 (5th place Western Division)
- Manager: Chuck Tanner
    1. Average: Pat Kelly (.280), Bill Melton (.277), Carlos May (.268)
    2. Home Runs: Bill Melton, Carlos May (20), Dick Allen (16)
    3. RBI's: Carlos May (96), Bill Melton (87), Pat Kelly (44)
    4. Pitching Wins: Wilbur Wood (24)*, Stan Bahnsen (18), Cy Acosta (10)
    5. ERA: Cy Acosta (2.23), Terry Forster (3.23), Wilbur Wood (3.46)
    6. Saves: Cy Acosta (18)

Season Attendance: 1,302,527

CUBS

- Final Record: 77-84 (5th place Eastern Division)
- Manager: Whitey Lockman
    1. Average: Jose Cardenal (.303), Billy Williams (.288), Rick Monday, Ron Santo (.267)
    2. Home runs: Rick Monday (26), Billy Williams, Ron Santo (20)
    3. RBI's: Billy Williams (86), Ron Santo (77), Jose Cardenal (68)
    4. Pitching Wins: Fergie Jenkins, Burt Hooton, Rick Reuschel (14)
    5. ERA: Bob Locker (2.55), Rick Reuschel (3.00), Bill Bonham (3.02)
    6. Saves: Bob Locker (18)

Season Attendance: 1,351,705

1974

WHITE SOX

- Final Record: 80-80 (4th place Western Division)
- Manager: Chuck Tanner
    1. Average: Jorge Orta (.316), Dick Allen (.301), Ken Henderson (.292)
    2. Home Runs: Dick Allen (32)*, Bill Melton (21), Ken Henderson (20)
    3. RBI's: Ken Henderson (95), Dick Allen (88), Jorge Orta (67)
    4. Pitching Wins: Jim Kaat (21), Wilbur Wood (20), Stan Bahnsen (12)
    5. ERA: Bart Johnson (2.73), Jim Kaat (2.92), Wilbur Wood (3.60)
    6. Saves: Terry Forster (24)

Season Attendance: 1,149,596

CUBS

- Final Record: 66-96 (6th place Eastern Division)
- Managers: Whitey Lockman (41-54), Jim Marshall (25-44)
    1. Average: Rick Monday (.294), Jose Cardenal (.293), Billy Williams (.280)
    2. Home Runs: Rick Monday (20), Billy Williams (16), Jerry Morales (15)
    3. RBI's: Jerry Morales (82), Jose Cardenal (72), Billy Williams (68)
    4. Pitching Wins: Rick Reuschel (13), Bill Bonham (11), Steve Stone (8)
    5. ERA: Bill Bonham (3.85), Ken Frailing (3.89), Steve Stone (4.13)
    6. Saves: Oscar Zamora (10)

Season Attendance: 1,015,378

1975

WHITE SOX

- Final Record: 75-86 (5th place Western Division)
- Manager: Chuck Tanner
    1. Average: Jorge Orta (.304), Pat Kelly (.274), Carlos May (.271)
    2. Home Runs: Deron Johnson (18), Bill Melton (15), Jorge Orta (11)
    3. RBI's: Jorge Orta (83), Deron Johnson (72), Bill Melton (70)
    4. Pitching Wins: Jim Kaat (20), Wilbur Wood (16), Rich Gossage (9)
    5. ERA: Rich Gossage (1.84), Jim Kaat (3.11), Wilbur Wood (4.11)
    6. Saves: Rich Gossage (26)

Season Attendance: 750,802

CUBS

- Final Record: 75-87 (5th place Eastern Division)
- Manager: Jim Marshall
    1. Average: Bill Madlock (.354)*, Jose Cardenal (.317), Andre Thornton (.293)
    2. Home Runs: Andre Thornton (18), Rick Monday (17), Jerry Morales (12)
    3. RBI's: Jerry Morales (91), Manny Trillo (70), Jose Cardenal (68)
    4. Pitching Wins: Ray Burris (15), Bill Bonham (13), Steve Stone (12)
    5. ERA: Rick Reuschel (3.73), Steve Stone (3.95), Ray Burris (4.12)
    6. Saves: Darold Knowles (15)

Season Attendance: 1,034,819

1976

WHITE SOX

- Final Record: 64-97 (6th place Western Division)
- Manager: Paul Richards
  1. Average: Ralph Garr (.300), Jorge Orta (.274), Bill Stein (.268)
  2. Home Runs: Jorge Orta, Jim Spencer (14), Jack Brohamer (7)
  3. RBI's: Jorge Orta (72), Jim Spencer (70), Bucky Dent (52)
  4. Pitching Wins: Ken Brett (10), Rich Gossage, Bart Johnson (9)
  5. ERA: Ken Brett (3.32), Rich Gossage (3.94), Francisco Barrios (4.31)
  6. Saves: Dave Hamilton (10)

Season Attendance: 914,651

CUBS

- Final Record: 75-87 (4th place Eastern Division)
- Manager: Jim Marshall
  1. Average: Bill Madlock (.339)*, Jose Cardenal (.299), Jerry Morales (.274)
  2. Home Runs: Rick Monday (32), Jerry Morales (16), Bill Madlock (15)
  3. RBI's: Bill Madlock (84), Rick Monday (77), Jerry Morales (67)
  4. Pitching Wins: Ray Burris (15), Rick Reuschel (14), Bill Bonham (9)
  5. ERA: Ray Burris (3.11), Rick Reuschel (3.46), Steve Renko (3.86)
  6. Saves: Bruce Sutter (10)

Season Attendance: 1,026,217

1977

- Final Record: 90-72 (3rd place Western Division)
- Manager: Bob Lemon
  1. Average: Ralph Gar (.300), Oscar Gamble (.297), Richie Zisk (.290)
  2. Home Runs: Oscar Gamble (31), Richie Zisk (30), Eric Soderholm (25)
  3. RBI's: Richie Zisk (101), Jorge Orta (84), Oscar Gamble (83)
  4. Pitching Wins: Steve Stone (15), Francisco Barrios (14), Chris Knapp (12)
  5. ERA: Lerrin LaGrow (2.45), Ken Kravec (4.10), Francisco Barrios (4.13)
  6. Saves: Lerrin LaGrow (25)

Season Attendance: 1,657,135

- Final Record: 81-81 (4th place Eastern Division)
- Manager: Herman Franks
  1. Average: Steve Ontiveros (.299), Larry Biittner (.298), Jerry Morales (.290)
  2. Home Runs: Bobby Murcer (27), Larry Biittner (12), Jerry Morales, Bill Buckner (11)
  3. RBI's: Bobby Murcer (89), Jerry Morales (69), Steve Ontiveros (68)
  4. Pitching Wins: Rick Reuschel (20), Ray Burris (14), Bill Bonham (10)
  5. ERA: Bruce Sutter (1.35), Rick Reuschel (2.79), Willie Hernandez (3.03)
  6. Saves: Bruce Sutter (31)

Season Attendance: 1,439,834

1978

- Final Record: 71-90 (5th place Western Division)
- Managers: Bob Lemon (34-40), Larry Doby (37-50)
    1. Average: Chet Lemon (.300), Ralph Garr (.275), Jorge Orta (.274)
    2. Home Runs: Eric Soderholm (20), Chet Lemon, Jorge Orta (13)
    3. RBI's: Lamar Johnson (72), Eric Soderholm (67), Chet Lemon (55)
    4. Pitching Wins: Steve Stone (12), Ken Kravec (11), Wilbur Wood (10)
    5. ERA: Jim Willoughby (3.86), Francisco Barrios (4.05), Ken Kravec (4.08)
    6. Saves: Lerrin LaGrow (16)

Season Attendance: 1,491,100

- Final Record: 79-83 (3rd place Eastern Division)
- Manager: Herman Franks
    1. Average: Bill Buckner (.323), Bobby Murcer (.281), Ivan DeJesus (.278)
    2. Home Runs: Dave Kingman (28), Bobby Murcer (9), Bill Buckner (5)
    3. RBI's: Dave Kingman (79), Bill Buckner (74), Bobby Murcer (64)
    4. Pitching Wins: Rick Reuschel (14), Mike Krukow, Donnie Moore (9)
    5. ERA: Bruce Sutter (3.18), Dennis Lamp (3.29), Rick Reuschel (3.41)
    6. Saves: Bruce Sutter (27)

Season Attendance: 1,525,311

1979

WHITE SOX

- Final Record: 73-87 (5th place Western Division)
- Managers: Don Kessinger (46-60), Tony LaRussa (27-27)
  1. Average: Chet Lemon (.318), Lamar Johnson (.309), Alan Bannister (.285)
  2. Home Runs: Chet Lemon (17), Jim Morrison (14), Claudell Washington (13)
  3. RBI's: Chet Lemon (86), Lamar Johnson (74), Claudell Washington (66)
  4. Pitching Wins: Ken Kravec (15), Richard Wortham (14), Ross Baumgarten (13)
  5. ERA: Ed Farmer (2.44), Ross Baumgarten (3.53), Francisco Barrios (3.60)
  6. Saves: Ed Farmer (14)

Season Attendance: 1,280,702

CUBS

- Final Record: 80-82
- Managers: Herman Franks (78-77), Joey Amalfitano (2-5)
  1. Average: Dave Kingman (.288), Steve Ontiveros (.285), Bill Buckner (.284)
  2. Home Runs: Dave Kingman (48)*, Jerry Martin (19), Barry Foote (16)
  3. RBI's: Dave Kingman (115), Jerry Martin (73), Bill Buckner (66)
  4. Pitching Wins: Rick Reuschel (18), Lynn McGlothlen (13), Dennis Lamp, Dick Tidrow (11)
  5. ERA: Bruce Sutter (2.23), Dick Tidrow (2.71), Dennis Lamp (3.51)
  6. Saves: Bruce Sutter (37)

Season Attendance: 1,648,587

Boxscores from Memorable Games in the 70's

May 12, 1970: Atlanta Braves vs. Chicago Cubs. *Ernie Banks hits 500th home run.*

Atlanta Braves	AB	R	H	RBI	Chicago Cubs	AB	R	H	RBI
Jackson ss	4	1	0	0	Kessinger ss	5	1	3	0
Milan 2b	5	1	1	0	Beckert 2b	5	0	1	0
Aaron rf	4	0	0	0	Williams lf	4	1	1	1
Carty lf	3	0	3	0	Santo 3b	5	1	2	1
Garr pr	0	0	0	0	Callison rf	4	0	0	0
Wilhelm p	0	0	0	0	Banks 1b	3	1	1	2
King ph	1	0	0	0	Hickman cf	3	0	0	0
Priddy p	0	0	0	0	Martin c	2	0	0	0
Cepeda 1b	4	0	0	0	Hall ph	1	0	0	0
Boyer 3b	4	1	2	0	Hiatt c	1	0	1	0
Gonzalez cf	4	0	0	0	Holtzman p	2	0	0	0
Tillman c	2	0	0	0	Smith ph	1	0	0	0
Lum lf	1	0	0	0	Abernathy p	0	0	0	0
Jarvis p	3	0	0	0	Popovich ph	1	0	0	0
Didier c	1	0	0	0	Regan p	0	0	0	0
	36	3	6	3		37	4	9	4

Atlanta	200	000	100	00 ---	3 6 0
Chicago	010	000	101	01 ---	4 9 1

Atlanta	IP	H	R	ER	BB	SO
Jarvis	8.0	4	2	2	1	6
Wilhelm	2.0	2	1	1	0	2
Priddy L (2-2)	0.0	3	1	1	1	0

Chicago	IP	H	R	ER	BB	SO
Holtzman	8.0	5	3	2	3	4
Abernathy	2.0	1	0	0	0	0
Regan W (2-0)	1.0	0	0	0	1	0

0 outs when winning run scored. E—Martin. DP—Atlanta 1, Chicago 2. 2B—Boyer (5), Santo (5), HR—Banks (3); Williams (12)CS—Cepeda. SF—Banks. T—2:45. A—5,264.

June 3, 1971. Cincinnati Reds vs. Chicago Cubs. *Ken Holtzman's second no-hitter.*

Chicago Cubs	AB	R	H	RBI	Cincinnati Reds	AB	R	H	RBI
Kessinger ss	4	0	1	0	McRae lf	3	0	0	0
Beckert 2b	4	0	2	1	Helms 2b	4	0	0	0
Williams lf	4	0	1	0	May 1b	3	0	0	0
Santo 3b	4	0	0	0	Bench c	3	0	0	0
Pepitone 1b	4	0	1	0	Perez 3b	3	0	0	0
Davis cf	4	0	0	0	Foster cf	3	0	0	0
Callison rf	3	0	1	0	Bradford rf	1	0	0	0
Breeden c	3	0	0	0	Concepcion ss	3	0	0	0
Holtzman p	3	1	0	0	Nolan p	2	0	0	0
					Ferrara ph	1	0	0	0
	33	1	6	1	Gibbon p	0	0	0	0
						26	0	0	0

```
Chicago        001  000  000  -- 1 6 0
Cincinnati     000  000  000  -- 0 0 1
```

Chicago	IP	H	R	ER	BB	SO
Holtzman W (4-6)	9	0	0	0	4	6

Cincinnati	IP	H	R	ER	BB	SO
Nolan L (5-6)	8	5	1	0	0	3
Gibbon	1	1	0	0	0	0

E—Perez (8). DP—Chicago, 1. SB—Kessinger (8), McRae (2). T—1:55. A—11,751.

September 30, 1971. Milwaukee Brewers vs. Chicago White Sox. *Bill Melton homers on the last game of the season to win home run title.*

Milwaukee Brewers	AB	R	H	RBI	Chicago White Sox	AB	R	H	RBI
Harper lf	2	0	0	0	Melton 3b	2	1	1	1
Auerbach ss	4	0	0	0	Williams 3b, rf	1	0	1	0
Cardenal rf	4	1	1	0	Kelly rf, cf	3	0	1	0
Briggs 1b	3	0	0	0	McKinney 2b	4	0	0	0
May cf	3	0	0	0	Hottman lf	4	0	1	0
Theolbald 2b	2	0	1	0	Johnstone cf	3	0	1	0
Schofield 2b	1	0	0	0	Morales ph, 3b	1	0	0	0
Kosco ph	1	0	0	0	Muser 1b	4	1	2	0
Porter c	3	0	0	1	Richard ss	3	0	0	0
Heise 3b	2	0	0	0	Brinkman c	2	0	1	1
Ratliff ph	1	0	0	0	Manuson p	0	0	0	0
Matchick 3b	1	0	0	0	Huntz ph	1	0	0	0
Parsons p	2	0	0	0	Hinton p	0	0	0	0
Morris p	0	0	0	0	Eddy p	1	0	1	0
Krausse p	0	0	0	0	May ph	0	0	0	0
Tepedino ph	1	0	0	0	Reichardt ph	1	0	0	0
Sanders p	0	0	0	0	O'Toole p	0	0	0	0
Pena ph	1	0	0	0	Perzanowski p	0	0	0	0
	31	1	2	1		30	2	9	2

```
Milwaukee    000  000  001  ---  1 2 1

Chicago      011  000  00x  ---  2 9 2
```

Milwaukee	IP	H	R	ER	BB	SO
Parsons L (13-17)	5.2	8	2	2	2	6
Morris	1.0	0	0	0	1	1
Krausse	0.1	0	0	0	0	0
Sanders	1.0	1	0	0	0	0

Chicago	IP	H	R	ER	BB	SO
Magnuson	2.0	0	0	0	0	0
Hinton W (3-4)	2.0	0	0	0	0	1
Eddy	2.0	1	0	0	3	1
O'Toole	2.0	0	0	0	1	2
Perzanowski S (1)	1.0	1	1	0	1	1

E—Heise (10), Muser (1), Richard (27). DP—Milwaukee 1. 2B—Eddy (1). 3B—Muser (1). HR—Melton (33). SH—Richard (5). CS—Kelly (9), Jonstone (5). T—2:27. A—2,814.

April 16, 1972. Philadelphia Phillies vs. Chicago Cubs. *Burt Hooton no-hits Phils.*

Philadelphia Phillies					Chicago Cubs				
Bowa ss	3	0	0	0	Cardenal rf	5	1	2	0
McCarver c	4	0	0	0	Beckert 2b	4	0	1	1
Montanez cf	2	0	0	0	Williams lf	5	1	3	0
Johnson 1b	4	0	0	0	Pepitone 1b	5	1	2	0
Luzinski lf	3	0	0	0	Santo 3b	5	1	3	0
Money 3b	1	0	0	0	Monday cf	2	0	0	0
Anderson rf	2	0	0	0	Kessinger ss	3	0	0	0
Doyle 2b	3	0	0	0	Hundley c	2	0	1	2
Brandon p	0	0	0	0	Hooton p	4	0	0	0
Reynolds p	0	0	0	0					
Selma p	1	0	0	0		35	4	12	3
Stone ph	0	0	0	0					
Short p	0	0	0	0					
Harmon 2b	1	0	0	0					
	24	0	0	0					

Philadelphia	000	000	000	---	0 0 1	
Chicago	000	100	21x	---	4 12 0	

Philadelphia	IP	H	R	ER	BB	SO
Selma L (0-1)	5.0	6	1	0	4	0
Short	1.2	4	2	2	1	2
Brandon	0.1	2	1	1	0	0
Reynolds	1.0	0	0	0	0	0

Chicago	IP	H	R	ER	BB	SO
Hooton W (1-0)	9.0	0	0	0	7	7

E—McCarver (1). DP—Philadelphia 1, Chicago 1. 2B—Santo (1). 3B—Cardenal (1). SH—Bowa (1), Kessinger (1). CS—Money (1). T—2:33. A—9,583.

June 4, 1972. New York Yankees vs. Chicago White Sox (Game 2). *Dick Allen's Pinch-hit 3 run walk-off homer off Sparky Lyle.*

New York Yankees	AB	R	H	RBI	Chicago White Sox	AB	R	H	RBI
Clarke 2b	4	0	1	0	Williams rf, lf	3	0	0	0
Torres rf	4	1	0	0	Alvarado 2b	4	0	0	0
Murcer cf	4	1	2	0	May lf	4	1	2	0
White lf	4	0	1	1	Acosta p	0	0	0	0
Alou 1b	4	0	1	1	Reichardt cf	3	0	0	1
Ellis c	4	0	1	0	Melton 3b	1	2	0	0
Lanier 3b	4	1	2	0	Andrews 1b	3	0	2	1
Michael ss	3	1	1	1	Orta pr	0	1	0	0
Kekich p	4	0	1	0	Morales ss	2	0	0	0
Lyle p	0	0	0	0	Allen ph	1	1	1	3
					Brinkman c	3	0	0	0
	35	4	11	2	Lemonds p	2	0	0	0
					Gossage p	0	0	0	0
					Kelly ph, rf	0	0	0	0
						26	5	5	5

New York   001 002 100 --- 4 11 0

Chicago   000 200 003 --- 5 5 2

New York	IP	H	R	ER	BB	SO
Kekich	8.1	4	4	4	7	6
Lyle L (2-1)	0.0	1	1	1	0	0

Chicago	IP	H	R	ER	BB	SO
Lemonds	5.0	7	3	3	0	2
Gossage	3.0	3	1	1	0	1
Acosta W (1-0)	1.0	1	0	0	0	0

E—Alvarado (3), Melton (10). DP—New York 2, Chicago 2. 2B—Michael (2), Andrews (5). 3B—May (1). HR—Allen (9). SF—Reichardt (1). SB—Lanier (1). Kelly (12). CS—Lanier (2). T—2:25. A—51,904.

July 31, 1972. Chicago White Sox vs. Minnesota Twins. *Dick Allen hits two inside-the-park home runs in the same game.*

Chicago White Sox	AB	R	H	RBI	Minnesota Twins	AB	R	H	RBI
Kelly rf	3	2	1	0	Tovar rf	4	0	0	0
Bradford cf	1	0	0	0	Thompson ss	4	0	1	0
Alvarado 2b, ss	5	2	2	1	Braun 2b	4	0	0	0
Allen 1b	4	2	2	5	Killebrew 1b	4	0	1	0
Muser pr, 1b	1	1	0	0	Reese lf	4	0	1	0
May lf	4	0	2	0	Darwin cf	4	1	1	0
Johnstone cf, rf	4	0	0	0	Soderholm 3b	3	0	0	0
Spiezio 3b	4	0	0	0	Borgmann c	3	0	1	0
Herrmann c	3	1	2	1	Blyleven p	1	0	0	0
Morales ss	0	0	0	0	Strickland p	0	0	0	0
Andrews 2b	4	0	0	0	Nettles ph	1	0	1	1
Bahnsen p	3	0	0	0	Gebhard p	0	0	0	0
					Brye ph	1	0	0	0
	36	8	9	7	Goltz p	0	0	0	0
						33	1	6	1

```
Chicago      3 0 0   0 3 1   1 0 0  —  8 9 1

Minnesota    0 0 0   0 1 0   0 0 0  —  1 6 2
```

Chicago	IP	H	R	ER	BB	SO
Bahnsen W (13-11)	9.0	6	1	0	0	6

Minnesota	IP	H	R	ER	BB	SO
Blyleven L (9-14)	4.1	5	6	6	3	3
Strickland	0.2	1	0	0	0	0
Gebhard	3.0	3	2	1	0	3
Goltz	1.0	0	0	0	0	0

E—Alvarado (7), Thompson (18), Darwin (5). 2B—Kelly (8), May (14). HR—Allen 2 (26, 27), Herrmann (5) SB—May (18). T—2:17. A—13,652.

September 2, 1972. San Diego Padres vs. Chicago Cubs. *Milt Pappas throws a no-hitter; one pitch away from a perfect game.*

San Diego Padres	AB	R	H	RBI	Chicago Cubs	AB	R	H	RBI
Hernandez ss	3	0	0	0	Kessinger ss	5	1	2	3
Jestadt ph	1	0	0	0	Cardenal rf	4	1	2	1
Roberts 3b	3	0	0	0	Williams lf	4	1	2	0
Lee lf	3	0	0	0	Santo 3b	3	1	0	0
Colbert 1b	3	0	0	0	Hickman 1b	4	1	3	1
Gaston rf	3	0	0	0	Fanzone 2b	3	1	0	1
Thomas 2b	3	0	0	0	Hundley c	4	1	2	0
Jeter cf	3	0	0	0	North cf	4	1	2	1
Kendall c	3	0	0	0	Pappas p	4	0	0	0
Caldwell p	2	0	0	0					
Stahl ph	0	0	0	0		35	8	13	7
	27	0	0	0					

San Diego   000 000 000 — 0 0 1
Chicago   202 000 04x — 8 13 0

San Diego	IP	H	R	ER	BB	SO
Caldwell L (6-8)	7.2	13	8	6	2	4
Severinsen	0.1	0	0	0	0	0

Chicago	IP	H	R	ER	BB	SO
Pappas W (12-7)	9.0	0	0	0	1	6

E—Hernandez (18). DP—San Diego 3. 2B—Hickman (12). Kessinger (16). T—2:03. A—11,144.

May 8, 1973. Chicago Cubs vs San Diego Padres. *Ernie Banks becomes the first black man to manage a major league baseball team after Whitey Lockman ejected.*

Chicago Cubs	AB	R	H	RBI	San Diego Padres	AB	R	H	RBI
Monday cf	5	1	1	2	Hernandez ss	5	1	1	0
Beckert 2b	6	0	1	0	Grubb cf	4	1	0	0
Cardenal rf	3	0	1	0	Lee lf	3	0	2	0
Hiser pr, rf	2	0	1	0	Morales pr, rf	2	0	0	0
Hickman 1b	3	0	0	0	Colbert 1b	6	0	1	2
Santo 3b	3	0	1	0	Gaston rf	6	0	2	0
James lf	4	0	0	0	Kendall c	5	0	1	0
Williams ph	1	0	0	0	Campbell 2b	5	0	3	0
Garrett lf	0	0	0	0	Hilton 3b	4	0	0	0
Rudolph c	5	1	2	0	Norman p	3	0	0	0
Kessinger ss	4	0	0	0	Marshall ph	0	0	0	0
Jenkins p	2	0	0	0	Romo p	0	0	0	0
Fanzone ph	0	1	0	0	Thomas ph	1	0	0	0
Locker p	1	0	1	0	Ross p	0	0	0	0
Pepitone ph	1	0	1	1	Troedson p	0	0	0	0
Bonham p	0	0	0	0					
	40	3	9	3		44	2	10	2

Chicago	000	000	020	001	---	3 9 0
San Diego	200	000	000	000	---	2 10 0

Chicago	IP	H	R	ER	BB	SO
Jenkins	7.0	7	2	2	5	5
Locker W (3-1)	4.0	3	0	0	3	4
Bonham S (2)	1.0	0	0	0	0	0

San Diego	IP	H	R	ER	BB	SO
Norman	8.0	5	2	2	2	5
Romo	2.0	1	0	0	2	0
Ross L (1-2)	1.1	2	1	1	1	1
Troedson	0.2	1	0	0	0	0

E—None. DP—Chicago 1, San Diego 3. 2B—Beckert (8), Rudolph (3), Pepitone (3), Kendall (7). HR—Monday (6). SB—Hiser (4), Locker (1), Hernandez 2 (3,4). CS—Hiser (1). T—3:12. A—4,554.

May 20, 1973. Minnesota Twins vs. Chicago White Sox. *Largest crowd ever to watch a game at old Comiskey Park.*

Minnesota Twins	AB	R	H	RBI	Chicago White Sox	AB	R	H	RBI
Carew 2b	5	0	2	1	Kelly rf	4	0	0	0
Hisle cf	4	0	1	0	May dh	5	0	1	0
Oliva dh	4	0	0	0	Allen, H pr, dh	0	0	0	0
Killebrew 1b	3	1	1	0	Muser 1b	5	0	2	0
Lis 1b	1	0	0	0	Melton 3b	4	0	1	0
Darwin rf	5	1	2	2	Henderson cf	3	0	0	0
Braun 3b	4	0	2	0	Reichardt lf	2	0	1	0
Thompson ss	4	0	2	0	Herrmann c	2	0	1	0
Holt lf	4	1	1	0	Orta 2b	1	0	0	0
Roof c	4	0	2	0	Allen, D ph	1	0	0	0
Mitterwald c	0	0	0	0	Alvarado ss	2	0	0	0
Corbin p	0	0	0	0	Leon ss	0	0	0	0
Sanders p	0	0	0	0	Andrews ph	1	0	0	0
					Morales 2b	1	0	0	0
	38	3	13	3	Fisher p	0	0	0	0
					Forster p	0	0	0	0
						31	0	6	0

Minnesota	000	010	200 ---	3 13 2
Chicago	000	000	000 ---	0 6 2

Minnesota	IP	H	R	ER	BB	SO
Corbin W (1-1)	6.2	4	0	0	5	4
Sanders S (6)	2.1	2	0	0	1	0

Chicago	IP	H	R	ER	BB	SO
Fisher L (4-3)	6.2	12	3	2	3	2
Forster	2.1	1	0	0	0	3

E—Braun (7), Thompson (9), Muser (1), Alvarado (4). DP—Minnesota 1, Chicago 1. 2B—Braun (9), Reichardt (4), Muser (2). HR—Darwin (5). SB—Hisle (5). CS—Kelly (6). T—2:44. *ATTENDANCE: 55,555.*

July 20, 1973. Chicago White Sox vs. New York Yankees. *Wilbur Wood starts both games of a double-header.*

Game 1

Chicago White Sox	AB	R	H	RBI	New York Yankees	AB	R	H	RBI
Kelly rf	4	0	1	0	Clarke 2b	6	3	2	1
Muser 1b	5	0	1	0	Alou, M. rf	3	1	3	1
May lf	5	0	2	0	White lf	5	1	2	3
Melton 3b	4	1	3	1	Murcer cf	4	1	2	1
Henderson dh	5	1	2	0	Munson c	5	1	2	1
Bradford cf	4	0	0	0	Nettles 3b	5	1	1	2
Herrmann c	4	0	1	0	Alou, F. 1b	5	2	3	0
Orta 2b	4	0	2	0	Sanchez dh	5	2	4	2
Leon ss	4	0	1	1	Lanier ss	5	0	1	1
Wood p	0	0	0	0	Medich p	0	0	0	0
Fisher p	0	0	0	0	McDaniel p	0	0	0	0
Gossage, p	0	0	0	0					
Geddes p	0	0	0	0		43	12	20	12
	39	2	13	2					

Chicago	0 00	002	000 ---	2 13 0
New York	8 00	010	2 1x ---	12 20 0

Chicago	IP	H	R	ER	BB	SO
Wood L (18-13)	0.0	4	6	5	1	1
Fisher	5.0	10	3	3	0	1
Gossage	2.0	3	2	2	2	1
Geddes	1.0	3	1	1	0	0

New York	IP	H	R	ER	BB	SO
Medich W (7-5)	5.2	10	2	2	1	0
McDaniel S (7)	3.1	3	0	0	0	0

E—None. 2B—White (11), Munson (17), Sanchez (3). HR—Melton (14). CS—Kelly (10). SB—Clarke (6).

T—2:31. A—34,587.

Game 2

Chicago White Sox	AB	R	H	RBI	New York Yankees	AB	R	H	RBI
Jeter rf	3	0	0	0	Clarke 2b	2	1	1	0
Alvarado 2b	3	0	0	0	Alou, M. rf	3	1	1	1
May dh	2	0	0	0	White lf	3	2	1	4
Melton 3b	2	0	0	0	Murcer cf	2	1	0	0
Henderson lf	2	0	1	0	Sanchez dh	3	0	1	0
Bradford cf	2	0	0	0	Nettles 3b	3	0	0	0
Allen, H. 1b	2	0	1	0	Alou, F. 1b	3	0	1	0
Leon ss	2	0	0	0	Moses c	3	1	0	0
Brinkman c	2	0	0	0	Michael ss	2	1	1	0
Wood p	0	0	0	0	McDowell p	0	0	0	0
Frailing p	0	0	0	0					
	20	0	2	0		24	7	6	5

Chicago   000   000 — 0 2 2

New York   000   250 — 7 6 0

Chicago	IP	H	R	ER	BB	SO
Wood L (18-14)	4.1	5	7	5	0	1
Frailing	1.0	1	0	0	1	2

New York	IP	H	R	ER	BB	SO
McDowell W (5-1)	6.0	2	0	0	1	8

E—Jeter (5), Melton (15). 2B—Michael (10). HR—White (11—grand slam). T—1:37. A—34,587.

John M. O'Donnell

September 28, 1974. St. Louis Cardinals vs. Chicago Cubs. *Billly Williams' final home run as a Chicago Cub.*

St. Louis Cardinals	AB	R	H	RBI	Chicago Cubs	AB	R	H	RBI
Brock lf	4	0	0	0	Monday cf	3	2	1	0
Sizemore 2b	4	0	1	0	Kessinger ss	3	2	0	0
Smith rf	3	0	0	0	Williams lf	3	1	2	2
Dwyer rf	0	0	0	0	Morales rf	0	0	0	0
Melendez ph, rf	1	0	0	0	Madlock 3b	3	0	1	3
Simmons c	3	1	0	0	Cardenal rf, lf	4	0	0	0
Torre 1b	2	1	0	0	LaCock 1b	3	0	0	0
McBride cf	3	1	0	0	Swisher c	4	0	0	0
Reitz 3b	4	0	1	2	Sperring 2b	4	1	1	0
Tyson ss	3	0	2	1	Reuschel p	1	0	0	0
Cruz ph	1	0	0	0	LaRoche p	2	2	2	0
McGlothen p	2	0	0	0	Zamora p	0	0	0	0
Hunt ph	1	0	0	0					
Siebert p	0	0	0	0		30	8	7	5
Hrabosky p	0	0	0	0					
Bare p	0	0	0	0					
	31	3	4	3					

St. Louis   000 300 000 --- 3 4 3

Chicago   000 103 400 --- 8 7 0

St. Louis	IP	H	R	ER	BB	SO
McGlothen L (16-12)	6.0	5	4	4	2	3
Siebert	0.0	1	1	0	0	0
Hrabosky	0,1	1	3	0	1	0
Bare	1.2	0	0	0	0	0
Chicago	IP	H	R	ER	BB	SO
Reuschel	3.2	1	2	2	2	4
LaRoche W (5-5)	4.1	3	1	1	1	3
Zamora	1.0	0	0	0	1	0

E—Sizemore (16), Torre (14), Hrabosky (3). DP—St. Louis 1. 2B—Tyson (14), Williams (21). 3B--

Madlock (5). HR—Williams (16). SF—Williams (2). T—2:18. A—13,867.

July 28, 1976. Chicago White Sox vs. Oakland Athletics. *Blue Moon Odom and Francisco Barrios combine to give up 11 walks but no hits to the A's.*

Chicago White Sox	AB	R	H	RBI	Oakland A's	AB	R	H	RBI
Hairston rf	3	0	2	0	North cf	3	0	0	0
Nordhagen ph, rf	2	0	0	0	Campaneris ss	2	0	0	0
Garr cf, lf	4	0	2	0	Rudi lf	3	0	0	0
Orta lf	3	0	0	0	Williams dh	1	1	0	0
Bannister cf	0	0	0	0	Lintz pr, dh	0	0	0	0
Kelly dh	2	0	0	0	Baylor ph, dh	1	0	0	0
Johnson ph, dh	1	0	0	0	Bando 3b	2	0	0	0
Stein 3b	4	0	2	0	Tenace c	3	0	0	0
Spencer 1b	3	2	2	1	Washington rf	3	0	0	0
Brohamer 2b	4	0	1	0	McMullen 1b	3	0	0	0
Dent ss	4	0	1	1	Garner 2b	3	0	0	0
Essian c	4	0	0	0	Torrez p	0	0	0	0
Odom p	0	0	0	0	Lindblad p	0	0	0	0
Barrios p	0	0	0	0	Fingers p	0	0	0	0
	34	2	10	2		24	1	0	0

Chicago   010 001 000 --- 2 10 1
Oakland   000 100 000 --- 1 0 1

Chicago	IP	H	R	ER	BB	SO
Odom W (2-0)	5.0	0	1	0	9	3
Barrios S (2)	4.0	0	0	0	2	2

Oakland	IP	H	R	ER	BB	SO
Torrez	5.0	7	1	1	1	2
Lindblad L (4-3)	2.1	2	1	1	0	0
Fingers	1.2	1	0	0	1	2

E—Essian (6), Bando (11). 2B—Spencer (9), Brohamer (8). SB—Kelly (9), North (51), Washington (26), Lintz (22). CS—Garr (4). T—2:31. A—3,367.

October 3, 1976. Montreal Expos vs. Chicago Cubs. *Bill Madlock goes 4-4 on the last day of the season to win the batting title.*

Montreal Expos	AB	R	H	RBI	Chicago Cubs	AB	R	H	RBI
Unser lf	3	0	0	1	Monday 1b	5	0	1	0
Garrett 2b	4	0	2	0	Wallis cf	4	2	3	0
Dawson cf	4	0	0	0	Madlock 3b	4	2	4	1
Valentine rf	4	0	2	0	Sperring ph, 3b	1	0	1	0
Jorgensen 1b	4	0	1	0	Morales rf	5	2	2	0
Parrish 3b	4	0	0	0	Trillo 2b	5	1	3	1
Williams c	4	1	1	1	Mitterwald c	4	0	2	3
Frias ss	4	1	1	0	Biittner lf	4	1	1	0
Fryman p	1	0	0	0	Kelleher ss	3	0	1	1
Lang p	0	0	0	0	Reuschel p	3	0	1	2
Atkinson p	0	0	0	0					
Cromartie ph	1	0	0	0		38	8	19	8
Murray p	0	0	0	0					
Taylor p	0	0	0	0					
Freed ph	1	0	1	0					
Carrithers p	0	0	0	0					
	34	2	8	2					

Montreal	001	010	000 -- 2 8 0
Chicago	005	102	00x -- 8 19 1

Montreal	IP	H	R	ER	BB	SO
Fryman L (13-13)	2.2	9	5	5	2	1
Lang	0.2	3	1	1	0	0
Atkinson	0.2	0	0	0	0	1
Murray	1.1	4	2	2	0	0
Taylor	1.2	1	0	0	0	1
Carrithers	1.0	2	0	0	0	0

Chicago	IP	H	R	ER	BB	SO
Reuschel W (14-12)	9.0	8	2	1	0	6

E—Reuschel (4). DP—Montreal 3, Chicago 1. 2B—Reuschel (4). 3B—Wallis (5). HR—Williams (17). SF—Unser (6). SB—Monday (5). T—1:57. A—9,486.

September 24, 1977. Chicago White Sox vs. Seattle Mariners. *Jack Brohamer hits for the cycle.*

Chicago White Sox	AB	R	H	RBI	Seattle Mariners	AB	R	H	RBI
Garr lf	4	1	3	0	Collins lf	3	0	1	2
Cruz, T. lf	1	0	0	0	Cruz, J. 2b	4	0	1	0
Lemon cf	4	1	1	0	Braun ph	1	0	0	0
Stillman dh	4	0	0	0	Fosse c	4	0	0	0
Gamble rf	5	2	2	1	Stanton rf	5	0	1	0
Cruz, H. pr, rf	0	0	0	0	Jones cf	4	0	1	0
Soderholm 3b	5	0	0	0	Stein 3b	3	0	1	0
Spencer 1b	4	2	2	0	Meyer 1b	4	1	1	0
Brohamer 2b	5	2	5	4	Bernhardt dh	4	1	2	0
Kessinger ss	3	0	0	0	Reynolds ss	4	1	2	1
Nahorodny c	4	0	1	2	Segui p	0	0	0	0
Kravec p	0	0	0	0	Erardi p	0	0	0	0
Verhoeven p	0	0	0	0	Galasso p	0	0	0	0
	39	8	14	7		36	3	10	3

```
Chicago    500  011  001 -- 8 14 0
Seattle    010  000  001 -- 3 10 1
```

Chicago	IP	H	R	ER	BB	SO
Kravec W (10-8)	8.0	10	3	3	3	3
Verhoeven	1.0	0	0	0	1	0

Seattle	IP	H	R	ER	BB	SO
Segui L (0-7)	0.1	3	3	3	0	1
Eradi	4.0	5	3	3	4	1
Galasso	4.2	6	2	2	2	1

E—Jones (9). DP—Chicago 1, Seattle 1. 2B—Lemon (38), Gamble (20), Brohamer 2 (8,9), Cruz (3), Collins (8). 3B—Brohamer (3), Reynolds (3). HR—Brohamer (2). SF—Nahorodny (1). T—2:45 A—17,636.

May 17, 1979. Philadelphia Phillies vs. Chicago Cubs. *The 23-22 game.*

Philadelphia Phillies					Chicago Cubs				
McBride rf	8	2	3	1	DeJesus ss	6	4	3	1
Bowa ss	8	4	5	1	Vail rf	5	2	3	1
Rose 1b	7	4	3	4	Burris p	0	0	0	0
Schmidt 3b	4	3	2	4	Thompson ph, rf	2	1	1	1
Unser lf	7	1	1	2	Buckner 1b	7	2	4	7
Maddox cf	4	3	4	4	Kingman lf	6	4	3	6
Gross pr, cf	2	1	1	1	Ontiveros 3b	7	2	1	1
Boone c	4	2	3	5	Martin cf	6	2	3	3
Meoli 2b	5	0	1	0	Sutter p	0	0	0	0
Lerch p	1	1	1	1	Foote c	6	1	3	1
Bird p	1	1	0	0	Sizemore 2b	4	2	2	1
Luzinski ph	0	0	0	0	Caudill p	0	0	0	0
Espinosa pr	1	1	0	0	Murcer rf, cf	2	0	1	0
McGraw p	0	0	0	0	Lamp p	0	0	0	0
Reed p	0	0	0	0	Moore p	1	0	1	1
McCarver ph	1	0	0	0	Hernandez p	1	0	0	0
Eastwick p	0	0	0	0	Dillard ph, 2b	1	2	1	0
					Biittner ph	1	0	0	0
	53	23	24	23	Kelleher 2b	1	0	0	0
						56	22	26	22

Philadelphia	708	240	100	1 —	23	24 2
Chicago	600	373	030	0 —	22	26 2

Philadelphia	IP	H	ER	R	BB	SO
Lerch	0.1	5	5	5	0	0
Bird	3.2	8	4	4	0	2
McGraw	0.2	4	7	4	3	1
Reed	3.1	9	6	6	0	0
Eastwick W (1-0)	2.0	0	0	0	0	1

Chicago	IP	H	ER	R	BB	SO
Lamp	0.1	6	6	6	0	0
Moore	2.0	6	7	7	2	1
Hernandez	2.2	7	8	6	7	1
Caudill	1.1	3	1	1	2	3
Burris	1.2	1	0	0	0	1
Sutter L (1-1)	2.0	1	1	1	1	1

E—Schmidt 2 (6, 7), DeJesus (7), Kingman (3). DP—Philadelphia 2. 2B—Bowa 2 (5, 6), Maddox 2 (9, 10), Rose 2 (13, 14), Boone (6), Martin (10), Foote (4), DeJesus (7). 3B—Gross (1), Moore (1). HR— Schmidt 2 (13, 14), Boone (2), Lerch (1), Maddox (6), Kingman 3 (10, 11, 12), Ontiveros (1), Buckner (4—grand slam), Martin (3). SF—Unser (2), Gross (1). SB—Bowa (6), Meoli (1). T—4:03. A—14,952.

July 12, 1979. Detroit Tigers vs. Chicago White Sox. Disco Demolition.

Game 1

Detroit Tigers	AB	R	H	RBI	Chicago White Sox	AB	R	H	RBI
LeFlore cf	5	0	2	0	Bannister 2b	4	0	1	0
Whitaker 2b	4	1	0	0	Moore lf	4	0	1	0
Staub dh	3	1	1	0	Lemon cf	3	0	1	0
Thompson 1b	4	0	0	0	Johnson 1b	3	0	0	0
Summers rf	3	1	2	0	Nordhagen dh	3	0	0	0
Morales lf	4	1	2	1	Orta ph, dh	1	0	0	0
Parrish c	4	0	1	1	Torres rf	3	1	1	0
Brookens 3b	4	0	1	1	Washington ph	1	0	0	0
Trammell ss	4	0	0	0	Morrison 3b	4	0	0	0
Underwood p	0	0	0	0	Pryor ss	3	0	1	1
Lopez p	0	0	0	0	Colbern c	3	0	0	0
					Howard p	0	0	0	0
	35	4	9	3	Farmer p	0	0	0	0
						32	1	5	1

Detroit   111 001 000 -- 4 9 0

Chicago   010 000 000 -- 1 5 2

Detroit	IP	H	R	ER	BB	SO
Underwood W (4-0)	7.2	5	1	1	2	3
Lopez S (5)	1.1	0	0	0	0	2

Chicago	IP	H	R	ER	BB	SO
Howard L (1-4)	5.1	6	4	2	2	4
Farmer	3.2	3	0	0	1	1

E—Morrison (1), Colbern (2). DP—Chicago 2. 2B—Bannister (14), Pryor (10), Moore (4). 3B—Brookens (1). SB—Staub (1), Morales (1), Summers (2), LeFlore (47). T—2:38. A—47,795.

Game 2: Game forfeited to Detroit due to unplayable field conditions.

July 14, 1979. Detroit Tigers vs. Chicago White Sox. *Claudell Washington homers three times in one game.*

Detroit Tigers	AB	R	H	RBI
Leflore cf	5	0	3	0
Whitaker 2b	5	0	1	0
Morales rf	4	1	1	0
Parrish c	4	0	0	0
Wockenfuss 1b	4	1	1	2
Staub dh	3	1	1	0
Jones lf	4	0	1	0
Brookens 3b	4	1	0	1
Trammell ss	4	0	1	1
Baker p	0	0	0	0
Wilcox p	0	0	0	0
Tobik p	0	0	0	0
	37	4	9	4

Chicago White Sox	AB	R	H	RBI
Bannister dh	4	1	1	1
Garr lf	4	2	2	2
Moore lf	1	1	1	1
Orta 2b	3	1	1	1
Johnson 1b	3	0	0	0
Squires 1b	1	0	0	0
Washington rf	5	3	3	5
Torres cf	5	1	2	1
May c	4	1	0	0
Morrisson 3b	3	2	2	1
Kessonger ss	2	0	1	1
Baumgarten p	0	0	0	0
Farmer p	0	0	0	0
	35	12	13	12

```
Detroit    020  000  020 -- 4  9 1
Chicago    101  103  33x -- 12 13 1
```

Detroit	IP	H	R	ER	BB	SO
Baker L (1-6)	4.2	5	3	3	5	5
Wilcox	1.1	5	5	5	0	2
Tobik	2.0	3	4	4	1	3

Chicago	IP	H	R	ER	BB	SO
Baumgarten W (9-5)	7.1	8	4	4	2	3
Farmer	1.2	1	0	0	0	1

E—Whitaker (4), Morrison (3). DP—Detroit 1. 2B—Trammell (6), Morales (16), Garr (7). 3B—Bannister (6). HR—Wockenfuss (6), **Washington 3 (8,9,10)**, Garr (6), Torres (3), Morrison (1). SB—Whitaker (12), LeFlore (48). T—2:54. A—23,887.

Acknowledgements

The author wishes to acknowledge the contributions from many parties in the production and publication of this book.

I wish to express sincere gratitude to Beth Bazan, for her expertise in editing and indexing, as well as her commitment to this endeavor. Thanks to Anthony Stanford for his friendship, sharing his deep knowledge on publishing, and referring me to Ms. Bazan. A thank you to my daughter Katie for her skill in formatting the images, and to my daughter Julie for her skills in the transmission of the appendices. I'd like to thank Patti Peterson with her help in image development. To the Pierces, Billy and Gloria, thank you for sharing your wisdom and your generous hospitality. To Randy Hundley, thank you for your perspective on the game and sharing your insights on teammates and opponents. I'd like to thank the two radio voices of Chicago baseball, Ed Farmer and Pat Hughes, for their support and their love of the game. To my two sons, Brian and Michael, thanks for your interest in the game so I don't have to constantly bombard your mom and your sisters with a subject they can scarcely tolerate. Thanks, Spike, for your electronic support in bringing this book to closure.

Finally, I'd like to thank the two that mean the most to me: my wife Betsy and my Lord, Jesus Christ.

Index

Yeager, Steve, 200-201
Young, Don, 32
Yount, Robin, 138-39

Zahn, Geoff, 130-31, 227
Zisk, Richie, 181, 189, 205, 218
Zimmer, Don, 97